Houghton Mifflin

Math

Chapter Intervention

Ways to Success Skill Sheets

- Chapter Prerequisites
- Chapter Objectives

GRADE

5

Introduction to Chapter Intervention

What is *Houghton Mifflin Math Chapter Intervention*?

Houghton Mifflin Math Chapter Intervention is a part of the complete intervention plan for *Houghton Mifflin Math.* This scaffolded math program is designed for students who need more time and support to develop math skills and acquire proficiency. Teachers may use the reproducible blackline masters in this book to help students on a skill-by-skill, chapter-by-chapter basis. Teachers may also use *Chapter Intervention* in conjunction with the *Ways to Success Intervention CD-Rom* and other *Houghton Mifflin Math* program resources outlined in the Teacher Notes for each skill.

Why is *Chapter Intervention* an essential teaching tool?

Chapter Intervention is an essential teaching tool for today's time-pressed teachers because it is a convenient, easy-to-implement, effective way to keep students moving forward in mathematics. This print-based program can be used as a supplement or alternative to the computer-based *Ways to Success Intervention* program with interactive teaching models and guided practice exercises for every lesson.

How do teachers use *Chapter Intervention*?

Houghton Mifflin Math Chapter Intervention provides support for the prerequisite skills and chapter objectives for every chapter in Grades 1–6. This flexible program allows teachers to help individual students or small groups of students on either an ongoing or an as-needed basis. Depending on students' needs, time available, and a teacher's preferred level of involvement, teachers have the option of giving students skill lessons to work on in the classroom or at home.

Although *Chapter Intervention* is designed to be used with *Houghton Mifflin Math* throughout the academic year, it is a highly versatile program that is equally well suited for use in after-school programs, summer school sessions, and one-on-one tutoring.

How does scaffolded instruction work?

Scaffolded instruction provides students who require intervention the support they need to successfully move from teacher-directed instruction to working independently. The structure of each skill lesson is especially designed to help a student with learning difficulties absorb, process, and practice math at a comfortable, individual pace.

Each skill lesson begins with either a stepped-out example or a scaffolded model for students to follow. There are also definitions, reminders, and references to guide students as they relearn and review important math skills and concepts.

As students move from one set of exercises to the next, models, scaffolding, and prompts are removed in a gradual and strategic way that enables students to learn and practice successfully.

For Grades 1–2, *Chapter Intervention* includes three types of intervention lessons—vocabulary, skill, and problem solving. For Grades 3–6, *Chapter Intervention* includes two types of intervention lessons—skill and problem solving.

Using Chapter Intervention

What is the best way to implement *Chapter Intervention*?

Chapter Intervention skill lessons cover both prerequisite and chapter-level skills. To assess students' understanding of the prerequisite skills necessary to succeed in a chapter, teachers should administer the Chapter Pretest from the *Houghton Mifflin Mathematics Assessment Guide* whenever the class starts a new chapter in *Houghton Mifflin Math*.

How a student performs on a Chapter Pretest will quickly identify areas of skill weakness. Teachers can then use this information to pinpoint appropriate prerequisite-level skill lessons for students to work on.

To assess students' understanding of chapter-level content, teachers should administer the Chapter Review/Test in *Houghton Mifflin Math* at the end of each chapter. Students whose test performance indicates areas of skill weakness are candidates for intervention and should be given appropriate chapter-level skill lessons.

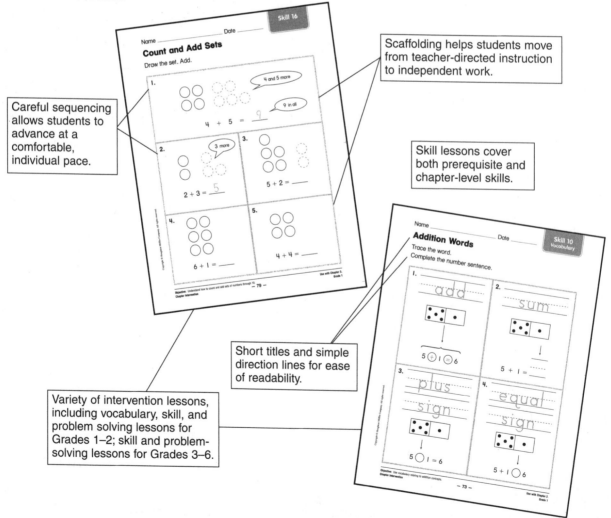

Scaffolding helps students move from teacher-directed instruction to independent work.

Careful sequencing allows students to advance at a comfortable, individual pace.

Skill lessons cover both prerequisite and chapter-level skills.

Short titles and simple direction lines for ease of readability.

Variety of intervention lessons, including vocabulary, skill, and problem solving lessons for Grades 1–2; skill and problem-solving lessons for Grades 3–6.

How are skill pages set up?

Skill pages are designed to maximize a student's opportunity for success and independent learning. There are just enough exercises to fill the page and to model the building blocks needed for mastering the skill. Titles and directions are written clearly and simply to minimize the need for verbal instruction. The different sections of the lesson pages are boxed to help students maintain focus.

How are Teacher Notes set up?

Teacher Notes are presented in a concise, easy-to-read format. They offer insight on Common Errors and Teaching Tips. Teacher Notes also detail resources available for more review, practice and/or intervention in *Ways to Success Intervention,* the *Teacher Edition,* and blackline masters for *Practice, Homework,* and/or *Problem Solving.*

Models and examples show students how to move step by step through a process.

Just enough exercises to fill the page and give students a sense of accomplishment.

Questions and prompts guide students through the thinking that will help them solve the problem.

Helpful reminders, reference boxes, and definitions help students review math skills and concepts.

Objectives are clearly stated at the bottom of each page.

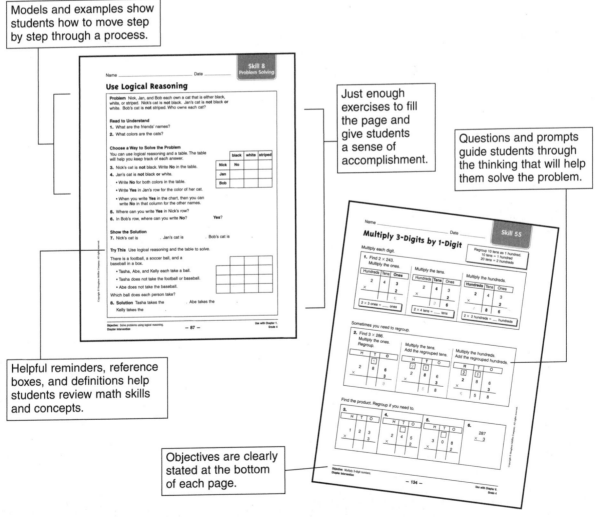

Table of Contents

Teacher Notes

Chapter 1: Place Value of Whole Numbers and Decimals

Skill 1

Objective Identify place value of whole numbers through hundred millions.

Answers

1. 40,000,000 2. 6,000,000
3. 300,000 4. 20,000
5. 1,000 6. 500 7. 80 8. 9
9. 6,000; 56 thousand, 98
10. 300,000,000;
392 million, 655 thousand, 835

Place Value
Prerequisite Skill from Grade 4

Common Error Students may make mistakes such as writing one million two thousand ten as 1,000,210.

- Use Skill 1 for scaffolded review of the concept.
- For more practice use *Ways to Success* 1a.

Teaching Tip Before students use the worksheet, you may wish to remind them that each period—ones, thousands, and millions—has a ones, tens, and hundreds place.

Skill 2

Objective Compare, order, and round whole numbers.

Answers

1. 309,564 > 307,421
2. 467, 398 < 467, 932
3. 950,443 = 950,443
4. 154,078 < 157,068
5. 68,754; 63,477; 61,538
6. 57,348; 54,637; 52,403
7. 3,000 8. 5,000 9. 9,000

Compare, Order, and Round
Prerequisite Skill from Grade 4

Common Error Students may incorrectly compare or order numbers because they misalign the digits.

- Use Skill 2 for scaffolded review of the concept.

Teaching Tip Before students use the worksheet, you may wish to review starting with the greatest place value and working down to the least place value to compare two numbers.

Skill 3

Objective Round decimals.

Answers

1. 73 2. 34 3. 27 4. 50
5. 136 6. 862 7. 14.2
8. 81.1 9. 38.9 10. 78.4
11. 273.5 12. 396.5 13. 12
14. 504 15. 708 16. 89
17. 36.8 18. 249.8 19. 89.5
20. 154.3

Round Decimals
Prerequisite Skill from Grade 4

Common Error Students may misidentify the place value they need to consider.

- Use Skill 3 for scaffolded review of the concept

Teaching Tip Before students use the worksheet, you may wish to have them round a number such as 7.35 to the nearest tenth and to the nearest whole number. (7.4; 7.0)

Skill 4

Objective Compare and order decimals.

Check that students have correctly aligned digits.

Answers
1. 0.15; 0.13; 0.15 > 0.13
2. 0.02; 0.21; 0.02 < 0.21
3. 13.65 = 13.65
4. 3.6 < 3.62 5. 0.28; 0.29; 0.31; 31; 0.28, 0.29, 0.31
6. 3.92; 5.01; 5.4
7. 6.7, 6.73, 6.84

Compare and Order Decimals *Prerequisite Skill from Grade 4*

Common Error Students may compare digits that are not in the same place.

- Use Skill 4 for scaffolded review of the concept.

Teaching Tip Before students use the worksheet, you may wish to have them use a number line and place the decimals 0.53, 0.7, and 0.09 in order from least to greatest. (0.09; 0.53; 0.7)

Skill 5

Objective Read and write numbers in standard and expanded form.

Answers
1. 60,000,000,000
2. 8,000,000,000 3. 400,000
4. 9,000 5. 15,281
6. 9,618,027,978
7. 15,000,528,000
8. 12,000,000
9. 20,900,000,000
10. 700,000,000,000

Read and Write Whole Numbers *Skill from Chapter 1*

Common Error Students may misinterpret the value of digits.

- Use Skill 5 for scaffolded review of the concept.
- For more practice use *Ways to Success* 1.3 or blackline masters Practice 1.3 or Homework 1.3.
- For small group intervention use the Intervention Activity, *Teacher Edition*, p. 9.

Teaching Tip Before students use the worksheet, you may wish to have them practice writing and reading the number that is one less than the number 100,000,000,000. (99,999,999,999; 99 billion, 999 million, 999 thousand, 999)

Skill 6

Objective Read and write decimals through thousandths.

Answers
1. 0.9 2. 0.016 3. 0.125
4. 0.12 5. 0.084 6. 0.406
7. 1.2 8. 31.279
9. fifty-three hundredths
10. two hundred forty-nine thousandths
11. four and twenty-seven hundredths
12. nine and two thousandths

Read and Write Decimals *Skill from Chapter 1*

Common Error Students may omit zeros when they are given the word form of a decimal and asked to write the standard form.

- Use Skill 6 for scaffolded review of the concept.
- For more practice use *Ways to Success* 1.5 or blackline masters Practice 1.5 or Homework 1.5.
- For small group intervention use the Intervention Activity, *Teacher Edition*, p. 15.

Teaching Tip Before students use the worksheet, you may wish to read aloud the following numbers and have students write them in standard form, 3 and 5 tenths; 305 thousandths; 35 hundredths. (3.5; 0.305; 0.35)

Skill 7

Objective Round, compare, and order whole numbers.

Check that students have correctly aligned digits.

Answers
1. $3,126,403 < 3,142,128$
2. $8,537,268$; $8,537,901$; $8,537,268 < 8,537,901$
3. $410,562$; $428,900$; $456,212$ 4. $924,963$; $936,100$; $976,405$ 5. $40,000$
6. $830,000$ 7. $130,000$
8. $9,160,000$

Compare and Round Whole Numbers *Skill from Chapter 1*

Common Error Students may incorrectly compare or order numbers because they misalign the digits of the numbers.

- Use Skill 7 for scaffolded review of the concept.
- For more practice use *Ways to Success* 1.4 or blackline masters Practice 1.4 or Homework 1.4.
- For small group intervention use the Intervention Activity, *Teacher Edition*, p. 12.

Teaching Tip Before students use the worksheet, you may wish to have them use a place-value chart to compare the numbers $856,775,659,050$ and $856,775,659,500$. Then have student round each number to the nearest thousand and compare them.

Skill 8

Objective Round, compare and order decimals.

Check that students have correctly aligned digits.

Answers
1. $0.78 > 0.63$
2. $0.149 < 0.170$ 3. 1.659; 1.682; $1.659 < 1.682$
4. 0.33; 0.48 5. 0.642; 0.671; 0.685 6. 0.26
7. 0.13 8. 6.03 9. 32.99

Compare and Round Decimals *Skill from Chapter 1*

Common Error Students may incorrectly round decimals to the nearest hundredth.

- Use Skill 8 for scaffolded review of the concept.
- For more practice use *Ways to Success* 1.7 or blackline masters Practice 1.7 or Homework 1.7.
- For small group intervention use the Intervention Activity, *Teacher Edition*, p. 22.

Teaching Tip Before students use the worksheet, you may wish to have them use a place-value chart to help them round the decimal 0.659 to the nearest hundredth. (0.66)

Skill 9

Objective Relate place value and exponents.

Answers
1. 10^3; 10^2; 10^1; 1 2. $7, 5; 5$; 10^3; 7×10^2; 5×10^1; 5
3. 10^2; 8×10^1; 9×1
4. 6×10^1; 7×1
5. 4×10^5; 3×10^4; 7×10^3; 2×10^2; 0×10^1; 3×1

Place Value and Exponents *Skill from Chapter 1*

Common Error Students may confuse the meanings of base and exponent.

- Use Skill 9 for scaffolded review of the concept.
- For more practice use *Ways to Success* 1.2 or blackline masters Practice 1.2 or Homework 1.2.
- For small group intervention use the Intervention Activity, *Teacher Edition*, p. 7.

Teaching Tip Before students use the worksheet, you may wish to have them practice writing $5 \times 5 \times 5 \times 5$ using its base and exponent. (5^4)

Skill 10

Objective Solve problems by finding patterns.

Answers
1. 5 minutes 2. 10 minutes
3. 15 minutes 4. *See student page.* 5. 5 minutes
6. 20 minutes 7. 12
8. 60 tulips

Problem Solving:
Find a Pattern

Skill from Chapter 1

Common Error Students may make computational errors, which might lead them to misinterpret a pattern.

- Use Skill 10 for scaffolded review of the concept.
- For more practice use *Ways to Success* 1.6 or blackline masters Problem Solving 1.6, Practice 1.6 or Homework 1.6.
- For small group intervention use the Intervention Activity, *Teacher Edition*, p. 18.

Teaching Tip Before students use the worksheet, you may wish to have them look at numeric patterns (3, 6, 9, 12…) (4, 12, 20, 28…) and determine how much they increase each time. (3; 8)

Chapter 2: Add and Subtract Whole Numbers

Skill 11

Objective Use addition properties.

Answers
1. $8 + 7 = 15$ 2. $2 + 9 = 11$ 3. $4 + 23 = 27$ 4. $10 + 16 = 26$ 5. $7 + 6 = 3 + 10$; $13 = 13$ 6. $26 + 8 = 29 + 5$; $34 = 34$ 7. $(11 + 8) + 20 = 11 + (8 + 20)$; $19 + 20 = 11 + 28$; $39 = 39$ 8. $125 + (15 + 10) = (125 + 15) + 10$; $125 + 25 = 140 + 10$; $150 = 150$ 9. 5 10. 10
11. 89 12. 276 13. 6; Associative Property 14. 14; Commutative Property
15. 156; Identity Property
16. 3; Identity Property

Use Addition Properties

Prerequisite Skill from Grade 4

Common Error Students may forget to add all of the addends. Have students place a dot next to each addend as they use it to create the sum.

- Use Skill 11 for scaffolded review of the concept.

Teaching Tip Before students use the worksheet, you may wish to have them use place-value blocks to model $8 + 5 = 13$ and $5 + 8 = 13$ to show the Commutative Property of Addition.

Skill 12

Objective Add and subtract up to 6-digit whole numbers.

Answers
1. 96,414 2. 36,129
3. 9,391 4. 68,273
5. 11,953 6. 102,088
7. 678,492 8. 61,215

Add and Subtract Greater Numbers

Prerequisite Skill from Grade 4

Common Error Students may forget to add regrouped numbers. Remind student to add from right to left, beginning with the digit with the least value.

- Use Skill 12 for scaffolded review of the concept.
- For more practice use *Ways to Success* 2d.

Teaching Tip Before students use the worksheet, you may wish to have them use a place-value chart to find the sum of the numbers 52,179 and 28,325. (80,504) Then have them use a place-value chart to find the difference of the same numbers. (23,854)

Skill 13

Objective Estimate sums and differences.

Answers
1. 4,000; 5,000; 9,000
2. 10,000; 2,000; 12,000
3. 5,300; 4,700; 600
4. 8,900; 5,500; 3,400
5. 9,330; 6,330; 3,000
6. 3,500; 2,300; 5,800
7. 4,000 8. 5,300 9. 1,200
10. 11,490

Estimate Sums and Differences

Prerequisite Skill from Grade 4

Common Error   Students may misunderstand the rules for rounding the number 5.

- Use Skill 13 for scaffolded review of the concept.
- For more practice use *Ways to Success* 2b.

Teaching Tip   Before students use the worksheet, you may wish to have them practice estimating the sum and difference of 4,359 and 2,125 by rounding to the nearest thousand, hundred, and ten.

Skill 14

Objective   Solve equations.

Answers
1. $n = 7$ 2. $x = 9$ 3. $c = 3$
4. $n = 6$ 5. $y = 2$ 6. $a = 5$
7. $d = 8$ 8. $n = 3$ 9. $p = 8$
10. $n = 7$

Equations

Prerequisite Skill from Grade 4

Common Error   Students may misinterpret models of equations.

- Use Skill 14 for scaffolded review of the concept.
- For more practice use *Ways to Success* 2e.

Teaching Tip   Before students use the worksheet, you may wish to have them use counters to solve the equations $n + 8 = 14$ and $12 - x = 4$.

Skill 15

Objective   Use addition properties to evaluate algebraic expressions.

Answers
1. 14 2. (7 + 3) + 2; 10 + 2; 12 3. 43 + (7 + 5); (43 + 7) + 5; 50 + 5; 55 4. 41 + 20; 61 5. 7 + (53 + 25); (7 + 53) + 25; 60 + 25; 85 6. 93 + (21 + 7); 93 + (7 + 21); (93 + 7) + 21; 100 + 21; 121 7. 56 + 0; 56 8. (8 + 15) −15; 8 + (15 − 15); 8 + 0; 8 9. (10 + 5) − 15; 15 − 15; 0

Addition Properties and Expressions

Skill from Chapter 2

Common Error   Students may reverse the number and variable in subtraction expressions. For each word phrase that describes subtraction, have students answer these questions; What is being decreased? What is being subtracted from?

- Use Skill 15 for scaffolded review of the concept.
- For more practice use *Ways to Success* 2.1 or blackline masters Practice 2.1 or Homework 2.1.
- For small group intervention use the Intervention Activity, *Teacher Edition*, p. 30.

Teaching Tip   Before students use the worksheet, you may wish to have them practice different ways to say the expressions 8 + 5 (eight plus five, five more than eight, etc.) and 12 − 7 (twelve minus seven, seven less than twelve, etc.).

Skill 16

Objective Estimate sums and differences.

Answers
1. $7,000 + 1,000 = 8,000$; 8,000 2. $9,000 + 6,000 = 15,000$; 15,000 3. $7,000 - 6,000 = 1,000$; 1,000
4. $9,000 - 3,000 = 6,000$; 6,000 5. $4,000 + 5,000 = 9,000$; 9,000 6. $7,000$; $6,000 + 3,000 = 9,000$; 7,000; 9,000 7. 15,000; 17,000

Estimate More Sums and Differences

Skill from Chapter 2

Common Error Students may round the numbers within an addition and subtraction exercise to different places.

- Use Skill 16 for scaffolded review of the concept.
- For more practice use *Ways to Success* 2.2 or blackline masters Practice 2.2 or Homework 2.2.
- For small group intervention use the Intervention Activity, *Teacher Edition*, p. 33.

Teaching Tip Before students use the worksheet, you may wish to have them practice estimating the sum and difference of 3,695 and 2,129 using rounding to the greatest place. (6,000; 2,000)

Skill 17

Objective Add and subtract up to 6-digit whole numbers.

Answers
1. 1; 1; 598,611 2. 7; 11; 1; 15; 621,089 3. 538,322
4. 336,980 5. 138,489
6. 312,189

Subtract and Add Greater Numbers *Skill from Chapter 2*

Common Error Students may add or subtract numbers that are not in the same place.

- Use Skill 17 for scaffolded review of the concept.
- For more practice use *Ways to Success* 2.3 or blackline masters Practice 2.3 or Homework 2.3.
- For small group intervention use the Intervention Activity, *Teacher Edition*, p. 36.

Teaching Tip Before students use the worksheet, you may wish to have them use a place-value chart to find the sum of the numbers 359,042 and 298,321. (657,363) Then have them use a place-value chart to find the difference of the same numbers. (60,721)

Skill 18

Objective Solve addition and subtraction equations using mental math.

Answers
1. $3 + m = 12$; 9
2. $x + 23 = 25$; 2
3. $17 - m = 9$; 8
4. $47 - k = 17$; 30 5. 75
6. 34 7. 35 8. 50

Use Mental Math *Skill from Chapter 2*

Common Error Students may misinterpret the models in order to solve the equations.

- Use Skill 18 for scaffolded review of the concept.
- For more practice use *Ways to Success* 2.5 or blackline masters Practice 2.5 or Homework 2.5.
- For small group intervention use the Intervention Activity, *Teacher Edition*, p. 41.

Teaching Tip Before students use the worksheet, you may wish to remind them that the total of the two lesser quantities is equal to the greater quantity.

Skill 19

Objective Solve problems by identifying relevant information in a word problem.

Answers
1. 5,212 **2.** 2,125
3. children **4.** *See student page.* **5.** 5,212 **6.** 3,087
7. *See student page.*; 204

Problem Solving:
Identify Relevant Information *Skill from Chapter 2*

Common Error Students may identify more information than they need to solve the problem.

- Use Skill 19 for scaffolded review of the concept.
- For more practice use *Ways to Success* 2.6 or blackline masters Problem Solving 2.6, Practice 2.6 or Homework 2.6.

Teaching Tip As students complete the worksheet, you may wish to have them circle the relevant information and cross out the extra information in each problem.

Chapter 3: Multiply Whole Numbers

Skill 20

Objective Use multiplication properties.

Answers
1. 27 **2.** $2 \times 4 = 8$ **3.** $3 \times 5 = 15$ **4.** $10 \times 8 = 80$
5. 8; $24 = 24$ **6.** 5; 9; $45 = 45$ **7.** 4×2; $4 \times 4 = 2 \times 8$; $16 = 16$ **8.** $(7 \times 5) \times 1$; $7 \times 5 = 35 \times 1$; $35 = 35$
9. 64 **10.** 48 **11.** 0 **12.** 0
13. 6; Associative Property
14. 26; Identity Property
15. 0; Zero Property **16.** 6; Commutative Property; Zero Property

Use Multiplication Properties *Prerequisite Skill from Grade 4*

Common Error In using multiplication properties, students may use the wrong operation when writing an expression for a word phrase.

- Use Skill 20 for scaffolded review of the concept.
- For more practice use *Ways to Success* 3b.

Teaching Tip Before students use the worksheet, you may wish to have them use graph paper to model arrays for $3 \times 9 = 27$ and $9 \times 3 = 27$ to show the Commutative Property of Multiplication.

Skill 21

Objective Multiply by one-digit numbers.

Answers
1. 735 **2.** 645 **3.** 926
4. 820 **5.** 816 **6.** 9,777
7. 6,524 **8.** 8,818 **9.** 7,660

Multiply by One-Digit Numbers *Prerequisite Skill from Grade 4*

Common Error Students may forget to record regrouping.

- Use Skill 21 for scaffolded review of the concept.
- For more practice use *Ways to Success* 3d.

Teaching Tip Before students use the worksheet, you may wish to have them use a place-value chart to multiply $1,259 \times 7$. (8,813)

Skill 22

Objective Estimate products.

Answers
1. 600 2. 800 3. 9,000
4. 30,000 5. 100; 700
6. 300; 600 7. 500; 3,000
8. 5,400 9. 6,000
10. 40,000 11. 6,000
12. 48,000

Estimate Products
Prerequisite Skill from Grade 4

Common Error Students may interpret an estimate as an exact answer.

- Use Skill 22 for scaffolded review of the concept.
- For more practice use *Ways to Success* 3f.

Teaching Tip Before students use the worksheet, you may wish to have them review the rules for rounding and practice rounding 4,359 to the greatest place. (4,000)

Skill 23

Objective Use multiplication properties to evaluate algebraic expressions.

Answers
1. 120 + 24; 144 2. 5; 20 × 7; 140 3. 5; 5; 150 + 25; 175 4. 2; 2; 16 × 10; 160 5. 57 6. 360 7. 0 8. 1,080 9. 63

Evaluate Expressions
Skill from Chapter 3

Common Error Students may use the wrong property when evaluating an expression.

- Use Skill 23 for scaffolded review of the concept.
- For more practice use *Ways to Success* 3.1, 3.2 or blackline masters Practice 3.1, 3.2 or Homework 3.1, 3.2.
- For small group intervention use the Intervention Activity, *Teacher Edition,* pp. 61 and 63.

Teaching Tip Before students use the worksheet, you may wish to have them use graph paper to model 7 × (3 + 4) to show the distributive property of multiplication.

Skill 24

Objective Multiply by two-digit numbers.

Answers
1. 972; 6,480; 7,452 2. 940; 7,050; 7,990 3. 254, 7,620; 7,874 4. 1,648; 8,240; 9,888

Multiply by Two-Digit Numbers
Skill from Chapter 3

Common Error While multiplying by two-digit numbers, students may misalign partial products or add regrouped digits twice.

- Use Skill 24 for scaffolded review of the concept.
- For more practice use *Ways to Success* 3.7 or blackline masters Practice 3.7 or Homework 3.7.
- For small group intervention use the Intervention Activity, *Teacher Edition,* p. 78.

Teaching Tip Before students use the worksheet, you may wish to have them use a place-value chart to multiply 153 × 38. (5,814)

Skill 25

Objective Estimate products of whole numbers.

Answers
1. 70; 30; 2,100 **2.** 40; 50; 2,000 **3.** 40; 2,800; 50; 4,000; 2,800, 4,000 **4.** 60; 4,200; 70; 5,600; 4,200, 5,600 **5.** $40 \times 50 = 2,000$; $50 \times 60 = 3,000$; 2,000, 3,000 **6.** $80 \times 20 = 1,600$; $90 \times 30 = 2,700$; 1,600, 2,700 **7.** $30 \times 20 = 600$; $40 \times 30 = 1,200$; 600, 1,200

Product Estimation
Skill from Chapter 3

Common Error Students may round factors incorrectly when estimating.

- Use Skill 25 for scaffolded review of the concept.
- For more practice use *Ways to Success* 3.6 or blackline masters Practice 3.6 or Homework 3.6.
- For small group intervention use the Intervention Activity, *Teacher Edition*, p. 75.

Teaching Tip Before students use the worksheet, you may wish to have them use front-end estimation to estimate the product of 38 and 21. (600)

Skill 26

Objective Solve problems by using logical reasoning.

Answers
1. Connor; Tina; Brad; Jolie **2.** drums; guitar; piano; bass **3.** See student page. **4.** No **5.** guitar; piano; bass **6.** drums; piano; bass; guitar **7.** bass; guitar; piano **8.** *See student page.* **9.** yellow, red

Problem Solving:
Logical Reasoning
Skill from Chapter 3

Common Error Students may use logical reasoning incorrectly and find a wrong answer.

- Use Skill 26 for scaffolded review of the concept.
- For more practice use *Ways to Success* 3.3 or blackline masters Problem Solving 3.3, Practice 3.3 or Homework 3.3.
- For small group intervention use the Intervention Activity, *Teacher Edition*, p. 66.

Teaching Tip Before students use the worksheet, you may wish to have them use manipulatives to act out a logical reasoning problem.

Chapter 4: Divide by One-Digit Numbers

Skill 27

Objective Estimate quotients.

Answers
1. 40 **2.** $2 \times 8 = 16$; $160 \div 8$; 20 **3.** $5 \times 6 = 30$; 50 **4.** $4 \times 7 = 28$; 40 **5.** $2 \times 7 = 14$; 20 **6.** $5 \times 8 = 40$; 50 **7.** $3 \times 5 = 15$; 30 **8.** $9 \times 3 = 27$; 90

Estimate Quotients
Prerequisite Skill from Grade 4

Common Error Students may write an incorrect number of zeros in the estimated quotient.

- Use Skill 27 for scaffolded review of the concept.
- For more practice use *Ways to Success* 4a.

Teaching Tip Before students use the worksheet, you may wish to have them practice using basic facts and multiples of ten to estimate the quotient of $357 \div 7$. ($35 \div 7 = 5$; $350 \div 7 = 50$)

Skill 28

Objective Divide 4-digit dividends by 1-digit divisors.

Answers
1. 900; 939 R1 **2.** 400; 446
3. 3,000 ÷ 5 = 600; 668 R1
4. 4,200 ÷ 7 = 600; 603 R5
5. 7,200 ÷ 9 = 800; 814
6. 2,400 ÷ 8 = 300; 313
7. 5,400 ÷ 9 = 600; 611 R5
8. 6,300 ÷ 7 = 900; 897 R4

Divide Whole Numbers *Prerequisite Skill from Grade 4*

Common Error Students may be confused when they encounter a zero in the dividend and may forget to bring down a zero as if it were any other digit.

- Use Skill 28 for scaffolded review of the concept.

Teaching Tip Before students use the worksheet, you may wish to have them use a place-value chart to divide 2,006 ÷ 4. (501 R2)

Skill 29

Objective Find factors and multiples of a number.

Answers
1. 12; 6; 4; 4; 6; 12 **2.** 20;
10; 5; 5; 10; 20 **3.** 24; 12; 8;
6; 3; 4; 6; 8; 12; 24 **4.** 8;
16; 24; 32 **5.** 10; 20; 30; 40
6. 4; 8; 12; 16

Find Factors and Multiples *Prerequisite Skill from Grade 4*

Common Error Students may mix up factors and multiples.

- Use Skill 29 for scaffolded review of the concept.

Teaching Tip Before students use the worksheet, you may wish to have them review the use of a multiplication table to find factors and multiples.

Skill 30

Objective Use mental math to divide multiples of 10.

Answers
1. 90; 900; 9,000; 900 **2.** 8;
80; 800; 8,000; 8,000 **3.** 3;
30; 300; 3,000; 30 **4.** 1; 10;
100; 1,000; 1,000 **5.** 4; 40;
400; 4,000; 4,000 **6.** 60
7. 300 **8.** 9,000 **9.** 500
10. 700 **11.** 40 **12.** 2,000
13. 5,000

Use Mental Math to Divide *Prerequisite Skill from Grade 4*

Common Error Students may confuse the number of zeros in the pattern of zeros when dividing multiples of 10.

- Use Skill 30 for scaffolded review of the concept.
- For more practice use *Ways to Success* 3e.

Teaching Tip Before students use the worksheet, you may wish to have them use basic facts to help them divide 56 ÷ 8; 560 ÷ 80; 5,600 ÷ 80; 56,000 ÷ 80. (7; 7; 70; 700)

Skill 31

Objective Estimate quotients.

Answers
1. 400
2. $2,100 \div 3$; $2,100 \div 3$; 700
3. $2,500 \div 5$; $2,500 \div 5$; 500
4. $2,400 \div 6$; $2,400 \div 6$; 400
5. $4,000 \div 8$; $4,000 \div 8$; 500
6. $2,700 \div 9$; $2,700 \div 9$; 300

Use Compatible Numbers
Skill from Chapter 4

Common Error Students may write an incorrect number of zeros in the estimated quotient.

- Use Skill 31 for scaffolded review of the concept.
- For more practice use *Ways to Success* 4.1 or blackline masters Practice 4.1 or Homework 4.1.
- For small group intervention use the Intervention Activity, *Teacher Edition*, p. 87.

Teaching Tip Before students use the worksheet, you may wish to have them use basic facts to find the place value of the first digit of the quotient for $4,350 \div 7$ ($6 \times 7 = 42$, so 6 is the first digit) and $3,875 \div 4$ ($4 \times 9 = 36$, so 9 is the first digit).

Skill 32

Objective Divide by 1-digit divisors.

Check students' work.
Answers
1. 73 2. 175 R2 3. 216 R1
4. 189 R1 5. 655 6. 629 R1

Divide by 1-Digit Divisors
Skill from Chapter 4

Common Error Students may misplace the first digit of the quotient.

- Use Skill 32 for scaffolded review of the concept.
- For more practice use *Ways to Success* 4.2 or blackline masters Practice 4.2 or Homework 4.2.
- For small group intervention use the Intervention Activity, *Teacher Edition*, p. 89.

Teaching Tip Before students use the worksheet, you may wish to have them review the steps for long division (divide, multiply, subtract, bring down).

Skill 33

Objective Determine when to put zeros in the quotient.

Answers
1. 106 R2 2. 605 R2
3. 3,077 R1 4. 830 R3
5. 408 R4 6. 4,062 R1
7. 750 R3 8. 704 R1

Zeros in the Quotient
Skill from Chapter 4

Common Error Students may write too many zeros in the quotient.

- Use Skill 33 for scaffolded review of the concept.
- For more practice use *Ways to Success* 4.5 or blackline masters Practice 4.5 or Homework 4.5.
- For small group intervention use the Intervention Activity, *Teacher Edition*, p. 97.

Teaching Tip Before students use the worksheet, you may wish to have them divide 425 by 4 (106 R1). Have students multiply the quotient by the divisor and then add the remainder to check their answers. ($106 \times 4 = 424 + 1 = 455$)

Skill 34

Objective Use the rules for divisibility.

Answers
Answers may vary. Check students' work.

Use Divisibility Rules
Skill from Chapter 4

Common Error Students may only check the last digit to see whether it is divisible by a given number.

- Use Skill 34 for scaffolded review of the concept.
- For more practice use *Ways to Success* 4.4 or blackline masters Practice 4.4 or Homework 4.4.
- For small group intervention use the Intervention Activity, *Teacher Edition*, p. 94.

Teaching Tip Before students use the worksheet, you may wish to have them find out if 150 can be divided by 2, 3, 4, 5, 9, and 10 without a remainder. Then introduce each divisibility rule and have students apply it to the number 150.

Skill 35

Objective Solve multiplication and division equations using mental math.

Answers
1. $y = 5$ **2.** $b = 7$
3. $a = 10$ **4.** $k = 8$
5. $p = 7$ **6.** $t = 9$ **7.** $y = 12$
8. $b = 3$ **9.** $p = 50$
10. $t = 48$ **11.** $k = 5$
12. $a = 4$

Mental Math Computation
Skill from Chapter 4

Common Error Students may forget their multiplication and division facts.

- Use Skill 35 for scaffolded review of the concept.
- For more practice use *Ways to Success* 4.7 or blackline masters Practice 4.7 or Homework 4.7.
- For small group intervention use the Intervention Activity, *Teacher Edition*, p. 104.

Teaching Tip Before students use the worksheet, you may wish to have them use a multiplication table to help them solve the equations.

Skill 36

Objective Solve problems by using guess and check.

Answers
1. 20 **2.** 3 times **3.** 3; 4
4. *Check students' tables.*
5. 3 **6.** 16 **7.** *Check students' tables.* **8.** 6 vests; 6 sweatshirts; 12 T-shirts
9. 8 and 4

Problem Solving:
Guess and Check
Skill from Chapter 4

Common Error Students may have difficulty narrowing down their guesses to come to a solution.

- Use Skill 36 for scaffolded review of the concept.
- For more practice use *Ways to Success* 4.6 or blackline masters Problem Solving 4.6, Practice 4.6 or Homework 4.6.
- For small group intervention use the Intervention Activity, *Teacher Edition*, p. 100.

Teaching Tip As students use the worksheet, you may wish to give students examples of reasonable guesses and unreasonable guesses for the problems given.

Chapter 5: Divide by 2-Digit Numbers

Skill 37

Objective Divide 3-digit dividends with 1- and 2-digit divisors.

Answers
1. 60; 61 R17; 61 × 21 = 1,281; 1,281 + 17 = 1,298 **2.** 40; 20; 21 R3; 21 × 42 = 882; 882 + 3 = 885 **3.** 1,800 ÷ 30 = 60; 61 R8; 61 × 31 = 1,891; 1,891 + 8 = 1,899 **4.** 1,600 ÷ 40 = 40; 41 R4; 41 × 41 = 1,681; 1,681 + 4 = 1,685

Divide Three-Digit Dividends   *Prerequisite Skill from Grade 4*

Common Error Students may use too many or too few zeros in the quotient.

- Use Skill 37 for scaffolded review of the concept.
- For more practice use *Ways to Success* 5b.

Teaching Tip Before students use the worksheet, you may wish to have them practice their basic facts by dividing 36 by 6, 360 by 6, 3600 by 6, 360 by 60, and 3600 by 60. (6; 60; 600; 6; 60)

Skill 38

Objective Use order of operations.

Answers
1. 8; 9; 72; 75 **2.** 20 × 3 + 10; 60 + 10; 70 **3.** 18 ÷ 9 + 5; 2 + 5; 7 **4.** 90 ÷ 3 − 8 × 2; 30 − 16; 14 **5.** 10 − 6 ÷ 2 + 16 × 2; 10 − 3 + 32; 39

Order of Operations   *Prerequisite Skill from Grade 4*

Common Error Students may work from left to right, rather than following the order of operations.

- Use Skill 38 for scaffolded review of the concept.
- For more practice use *Ways to Success* 5f.

Teaching Tip Before students use the worksheet, you may wish to have them solve 6 + 4 ÷ 2 × (7 + 3) using the order of operations. (26)

Skill 39

Objective Divide by 2-digit divisors.

Check students' work.
Answers
1. 8 R2; 338 **2.** 3 R2 **3.** 3 R14 **4.** 5 R71 **5.** 4 R3

Divide by Two-Digit Divisors   *Skill from Chapter 5*

Common Error Students may forget to record the remainder, or forget to add in the remainder when they are checking their answer.

- Use Skill 39 for scaffolded review of the concept.
- For more practice use *Ways to Success* 5.2 or blackline masters Practice 5.2 or Homework 5.2.
- For small group intervention use the Intervention Activity, *Teacher Edition,* p. 113.

Teaching Tip Before students use the worksheet, you may wish to remind them to compare the remainder to the divisor.

Skill 40

Objective Adjust the quotient.

Answers
1. 30; 23 R5 **2.** 40; 32 R15
3. 10; 40; 31 R2 **4.** 40;
51 R3 **5.** 30; 38 R14 **6.** 20;
40; 48 R2

Adjust the Quotient
Skill from Chapter 5

Common Error Students may not adjust their estimates.

- Use Skill 40 for scaffolded review of the concept.
- For more practice use *Ways to Success* 5.4 or blackline masters Practice 5.4 or Homework 5.4.
- For small group intervention use the Intervention Activity, *Teacher Edition*, p. 119.

Teaching Tip Before students use the worksheet, you may wish to have them decide if the following estimates are too large or too small: $65 \div 22 = 4$, $158 \div 25 = 5$, $356 \div 38 = 10$. (too large; too small; too large)

Skill 41

Objective Divide with greater numbers.

Answers
1. 57 R15 **2.** 224 R8
3. 84 R4 **4.** 93 R14
5. 386 R3

Divide With Greater Numbers
Skill from Chapter 5

Common Error Students may have difficulty lining up the first digit of the quotient.

- Use Skill 41 for scaffolded review of the concept.
- For more practice use *Ways to Success* 5.5 or blackline masters Practice 5.5 or Homework 5.5.
- For small group intervention use the Intervention Activity, *Teacher Edition*, p. 122.

Teaching Tip Before students use the worksheet, you may wish to have them estimate and determine the place value of the first digit of the quotient for the following equations: $3,598 \div 25$; $67,854 \div 85$.
(1, hundreds place; 7, hundreds place)

Skill 42

Objective Use the correct order of operations.

Answers
1. 2; $64 + 15 \times 2$; $64 + 30$;
94 **2.** 5 + $7^2 \div 7$; 5 + 49
$\div$ 7; 5 + 7; 12 **3.** $5^2 - 12$
$\div 4 + 4$; $25 - 12 \div 4 + 4$,
$25 - 3 + 4$; 26 **4.** $3^2 + 5^2$
$\times 2$; $9 + 25 \times 2$; $9 + 50$;
59 **5.** $12 \div 2^2 + 3^2 - 6$; 12
$\div 4 + 9 - 6$; $3 + 9 - 6$; 6

Use Order of Operations
Skill from Chapter 5

Common Error Students may ignore the rules for order of operations and simplify all expressions by performing the operations from left to right.

- Use Skill 42 for scaffolded review of the concept.
- For more practice use *Ways to Success* 5.6 or blackline masters Practice 5.6 or Homework 5.6.
- For small group intervention use the Intervention Activity, *Teacher Edition*, p. 126.

Teaching Tip Before students use the worksheet, you may wish to have them use a mnemonic device such as "Please Excuse My Dear Aunt Sally" to help them remember the order of operations. (Parentheses, Exponents, Multiplication, Division, Addition, Subtraction)

Skill 43

Objective Solve a problem by interpreting remainders.

Answers
1. 32 2. 7 3. *See student page.* 4. divide 5. 4 6. No; Yes 7. No 8. No 9. 5; 5 10. 15 full bags 11. 4 books

Problem Solving:
Interpret Remainders
Skill from Chapter 5

Common Error Students may have difficulty deciding when to use the remainder as the answer.

- Use Skill 43 for scaffolded review of the concept.
- For more practice use *Ways to Success* 5.7 or blackline masters Problem Solving 5.7, Practice 5.7 or Homework 5.7.
- For small group intervention use the Intervention Activity, *Teacher Edition,* p. 130.

Teaching Tip Before students use the worksheet, you may wish to have them think of a word problem for the equation $305 \div 25$ and determine how to interpret the remainder. (*For example:* 25 students are going to share 305 cookies. How many cookies will be left over? 5 cookies will be left over, the answer is the remainder.)

Chapter 6: Units of Measure

Skill 44

Objective Convert units of capacity and mass.

Answers
1. $6 \times 1,000 = 6,000$; 6,000 kg
2. $7 \times 1,000 = 7,000$; 7,000 mL
3. $8,000 \div 1,000 = 8$; 8 L
4. $5,000 \div 1,000 = 5$; 5 L
5. $8 \times 1,000 = 8,000$; 8,000 g
6. $2,000 \div 1,000 = 2$; 2 kg
7. $9,000 \div 1,000 = 9$; 9 L
8. 2,000 mL 9. 5,000 mL
10. 7 kg

Convert Units of Measure
Prerequisite Skill from Grade 4

Common Error Students may have difficulty identifying which is the larger unit.

- Use Skill 44 for scaffolded review of the concept.
- For more practice use *Ways to Success* 6c.

Teaching Tip As students use the worksheet, you may wish to have them decide which unit is smaller for each of the following examples: milliliters and liters (milliliters are smaller); grams and kilograms (grams are smaller).

Skill 45

Objective Determine elapsed time.

Answers
1. 2 h; 30 min; 2 h + 30 min = 2 h 30 min
2. 2 h; 15 min; 2 h 15 min
3. 1; 50 min; 1 h 50 min
4. 3 h 20 min 5. 5 h 25 min
6. 7 h 15 min 7. 4 h 40 min

Find Elapsed Time
Prerequisite Skill from Grade 4

Common Error Students may forget to notice if the start time or end time is A.M. or P.M.

- Use Skill 45 for scaffolded review of the concept.

Teaching Tip Before students use the worksheet, you may wish to have them highlight the A.M. times with yellow and the P.M. times with blue.

Skill 46

Objective Convert between customary units of length, capacity, and weight.

Answers
1. 16 oz; 4 × 16 = 64; 64 oz **2.** 4 qt; 5 × 4 = 20; 20 qt **3.** 3 ft; 18 ÷ 3 = 6; 6 yd
4. 2,000 lb; 6,000 ÷ 2,000 = 3; 3T
5. 2 × 5,280 = 10,560; 10,560 ft **6.** 96 ÷ 16 = 6; 6 lb **7.** 52 ÷ 4 = 13; 13 gal
8. 80 oz **9.** 4 ft **10.** 11 pt

Convert Customary Units   *Skill from Chapter 6*

Common Error Students may be unsure whether to multiply or divide.

- Use Skill 46 for scaffolded review of the concept.
- For more practice use *Ways to Success* 6.2, 6.3, or blackline masters Practice 6.2, 6.3 or Homework 6.2, 6.3.
- For small group intervention use the Intervention Activity, *Teacher Edition,* pp. 151 and 154.

Teaching Tip Before students use the worksheet, you may wish to have them decide whether to multiply or divide for the following examples: 24 inches equals how many feet? (divide) 3 pounds equals how many ounces? (multiply)

Skill 47

Objective Convert between metric units of length, capacity, and mass.

Answers
1. 1,000; 12; 12,000; 12,000 **2.** 10, 15; 150; 150 **3.** 100; 2,300; 23; 23 **4.** 1,000; 7,000; 7; 7 **5.** 4 × 10 = 40; 40 **6.** 8,000 ÷ 1,000 = 8; 8 **7.** 500 ÷ 10 = 50; 50
8. 20,000 **9.** 35 **10.** 18,000

Convert Metric Units   *Skill from Chapter 6*

Common Error Students may use the wrong operations to convert measurements.

- Use Skill 47 for scaffolded review of the concept.
- For more practice use *Ways to Success* 6.4, 6.5, or blackline masters Practice 6.4, 6.5 or Homework 6.4, 6.5.
- For small group intervention use the Intervention Activity, *Teacher Edition,* pp. 159 and 162.

Teaching Tip Before students use the worksheet, you may wish to remind them of how to convert measurements: smaller unit to larger unit you divide; larger unit to smaller unit you multiply.

Skill 48

Objective Add and subtract measurements.

Answers
1. 6 ft, 4 in. **2.** 13 lb, 1 oz **3.** 15 gal, 2 qt **4.** 2 h, 35 min **5.** 2 h, 51 min **6.** 7 ft, 5 in. **7.** 4 h, 33 min

Add and Subtract Measurements   *Skill from Chapter 6*

Common Error Students may rename smaller units without changing larger units.

- Use Skill 48 for scaffolded review of the concept.
- For more practice use *Ways to Success* 6.6 or blackline masters Practice 6.6 or Homework 6.6.
- For small group intervention use the Intervention Activity, *Teacher Edition,* p. 165.

Teaching Tip Before students use the worksheet, you may wish to have them find the sum of 3 feet 8 inches and 2 feet 10 inches. Lead them through the regrouping of feet and inches. Then have them find the difference. (6 feet 6 inches; 10 inches)

Skill 49

Objective Solve multi-step problems.

Answers
1. 15 min 2. 7:40 A.M.
3. 8:05 A.M. 4. *See student page.* 5. 25 min + 15 min = 40 min 6. 40 min
7. 55 min 8. 1 hr, 5 min

Problem Solving:
Solve Multi-Step Problems
Skill from Chapter 6

Common Error Students may perform operations in the wrong order.

- Use Skill 49 for scaffolded review of the concept.
- For more practice use *Ways to Success* 6.7 or blackline masters Problem Solving 6.7, Practice 6.7 or Homework 6.7.

Teaching Tip As students use the worksheet, you may wish to have them use a demonstration clock to help them solve each problem.

Chapter 7: Graph Data

Skill 50

Objective Read and interpret a bar graph.

Answers
1. Favorite Winter Activity
2. 2 3. Snowboarding
4. Snowboarding 5. Ice Skating 6. 12 7. Sledding
8. 4 9. 40

Bar Graphs
Prerequisite Skill from Grade 4

Common Error Students may misread the lengths of the bars on the graph.

- Use Skill 50 for scaffolded review of the concept.
- For more practice use *Ways to Success* 7a.

Teaching Tip As students use the worksheet, you may wish to give them an index card to line up the end of the bar with the number on the scale.

Skill 51

Objective Read and interpret a line graph.

Answers
1. Daily Temperatures at Noon 2. 5 3. Fahrenheit, or °F 4. fell 5. rose 6. fell
7. Wednesday; 15°F
8. Friday; 35°F

Line Graphs
Prerequisite Skill from Grade 4

Common Error Students may misread intervals.

- Use Skill 51 for scaffolded review of the concept.
- For more practice use *Ways to Success* 7c.

Teaching Tip Before students use the worksheet, you may wish to help them see that all horizontal lines are parallel to one another, as are the vertical lines. Therefore, the difference in the temperature from one line to the next is the same.

Skill 52

Objective Analyze different types of graphs.

Answers
1. Wednesday 2. Tuesday
3. Wednesday 4. 2
5. 3:00 P.M.. 6. 20° F
7. rose 8. fell 9. playing
soccer 10. homework
11. about $\frac{1}{8}$

Analyze Graphs
Prerequisite Skill from Grade 4

Common Error Students may misread the circle graph.

- Use Skill 52 for scaffolded review of the concept.
- For more practice use *Ways to Success* 7d.

Teaching Tip Before students use the worksheet, you may wish to review how to interpret circle graphs. Provide students with labeled models of circle graphs that show $\frac{1}{2}$, $\frac{1}{4}$, and $\frac{1}{8}$.

Skill 53

Objective Use a double bar graph to compare data.

Answers
1. Music Lessons
2. Number of Students
3. 10 4. instrument 5. boys;
girls 6. 70; 50 7. flute
8. 20 9. 120 10. 60

Double Bar Graphs
Skill from Chapter 7

Common Error Students may transpose data sets.

- Use Skill 53 for scaffolded review of the concept.
- For more practice use *Ways to Success* 7.1 or blackline masters Practice 7.1 or Homework 7.1.
- For small group intervention use the Intervention Activity, *Teacher Edition*, p. 175.

Teaching Tip As students use the worksheet, you may wish to have them make a table of the data for each category.

Skill 54

Objective Make and use histograms.

Answers
1. 10 2. 0–4, 5–9, 10–14,
15–19 3. 0–4 4. 15–19
5. 2 6. No. *Check students'
answers.* 7. 4 8. $20–$29

Histograms
Skill from Chapter 7

Common Error Students may confuse the scale and the intervals.

- Use Skill 54 for scaffolded review of the concept.
- For more practice use *Ways to Success* 7.2 or blackline masters Practice 7.2 or Homework 7.2.
- For small group intervention use the Intervention Activity, *Teacher Edition*, p. 177.

Teaching Tip Before students use the worksheet, you may wish to label the scale on the vertical axis and the intervals on the horizontal axis.

Skill 55

Objective Use double line graphs.

Answers
1. Distance Traveled
2. Distance in miles
3. Frank's data **4.** 10; 5; Brett **5.** 25 miles; 20 miles; 5 miles **6.** 10 miles

Double Line Graphs
Skill from Chapter 7

Common Error Students may read the wrong line on a double line graph.

- Use Skill 55 for scaffolded review of the concept.
- For more practice use *Ways to Success* 7.3 or blackline masters Practice 7.3 or Homework 7.3.
- For small group intervention use the Intervention Activity, *Teacher Edition,* p. 180.

Teaching Tip Before students use the worksheet, you may wish to highlight each line in a different color on the graph and in the key.

Skill 56

Objective Decide which graph is most appropriate to display data.

Answers
1. pictograph **2.** bar graph
3. line graph **4.** circle graph
5. histogram

Choose Appropriate Graphs
Skill from Chapter 7

Common Error Students may choose an inappropriate graph.

- Use Skill 56 for scaffolded review of the concept.
- For more practice use *Ways to Success* 7.4 or blackline masters Practice 7.4 or Homework 7.4.
- For small group intervention use the Intervention Activity, *Teacher Edition,* p. 183.

Teaching Tip Before students use the worksheet, you may wish to have them think about the type of graph they would use to show temperature changes over time, students' favorite pets, and the heights of students in the fifth grade. (line graph, bar or circle graph, histogram)

Skill 57

Objective Identify and analyze misleading graphs.

Answers
1. No **2.** No; Yes **3.** 25
4. 25 **5.** No **6.** Graph A

Misleading Graphs
Skill from Chapter 7

Common Error Students may think that increasing the interval makes the differences in data seem greater.

- Use Skill 57 for scaffolded review of the concept.
- For more practice use *Ways to Success* 7.5 or blackline masters Practice 7.5 or Homework 7.5.
- For small group intervention use the Intervention Activity, *Teacher Edition,* p. 185.

Teaching Tip Before students use the worksheet, you may wish to have them graph the following data set using intervals of 2 and then graph the same data using intervals of 20. Data set: 3, 25, 38, 40.

Skill 58

Objective Solve problems by identifying relevant information in a graph.

Answers
1. Grades 5 and 6
2. *See students' page.*
3. *See students' page.*
4. 12; 14; 26 **5.** 26; Jupiter
6. 26; 30; 28 **7.** Peg; 30

Problem Solving:
Identify Information in a Graph   *Skill from Chapter 7*

Common Error Students may read the wrong bar when interpreting the double bar graph.

- Use Skill 58 for scaffolded review of the concept.
- For more practice use *Ways to Success* 7.6 or blackline masters Problem Solving 7.6, Practice 7.6 or Homework 7.6.

Teaching Tip As students use the worksheet, you may wish to have them highlight the question being asked and the relevant information from the graph.

Chapter 8: Data and Statistics

Skill 59

Objective Read and interpret line plots and stem-and-leaf plots.

Answers
1. 7 **2.** 7 **3.** 4 **4.** 4 **5.** 19
6. 31 **7.** 31 **8.** 10

Line Plots and Stem-and-Leaf Plots   *Prerequisite Skill from Grade 4*

Common Error When using stem-and-leaf plots to find the mean or median, Students may count the stems as outcomes.

- Use Skill 59 for scaffolded review of the concept.
- For more practice use *Ways to Success* 8c.

Teaching Tip As students use the worksheet, you may wish to have them circle or color-code the stems to differentiate them from the leaves.

Skill 60

Objective Find median, mode, and range.

Answers
1. 20, 20, 25, 30, 35, 35, 35, 35, 40, 45, 50 **2.** 11; 35
3. 35 **4.** 35 **5.** 50; 20 **6.** 30
7. 12, 15, 15, 15, 17, 18, 18, 20, 23 **8.** Median: 17; Mode: 15; Range: 11

Median, Mode, and Range   *Prerequisite Skill from Grade 4*

Common Error Students may confuse the meanings of the words median, mode, and range.

- Use Skill 60 for scaffolded review of the concept.
- For more practice use *Ways to Success* 8b.

Teaching Tip Before students use the worksheet, you may wish to have them practice finding the median, mode and range for the data set: 12, 4, 8, 1, 21, 19, 4, 39. (median: 12; mode: 4; range: 38)

Skill 61

Objective Use a stem-and-leaf plot to display data.

Answers
1. 17, 19, 23, 25, 25, 28, 28, 28, 30, 30, 32, 35, 51
2. *Check students' stem-and-leaf plots.* 3. 51 4. 1, 2, 3, 5
5. 0, 1, 2, 3, 5, 7, 8, 9 6. 28
7. 28 8. 34 9. 32, 33, 37, 38, 45, 48, 48, 48, 53, 58, 59
10. *Check students' stem-and-leaf plots.* 11. Mode: 48, Median: 48; Range: 27

Use Stem-and-Leaf Plots   *Skill from Chapter 8*

Common Error Students may forget to use the stem as the tens place for the data.

- Use Skill 61 for scaffolded review of the concept.
- For more practice use *Ways to Success* 8.3 or blackline masters Practice 8.3 or Homework 8.3.
- For small group intervention use the Intervention Activity, *Teacher Edition,* p. 199.

Teaching Tip Before students use the worksheet, you may wish to have them practice reading aloud the data from a stem-and-leaf plot.

Skill 62

Objective Find the mean, median, mode, and range of a set of data.

Answers
1. 0, 1, 1, 2, 2, 2, 2, 3, 3, 4
2. 20 3. 10 4. 2 5. 2; 2
6. 2 7. 2 8. 4; 0 9. 4

Mean, Median, Mode and Range   *Skill from Chapter 8*

Common Error Students may forget to arrange the data from least to greatest before finding the median.

- Use Skill 62 for scaffolded review of the concept.
- For more practice use *Ways to Success* 8.2 or blackline masters Practice 8.2 or Homework 8.2.
- For small group intervention use the Intervention Activity, *Teacher Edition,* p. 196.

Teaching Tip Before students use the worksheet, you may wish to have them find the mean, median, mode, and range for the data set: 12, 16, 4, 8, 32, 1, 32. (mean: 15; median: 12; mode: 32; range 31)

Skill 63

Objective Draw conclusions from data displays.

Answers
1. 5.8; 6; 6 2. 6 3. mean, median, mode 4. mean; median; mode; 6; $6 5. 4; 3.5; 2 6. No 7. mode; 2

Draw Conclusions   *Skill from Chapter 8*

Common Error Students may always choose the mode as the best representation for every set of data, because it occurs most often.

- Use Skill 63 for scaffolded review of the concept.
- For more practice use *Ways to Success* 8.5 or blackline masters Practice 8.5 or Homework 8.5.
- For small group intervention use the Intervention Activity, *Teacher Edition,* p. 206.

Teaching Tip Before students use the worksheet, you may wish to have them show the following numbers on a line plot: 2, 2, 3, 3, 4, 4, 10, 10, 10. Then use questioning to help them see that since 6 of 9 data cluster around a point that is not close to the mode, the mode is not always the best representation of data.

Skill 64

Objective Solve problems by making a table.

Answers
1. 0−9, 10−19, 20−29, 30−35 **2−4.** *See students' page.* **5.** 2; 3; 4; 3 **6.** 20−29 **7.** *Check students' work.*
8. 3 **9.** 155; 159

Problem Solving:
Make a Table
Skill from Chapter 8

Common Error Students may exclude some data from their table.

- Use Skill 64 for scaffolded review of the concept.
- For more practice use *Ways to Success* 8.4 or blackline masters Problem Solving 8.4, Practice 8.4 or Homework 8.4.
- For small group intervention use the Intervention Activity, *Teacher Edition*, p. 202.

Teaching Tip As students use the worksheet, you may wish to have them cross out the data they have used as they list it on a table.

Chapter 9: Number Theory and Fraction Concepts

Skill 65

Objective Identify prime and composite numbers.

Answers
1. 11 **2.** 1; 2; 3; 4; 6; 12
3. 1; 7; prime; 1; 5; prime
4. 1; 3; 9; composite; 1; 13; prime **5.** 1; 3; 5; 15; composite **6.** 1; 2; 3; 6; 9; 18; composite

Prime and Composite Numbers
Prerequisite Skill from Grade 4

Common Error Students may misidentify prime and composite numbers.

- Use Skill 65 for scaffolded review of the concept.
- For more practice use *Ways to Success* 9a.

Teaching Tip Before students use the worksheet, you may wish to have them review the divisibility rules.

Skill 66

Objective Find factors and multiples of a number.

Answers
1. *Check students' answers.*
2. 4, 6 **3−8.** *Check students' answers.*

Factors and Multiples
Prerequisite Skill from Grade 4

Common Error Students may forget to list all factors.

- Use Skill 66 for scaffolded review of the concept.
- For more practice use *Ways to Success* 9b.

Teaching Tip Before students use the worksheet, you may wish to have them use a multiplication table to list all of the factors of 48.
(1, 2, 3, 4, 6, 8, 12, 16, 24, 48)

Skill 67

Objective Represent a fraction of a region, set, and a number.

Answers

1. $\frac{5}{9}$ 2. $\frac{1}{6}$ 3. $\frac{2}{5}$ 4. $\frac{6}{10}$ 5. $\frac{5}{6}$
6. $\frac{3}{5}$

Represent Fractions   *Prerequisite Skill from Grade 3*

Common Error Students may transpose the numerator and the denominator of a fraction.

- Use Skill 67 for scaffolded review of the concept.
- For more practice use *Ways to Success* 9c.

Teaching Tip Before students use the worksheet, you may wish to have them review that the denominator is always the total number of equal parts and that it is always written under the fraction bar.

Skill 68

Objective Compare and order fractions.

Answers

1. $<$ 2. $=$ 3. $<$ 4. $\frac{8}{12}$; $<$
5. $\frac{2}{3}$; $\frac{7}{9}$; $\frac{8}{9}$ 6. $\frac{5}{12}$, $\frac{3}{4}$; $\frac{11}{12}$

Compare and Order Fractions *Prerequisite Skill from Grade 4*

Common Error Students may use incorrect models.

- Use Skill 68 for scaffolded review of the concept.
- For more practice use *Ways to Success* 9g.

Teaching Tip Before students use the worksheet, you may wish to have them make and cut out models for halves, fourths, sixths, eighths and tenths.

Skill 69

Objective Write the prime factorization of numbers.

Answers

1. $20 = 5 \times 2 \times 2$
2. $54 = 2 \times 3 \times 3 \times 3$
3. $56 = 2 \times 2 \times 2 \times 7$
4. $50 = 5 \times 5 \times 2$

Prime Factorization   *Skill from Chapter 9*

Common Error Students may begin with numbers that are not factors of the given number.

- Use Skill 69 for scaffolded review of the concept.
- For more practice use *Ways to Success* 9.2 or blackline masters Practice 9.2 or Homework 9.2.
- For small group intervention use the Intervention Activity, *Teacher Edition*, p. 227.

Teaching Tip Before students use the worksheet, you may wish to have them use a factor tree to find the prime factorization of 24. $(2 \times 2 \times 2 \times 3)$

Skill 70

Objective Find common factors and the greatest common factor of two numbers.

Answers
1. 6 **2.** 8 **3.** 7 **4.** 6, 8, 12; 6, 10, 15; 6 **5.** 3, 9; 3, 5, 9, 15; 9 **6.** 1, 3, 7, 21; 1, 2, 4, 7, 8, 14, 28, 56; 1 **7.** 1, 2, 4, 8, 16, 32; 1, 2, 3, 4, 6, 8, 12, 16, 24, 48; 16

Greatest Common Factor
Skill from Chapter 9

Common Error Students may only list one of a pair of factors.

- Use Skill 70 for scaffolded review of the concept.
- For more practice use *Ways to Success* 9.3 or blackline masters Practice 9.3 or Homework 9.3.
- For small group intervention use the Intervention Activity, *Teacher Edition,* p. 230.

Teaching Tip Before students use the worksheet, you may wish to have them practice using a multiplication chart to list all of the factors for the following number pairs: 12 and 15; 35 and 49; 60 and 72. Then have students circle the greatest common factors for each pair. (3; 7; 12)

Skill 71

Objective Find common multiples and the least common multiple of two numbers.

Check students' answers.
Answers
1. 4 **2.** 18 **3.** 8 **4.** 48, 60, 72; 12 **5.** 20, 25, 30; 40, 50, 60; 10 **6.** 15, 30, 45, 60, 75, 90; 20, 40, 60, 80, 100, 120; 60 **7.** 16, 32, 48, 64, 80, 96; 24, 48, 72, 96, 120, 144; 48

Least Common Multiple
Skill from Chapter 9

Common Error Students may confuse the Greatest Common Factor and the Least Common Multiple.

- Use Skill 71 for scaffolded review of the concept.
- For more practice use *Ways to Success* 9.4 or blackline masters Practice 9.4 or Homework 9.4.
- For small group intervention use the Intervention Activity, *Teacher Edition,* p. 234.

Teaching Tip Before students use the worksheet, you may wish to have them practice using a 12 × 12 multiplication chart to list all of the multiples for the following number pairs: 3 and 4; 5 and 10; 4 and 6. Then have students circle the least common multiple for each pair. (12; 10; 12)

Skill 72

Objective Find equivalent fractions and write fractions in simplest form.

Answers
1. $\frac{6}{15}$ **2.** $\frac{6}{14}$ **3.** $\frac{15}{24}$ **4.** $\frac{2}{3}$ **5.** $\frac{6}{8}$
6. $\frac{5}{7}$ **7.** 2; $\frac{3}{5}$ **8.** 8; $\frac{3}{4}$

Equivalent Fractions and Simplest Form
Skill from Chapter 9

Common Error Students sometimes forget to list all the factors before choosing the GCF.

- Use Skill 72 for scaffolded review of the concept.
- For more practice use *Ways to Success* blackline masters 9.6 and Practice and Homework 9.6.
- For small group instruction use the Intervention Activity, *Teacher Edition,* p. 241.

Teaching Tip Before students use the worksheet, you may wish to have them write the prime factorization of the numerator and denominator and use this to make sure the fraction is in simplest form.

Skill 73

Objective Relate fractions, mixed numbers, and decimals.

Answers

1. 0.25 **2.** $\frac{79}{100}$; 0.79 **3.** $\frac{45}{100}$; 0.45 **4.** 2.33 **5.** $1\frac{50}{100}$; 1.5 **6.** $2\frac{18}{100}$; 2.18 **7.** $1\frac{20}{100}$; 1.2

Fractions, Mixed Numbers, and Decimals   *Skill from Chapter 9*

Common Error Students may mix up tenths and hundredths when changing fractions to decimals.

- Use Skill 73 for scaffolded review of the concept.

Teaching Tip Before students use the worksheet, you may wish to have them write the following fractions as both fractions and decimals: 5 tenths, 5 hundredths, 9 tenths, 9 hundredths. ($\frac{5}{10}$; 0.5; $\frac{5}{100}$; 0.05; $\frac{9}{10}$; 0.9; $\frac{9}{100}$; 0.09)

Skill 74

Objective Change decimals to fractions and change fractions to decimals.

Answers

1. 4; $\frac{4}{5}$ **2.** $\frac{13}{20}$ **3.** $\frac{6}{25}$ **4.** $\frac{9}{25}$; $4\frac{9}{25}$ **5.** $6\frac{2}{5}$ **6.** 0.75 **7.** 0.35 **8.** 0.26 **9.** 0.48

Change Decimals and Fractions   *Skill from Chapter 9*

Common Error Students may forget to multiply the numerator and the denominator by the same number to find equivalent fractions.

- Use Skill 74 for scaffolded review of the concept.
- For more practice use *Ways to Success* 9.8 or blackline masters Practice 9.8 or Homework 9.8.
- For small group instruction use the Intervention Activity, *Teacher Edition*, p. 247.

Teaching Tip Before students use the worksheet, you may wish to have them write the following decimals as mixed numbers: 3.1; 3.01; 15.5; 15.05. ($3\frac{1}{10}$; $3\frac{1}{100}$; $15\frac{5}{10}$; $15\frac{5}{100}$)

Skill 75

Objective Compare and order fractions and decimals.

Answers

1. $0.55 < 0.67$; $\frac{11}{20} < 0.67$ **2.** $\frac{60}{100}$; $\frac{60}{100} = 0.60$; $0.60 > 0.51$; $\frac{3}{5} > 0.51$ **3.** $0.25 < 0.3 < \frac{3}{5}$ **4.** $\frac{35}{100}$; 0.35; $0.2 < 0.33 < \frac{7}{20}$

Compare Decimals and Fractions   *Skill from Chapter 9*

Common Error Students may have difficulty changing a fraction to a decimal.

- Use Skill 75 for scaffolded review of the concept.
- For more practice use *Ways to Success* 9.9 or blackline masters Practice 9.9 or Homework 9.9.
- For small group instruction use the Intervention Activity, *Teacher Edition*, p. 250.

Teaching Tip Before students use the worksheet, you may wish to have them write $\frac{4}{5}$ and $\frac{9}{20}$ as decimals. (0.80; 0.45)

Skill 76

Objective Solve problems using logical reasoning.

Answers
1. 90 **2.** 6 **3.** *Check students' work.* **4.** 3, 5, 6, 9, 10 **5.** 18, 30 **6.** 18, 30 **7.** 18, 30 **8.** 2, 3, 6, 9, 18 **9.** 6, 9, 18 **10.** 6, 9

Problem Solving:
Use Logical Reasoning
Skill from Chapter 9

Common Error Students may neglect to check that their answer is reasonable.

- Use Skill 76 for scaffolded review of the concept.
- For more practice use *Ways to Success* blackline 9.7 and Problem Solving 9.7.
- For small group instruction use the Intervention Activity, *Teacher Edition*, p. 244.

Teaching Tip As students use the worksheet, you may wish to have them check if their answer is reasonable by rereading the problem.

Chapter 10: Add and Subtract Fractions

Skill 77

Objective Estimate sums of fractions.

Answers
1. $\frac{1}{3} < \frac{1}{2}; \frac{2}{5} < \frac{1}{2}$; The sum is less than 1.
2. $\frac{4}{9} < \frac{1}{2}; \frac{3}{10} < \frac{1}{2}$; The sum is less than 1.
3. $\frac{3}{4} > \frac{1}{2}; \frac{4}{8} = \frac{1}{2}$; The sum is greater than 1.

Estimate Fraction Sums
Prerequisite Skill from Grade 4

Common Error Students may incorrectly compare a fraction to $\frac{1}{2}$.

- Use Skill 77 for scaffolded review of the concept.
- For more practice use *Ways to Success* 10c.

Teaching Tip Before students use the worksheet, you may wish to have them review the concept that the numerator for a fraction equivalent to $\frac{1}{2}$ will have a numerator that is half its denominator.

Skill 78

Objective Add and subtract fractions with like denominators.

Answers
1. $\frac{7}{8}$ **2.** $\frac{6}{9}; \frac{2}{3}$ **3.** $\frac{5}{6}$ **4.** $\frac{5}{10}; \frac{1}{2}$
5. $\frac{1}{5}$ **6.** $\frac{2}{6}; \frac{1}{3}$ **7.** $\frac{4}{9}$ **8.** $\frac{3}{12}; \frac{1}{4}$

Fractions With Like Denominators
Prerequisite Skill from Grade 4

Common Error Students may add or subtract the denominators of the fractions.

- Use Skill 78 for scaffolded review of the concept.
- For more practice use *Ways to Success* 10b.

Teaching Tip Before students use the worksheet, you may wish to have them think of $\frac{3}{4}$ as 3 fourths, $\frac{2}{5}$ as 2 fifths, and $\frac{5}{6}$ as 5 sixths to focus them on the numerators and avoid adding the denominators.

Skill 79

Objective Add and subtract fractions with unlike denominators.

Answers

1. $\frac{2}{8}; \frac{1}{8}; \frac{3}{8}$ 2. $1\frac{1}{4}$

3. $\frac{8}{12}; \frac{4}{12}; \frac{4}{12}; \frac{1}{3}$ 4. $\frac{1}{6}$

Fractions With Unlike Denominators

Prerequisite Skill from Grade 4

Common Error Students may forget to first find equivalent fractions before adding or subtracting.

- Use Skill 79 for scaffolded review of the concept.
- For more practice use *Ways to Success* 10c, 10d.

Teaching Tip Before students use the worksheet, you may wish to have them review finding equivalent fractions for $\frac{2}{3}$ and $\frac{3}{4}$; $\frac{5}{6}$ and $\frac{4}{5}$; $\frac{3}{9}$ and $\frac{2}{3}$. ($\frac{8}{12}$ and $\frac{9}{12}$; $\frac{25}{30}$ and $\frac{24}{30}$; $\frac{3}{9}$ and $\frac{6}{9}$)

Skill 80

Objective Estimate fraction sums and differences.

Answers

1. $1\frac{1}{2}$ 2. $1; 1$ 3. $1 + 1 = 2;$ 2 4. $\frac{1}{2}; \frac{1}{2}$ 5. $1 - 1 = 0; 0$

Estimate with Fractions

Skill from Chapter 10

Common Error Students may use incorrect benchmarks to estimate a fraction sum or difference.

- Use Skill 80 for scaffolded review of the concept.
- For more practice use *Ways to Success* blackline masters 10.1 and Practice and Homework 10.1.
- For small group instruction, use the Intervention Activity, *Teacher Edition,* p. 257.

Teaching Tip Before students use the worksheet, you may wish to have them use a number line to help them decide whether the following fractions are closest to 0, $\frac{1}{2}$ or 1: $\frac{3}{5}; \frac{1}{6}; \frac{11}{12}$. ($\frac{1}{2}; 0; 1$)

Skill 81

Objective Add fractions and mixed numbers with like and unlike denominators.

Answers

1. $\frac{8}{12}; \frac{8}{12} + \frac{3}{12} = \frac{11}{12};$ $\frac{8}{12} + \frac{3}{12} = \frac{11}{12}$

2. $\frac{4}{10} + \frac{5}{10} = \frac{9}{10}$

3. $\frac{11}{12}$ 4. $\frac{11}{12}$ 5. $\frac{6}{15}; \frac{5}{15};$ $2\frac{6}{15} + 4\frac{5}{15} = 6\frac{11}{15}$ 6. $7\frac{17}{20}$

Add Fractions and Mixed Numbers

Skill from Chapter 10

Common Error Students may neglect to add the whole number to the whole-number sum after regrouping the sum of the fractions.

- Use Skill 81 for scaffolded review of the concept.
- For more practice use *Ways to Success* blackline masters 10.3 and Practice and Homework 10.3.
- For small group instruction, use the Intervention Activity, *Teacher Edition,* p. 261.

Teaching Tip Before students use the worksheet, you may wish to have them write the fractional sum as a mixed number first. Then have them add it to the whole-number sum.

Skill 82

Objective Subtract fractions and mixed numbers with like denominators.

Answers

1. $\frac{6}{8}$; $\frac{3}{4}$ 2. $\frac{4}{12}$; $\frac{1}{3}$ 3. $\frac{4}{10}$; $\frac{2}{5}$
4. $\frac{2}{6}$; $4\frac{2}{6}$; $4\frac{1}{3}$ 5. $6\frac{1}{3}$
6. $8\frac{11}{8}$; $5\frac{3}{4}$ 7. $3\frac{5}{5}$; $2\frac{2}{5}$

Subtract Fractions: Like Denominators
Skill from Chapter 10

Common Error Students may neglect to rename the whole number in order to subtract.

- Use Skill 82 for scaffolded review of the concept.
- For more practice use *Ways to Success* 10.5 or blackline masters Practice 10.5 or Homework 10.5.
- For small group instruction, use the Intervention Activity, *Teacher Edition,* p. 264.

Teaching Tip As students use the worksheet, you may wish to have them highlight the mixed numbers from which they are subtracting. Ask students if they need to rename these numbers to subtract.

Skill 83

Objective Subtract fractions and mixed numbers with unlike denominators.

Answers

1. 15; 8; $\frac{15}{20}$; $\frac{8}{20}$; $\frac{15}{20}$; $\frac{8}{20}$; $\frac{7}{20}$
2. 12, 10; 2 3. $\frac{7}{12}$ 4. $\frac{1}{10}$
5. 16; 15; 16; 15; 1 6. $3\frac{13}{30}$

Subtract With Unlike Denominators
Skill from Chapter 10

Common Error Students may write incorrect equivalent fractions once they find a common denominator or the LCD.

- Use Skill 83 for scaffolded review of the concept.
- For more practice use *Ways to Success* 10.6 or blackline masters Practice 10.6 or Homework 10.6.
- For small group intervention use the Intervention Activity, *Teacher Edition,* p. 269.

Teaching Tip As students use the worksheet, you may wish to remind them to rewrite fractions by multiplying both the numerator and the denominator by the same factor. Provide this example:

$$\frac{5}{8} - \frac{2}{4}; \frac{2}{4} \times \frac{2}{2} = \frac{4}{8}; \frac{5}{8} - \frac{4}{8} = \frac{1}{8}.$$

Skill 84

Objective Solve problems by drawing a diagram.

Answers

1. $\frac{1}{2}$ pound 2. 4 times greater 3. *See student page.*
4. 5 5. $2\frac{1}{2}$ pounds 6. $2\frac{1}{2}$
7. $1\frac{1}{2}$ miles; $\frac{3}{4}$ miles

Draw a Diagram
Skill from Chapter 10

Common Error Students may incorrectly model fractions.

- Use Skill 84 for scaffolded review of the concept.
- For more practice use *Ways to Success* blackline masters 10.7 and Practice and Homework 10.7.
- For small group instruction, use the Intervention Activity, *Teacher Edition,* p. 272.

Teaching Tip Before students use the worksheet, you may wish to have them use fraction strips to model fractions twice as long as $\frac{1}{4}$, 3 times as long as $\frac{1}{3}$, and 4 times as long as $\frac{1}{8}$. ($\frac{1}{2}$; 1; $\frac{1}{2}$)

Chapter 11: Add and Subtract Decimals

Skill 85

Objective Write fractions and mixed numbers as decimals and vice-versa.

Answers

1. $\frac{90}{100}$ or $\frac{9}{10}$; 0.9 2. $\frac{63}{100}$; 0.63 3. $1\frac{42}{100}$ or $1\frac{21}{50}$; 1.42
4. 0.8 5. 0.79 6. 7.1 7. $\frac{5}{10}$ or $\frac{1}{2}$ 8. $\frac{27}{100}$ 9. $5\frac{45}{100}$ or $5\frac{9}{20}$

Fractions and Decimals *Prerequisite Skill from Chapter 10*

Common Error Students may write incorrect decimals for the shaded part of models.

- Use Skill 85 for scaffolded review of the concept.
- For more practice use *Ways to Success* 10.1 or blackline masters Practice 10.1 or Homework 10.1.
- For small group instruction, use the Intervention Activity, *Teacher Edition,* p. 257.

Teaching Tip Before students use the worksheet, you may wish to remind them that a 10×10 grid consists of 100 squares. Each square represents $\frac{1}{100}$ or 0.01 of the grid, and each column of squares represents $\frac{1}{10}$ or 0.1 of the grid.

Skill 86

Objective Add and subtract decimals.

Answers

1. *Check students' work.*
2. 7, 1, 3 3. 3.17 4. 8.46
5. 2.1 6. 7.55 7. 0.47

Add and Subtract Decimals *Prerequisite Skill from Grade 4*

Common Error Students may not remember to write decimal points in their answers.

- Use Skill 86 for scaffolded review of the concept.
- For more practice use *Ways to Success* 11a.

Teaching Tip As students use the worksheet, you may wish to have them write the decimal point in their answer before they add or subtract.

Skill 87

Objective Estimate decimal sums and differences.

Answers

1. 3, 4; 0.7 2. 4, 8; 3.2 3. 8, 2; 6 4. 12, 6; 6 5. 2.6 6. 35
7. 0.4 8. 7 9. 1.5 10. 101
11. 3.8 12. 8

Estimate Decimals *Prerequisite Skill from Grade 4*

Common Error Students may round to the incorrect place.

- Use Skill 87 for scaffolded review of the concept.

Teaching Tip As students use the worksheet, you may wish to have them read each direction line carefully to help them find the place to which they should round. Have students highlight these numbers before they round.

Skill 88

Objective Relate addition and subtraction of fractions and decimals.

Answers

1. $\frac{49}{100}$; $\frac{7}{100}$; $\frac{56}{100}$; 0.49; 0.07; 0.56 **2.** $\frac{22}{100}$; $\frac{19}{100}$; $\frac{41}{100}$; 0.22; 0.19; 0.41 **3.** $\frac{9}{100}$; $\frac{20}{100}$; $\frac{11}{100}$; 0.20; 0.2; 0.11; 0.09

4. $\frac{59}{100}$; $\frac{14}{100}$; $\frac{45}{100}$; 0.59; 0.14; 0.45

Relate Fractions and Decimals
Skill from Chapter 11

Common Error Students may have difficulty changing fractions to decimals.

- Use Skill 88 for scaffolded review of the concept.
- For more practice use *Ways to Success* 11.1 or blackline masters Practice 11.1 or Homework 11.1.
- For small group intervention use the Intervention Activity, *Teacher Edition,* p. 283.

Teaching Tip Before students use the worksheet, you may wish to have them use a place-value chart to change $\frac{7}{10}$ and $\frac{4}{100}$ to decimals. (0.7; 0.04) Point out that 7 is written in the tenths place and 4 is written in the hundredths place.

Skill 89

Objective Add decimals through thousandths.

Answers

1. 10.73 **2.** 5.59 **3.** 5.53
4. 12.35 **5.** 5.181 **6.** 3.957
7. 2.984 **8.** 3.99 **9.** 7.045
10. 5.633

Add Decimals
Skill from Chapter 11

Common Error Students may align addends incorrectly when the numbers of digits in the addends differ.

- Use Skill 89 for scaffolded review of the concept.
- For more practice use *Ways to Success* 11.2 or blackline masters Practice 11.2 or Homework 11.2.
- For small group intervention use the Intervention Activity, *Teacher Edition,* p. 285.

Teaching Tip Before students use the worksheet, you may wish to have them use a place-value chart to align the addends 3.05 and 6.873. Remind students to use the decimal point to line up the digits.

Skill 90

Objective Subtract decimals through thousandths.

Answers

1. 4.121 **2.** 2.91 **3.** 6.56
4. 4.579 **5.** 3.134 **6.** 6.109
7. 6.77 **8.** 3.558 **9.** 3.529

Subtract Decimals
Skill from Chapter 11

Common Error Students may regroup incorrectly.

- Use Skill 90 for scaffolded review of the concept.
- For more practice use *Ways to Success* 11.3 or blackline masters Practice 11.3 or Homework 11.3.
- For small group instruction, use the Intervention Activity, *Teacher Edition,* p. 288.

Teaching Tip As students use the worksheet, you may wish to have them write each regrouping step on a separate piece of paper. For example, 6 tenths = 5 tenths 10 hundredths.

Skill 91

Objective Estimate decimal sums and differences.

Answers
1. 6; 3; 6.9 2. 2; 3; 8.5
3. 15; 9; 6 4. 45; 25; 20
5. 9; 0.5; 0.4 6. 20; 44; 64;
64 7. 17.4; 9.4; 8; 8

Estimate With Decimals
Skill from Chapter 11

Common Error Students may round to an incorrect place when estimating decimal sums and differences.

- Use Skill 91 for scaffolded review of the concept.
- For more practice use *Ways to Success* 11.4 or blackline masters Practice 11.4 or Homework 11.4.
- For small group instruction, use the Intervention Activity, *Teacher Edition,* p. 291.

Teaching Tip As students use the worksheet, you may wish to have them highlight the place value to which they need to round.

Skill 92

Objective Solve problems by deciding which computation method to use.

Answers
1. 26.42 2. 19.78
3. 26.42 − 19.78
4. 6.64 5. 7.5
6–7. *Check students' answers.*

Problem Solving:
Choose a Computation Method
Skill from Chapter 11

Common Error Students may choose an inefficient computation method.

- Use Skill 92 for scaffolded review of the concept.
- For more practice use *Ways to Success* 11.5 or blackline masters Problem Solving 11.5, Practice 11.5, or Homework 11.5.

Teaching Tip Before students use the worksheet, you may wish to have them choose which of the following expressions is best evaluated using mental math, $357.08 − 125.12$ or $3.50 − 2.25$. Guide students to recognize which expression has numbers that are easier to compute mentally. ($3.50 − 2.25$ is best solved using mental math.)

Chapter 12: Multiply and Divide Fractions

Skill 93

Objective Convert fractions and mixed numbers.

Answers
1. $\frac{10}{16}$ 2. 4 3. 12 4. 3 5. $\frac{19}{8}$
6. $\frac{29}{6}$ 7. $3\frac{1}{3}$ 8. 4 9. $6\frac{1}{2}$
10. $6\frac{3}{4}$

Fractions and Mixed Numbers
Prerequisite Skill from Grade 4

Common Error Students may not add the numerator when they change mixed numbers to improper fractions.

- Use Skill 93 for scaffolded review of the concept.

Teaching Tip Before students use the worksheet, you may wish to have them change $3\frac{1}{4}$ and $2\frac{2}{5}$ to improper fractions. ($\frac{13}{4}$; $\frac{12}{5}$) Remind students that they need to multiply the denominator and whole number first; then they add the numerator.

Skill 94

Objective Find part of a number.

Answers

1. 4 2. 6 3. 2 4. 4 5. 8
6. 15 7. 12 8. 28

Part of a Number

Common Error Students may forget to multiply after dividing to find part of a number.

- Use Skill 94 for scaffolded review of the concept.

Teaching Tip Before students use the worksheet, you may wish to remind them that sometimes they need to perform 2 steps in order to find part of a number. (divide or multiply)

Skill 95

Objective Find the product of two fractions.

Answers

1. $\frac{10}{18}$; $\frac{5}{9}$ 2. $\frac{6}{8}$; $\frac{3}{4}$ 3. $\frac{5}{24}$
4. $\frac{12}{40}$; $\frac{3}{10}$ 5. $\frac{1}{8}$ 6. $\frac{7}{10}$ 7. $\frac{1}{9}$
8. $\frac{5}{8}$ 9. $\frac{3}{4}$

Multiply Fractions

Common Error Students may not recall how to write a fraction in simplest form.

- Use Skill 95 for scaffolded review of the concept.

Teaching Tip Before students use the worksheet, you may wish to have them simplify the fractions $\frac{12}{16}$ and $\frac{15}{45}$. ($\frac{3}{4}$; $\frac{1}{3}$)

Skill 96

Objective Find products of fractions and mixed numbers.

Answers

1–4. *Check students' work.*

1. $\frac{3}{4}$ 2. $\frac{5}{3}$, $\frac{5}{3}$, $\frac{5}{15}$; $\frac{1}{3}$
3. $\frac{5}{4}$, $\frac{5}{4}$, $\frac{5}{8}$, $\frac{5}{5}$ 4. $\frac{7}{2}$, $\frac{7}{2}$, $\frac{7}{10}$, $\frac{7}{10}$

Multiply with Mixed Numbers

Common Error Students may not write fractions in simplest form.

- Use Skill 96 for scaffolded review of the concept.
- For more practice use *Ways to Success* 12.3 or blackline masters Practice 12.3 or Homework 12.3.
- For small group intervention use the Intervention Activity, *Teacher Edition,* p. 318.

Teaching Tip Before students use the worksheet, you may wish to have them write the fractions $\frac{15}{18}$ and $\frac{9}{27}$ in simplest form. ($\frac{5}{6}$, $\frac{1}{3}$)

Skill 97

Objective Use the reciprocal to divide fractions.

Answers

1. 10 2. 3; 2; 18; 2; 9 3. 3; 10; $\frac{9}{10}$ 4. $\frac{1}{8}$ 5. 10; 2; 30; $\frac{1}{15}$ 6. 1; 8; 4; 40; $\frac{1}{10}$ 7. $\frac{8}{11}$ 8. 5; 6; $\frac{5}{9}$

Divide Fractions
Skill from Chapter 12

Common Error Students may write the reciprocal of the dividend rather than the reciprocal of the divisor.

- Use Skill 97 for scaffolded review of the concept.
- For more practice use *Ways to Success* 12.5 or blackline masters Practice 12.5 or Homework 12.5.
- For small group instruction, use the Intervention Activity, *Teacher Edition*, p. 323.

Teaching Tip As students use the worksheet, you may wish to have them make sure they are using the correct reciprocal by checking to see that the product of the divisor and its reciprocal is 1.

Skill 98

Objective Use the reciprocal to divide fractions.

Answers

1. $\frac{11}{14}$ 2. $\frac{3}{8}$; $\frac{9}{16}$ 3. $\frac{5}{2}$; $\frac{10}{3}$; $\frac{5}{2}$; $\frac{3}{10}$; $\frac{3}{4}$ 4. $\frac{4}{5}$ 5. $\frac{3}{8}$; $\frac{6}{8}$; $\frac{3}{4}$ 6. $\frac{3}{5}$; $\frac{9}{4}$; $\frac{3}{5}$; $\frac{4}{9}$; $\frac{4}{15}$ 7. $\frac{2}{3}$; $\frac{2}{6}$; $\frac{1}{3}$ 8. $\frac{4}{5}$; $\frac{12}{5}$; $\frac{4}{5}$; $\frac{5}{12}$; $\frac{1}{3}$

Divide Mixed Numbers
Skill from Chapter 12

Common Error Students may not recall that the denominator of the improper fraction is the same as the denominator of the fraction part of the mixed number.

- Use Skill 98 for scaffolded review of the concept.
- For more practice use *Ways to Success* 12.6 or blackline masters Practice 12.6 or Homework 12.6.
- For small group instruction, use the Intervention Activity, *Teacher Edition*, p. 326.

Teaching Tip Before students use the worksheet, you may wish to have them review changing $3\frac{4}{5}$ from a mixed number to an improper fraction. ($\frac{19}{5}$)

Skill 99

Objective Solve problems by choosing the correct operation.

Answers

1. $5\frac{3}{4}$ 2. $\frac{1}{3}$ 3. *Check students' work.* 4. No 5. No 6. Yes 7. No 8. $5\frac{3}{4} \times \frac{1}{3} = 1\frac{11}{12}$ 9. $1\frac{11}{12}$ 10. division; $\frac{3}{4}$ hours

Problem Solving:
Choose the Operation
Skill from Chapter 12

Common Error Students may decide to multiply when they should divide.

- Use Skill 99 for scaffolded review of the concept.
- For more practice use *Ways to Success* 12.7 or blackline masters Problem Solving 12.7, Practice 12.7 or Homework 12.7.

Teaching Tip Before students use the worksheet, you may wish to have them review the language in a word problem that indicates multiplication, such as "$\frac{1}{2}$ of 350," and the language that indicates division, such as "students *share equally*."

Chapter 13: Multiply Decimals

Skill 100

Objective Multiply by 1-digit numbers.

Answers
1. 270 **2.** 864 **3.** 804
4. 3,234 **5.** 981 **6.** 1,728
7. 4,581 **8.** 1,332

Multiply by 1- and 3-Digit Numbers
Prerequisite Skill from Grade 4

Common Error Students may forget to add regrouped numbers.

- Use Skill 100 for scaffolded review of the concept.
- For more practice use *Ways to Success* 13a.

Teaching Tip Before students use the worksheet, you may wish to have them find 3×278. (834)

Skill 101

Objective Estimate products by rounding decimals.

1. 48; 48 **2.** 7; 28; 28 **3.** 3; 66; 66 **4.** 4; 44; 44 **5.** 6; 18; 18 **6.** 4; 80; 80 **7.** 7; 77; 77 **8.** 36 **9.** 30 **10.** 35 **11.** 130 **12.** 42 **13.** 72

Estimate More Products
Prerequisite Skill from Grade 4

Common Error Students may round incorrectly.

- Use Skill 101 for scaffolded review of the concept.
- For more practice use *Ways to Success* 13c.

Teaching Tip Before students use the worksheet, you may wish to have them review the rounding rules. Then have them round 8.24, 3.71, and 5.95 to the nearest whole number. (8, 4, 6)

Skill 102

Objective Relate multiplication of fractions to multiplication of decimals.

Answers
1. 3; 12; 12; 0.12 **2.** 5; 7; 35; 0.35 **3.** 12; 2; 2 **4.** 8; 10; 56; 10; 5.6 **5.** 12; 48; 48; 0.48 **6.** 2; 10; 28; 100; 28; 0.28

Relate Fraction and Decimal Products
Skill from Chapter 13

Common Error Students may incorrectly write the decimal as a fraction.

- Use Skill 102 for scaffolded review of the concept.
- For more practice use *Ways to Success* 13.1 or blackline masters Practice 13.1 or Homework 13.1.
- For small group intervention use the Intervention Activity, *Teacher Edition*, p. 335.

Teaching Tip Before students use the worksheet, you may wish to have them review writing decimals as fractions.

Skill 103

Objective Estimate decimal products.

Answers
1. 14.0; 14 **2.** 30; 0.5; 15.0; 15 **3.** 320; 320 **4.** 2; 20; 40 **5.** 2; 30; 60; 60 **6.** 60; 4; 240; 240

Estimate Decimal Products
Skill from Chapter 13

Common Error Students may not realize that the estimated product can be a whole number.

- Use Skill 103 for scaffolded review of the concept.
- For more practice, use *Ways to Success* 13.3 or blackline masters Practice 13.3 or Homework 13.3.
- For small group intervention use the Intervention Activity, *Teacher Edition*, p. 339.

Teaching Tip Before students use the worksheet, you may wish to have them use rounding to estimate the product of 0.24×80. (16)

Skill 104

Objective Find the product of a whole number and a decimal.

Answers
1. 23.2 **2.** 73.68 **3.** 15.555 **4.** 7.8 **5.** 38.25 **6.** 11.622 **7.** 8.1 **8.** 16.52 **9.** 31.178 **10.** 23.64 **11.** 14.769 **12.** 45.5

Multiply Whole Numbers and Decimals
Skill from Chapter 13

Common Error Students may forget to place a decimal point in the product.

- Use Skill 104 for scaffolded review of the concept.
- For more practice use *Ways to Success* 13.2 or blackline masters Practice 13.2 or Homework 13.2.
- For small group instruction, use the Intervention Activity, *Teacher Edition*, p. 337.

Teaching Tip Before students use the worksheet, you may wish to review that the product of a whole number and a decimal will have the same number of decimal places as the decimal. Then have students determine the number of decimal places in the products of 6.79 and 5, and of 3.7 and 2. (2 decimal places, 1 decimal place)

Skill 105

Objective Find the product of two decimals.

Answers
1. 1.56 **2.** 3.12 **3.** 0.12 **4.** 1.328 **5.** 0.5616 **6.** 0.312 **7.** 1.638 **8.** 3.168

Multiply Decimals
Skill from Chapter 13

Common Error Students may incorrectly place the decimal point in the product.

- Use Skill 105 for scaffolded review of the concept.
- For more practice use *Ways to Success* 13.4 or blackline masters Practice 13.4 or Homework 13.4.
- For small group instruction, use the Intervention Activity, *Teacher Edition*, p. 342.

Teaching Tip As students use the worksheet, you may wish to have them underline each digit to the right of the decimal point in each factor and count the underlined digits, before placing the decimal point in the product.

Skill 106

Objective Decide when to write zeros in the product.

Answers
1. 0.08 2. 0.024 3. 0.0028
4. 0.0035 5. 0.049
6. 0.0254 7. 0.016
8. 0.0025 9. 0.0942

Zeros in the Product

Skill from Chapter 13

Common Error Students may forget to write a zero, or may write an incorrect number of zeros in the product.

- Use Skill 106 for scaffolded review of the concept.
- For more practice use *Ways to Success* 13.5 or blackline masters Practice 13.5 or Homework 13.5.
- For small group instruction, use the Intervention Activity, *Teacher Edition,* p. 345.

Teaching Tip Before students use the worksheet, you may wish to have them multiply 0.8 by 1.04 using a place-value chart. (0.728)

Skill 107

Objective Solve problems by deciding whether the solution is reasonable.

Answers
1. 200 2. 50 3. 0.4
4. *See student page.*
5. multiplication
6. $200 \times 0.4 = 80$
7–8. *Check students' work.*

Problem Solving:
Reasonable Solutions

Skill from Chapter 13

Common Error Students may not know how to decide if an answer is or is not reasonable.

- Use Skill 107 for scaffolded review of the concept.
- For more practice use *Ways to Success* 13.6 or blackline masters Problem Solving 13.6, Practice 13.6 or Homework 13.6.

Teaching Tip Before students use the worksheet, you may wish to have them review problems for which the answer is reasonable and for which the answer is not reasonable.

Chapter 14: Divide Decimals

Skill 108

Objective Divide by whole numbers.

Answers
1. 73 R3 2. 36 R6 3. 18 R3
4. 54 R9 5. 17 6. 14 R47
7. 958 R1 8. 997 R1
9. 7 R61 10. 5 R10

Divide by Whole Numbers

Prerequisite Skill from Grade 4

Common Error Students may write an incorrect remainder.

- Use Skill 108 for scaffolded review of the concept.
- For more practice use *Ways to Success* 14c.

Teaching Tip Before students use the worksheet, you may wish to have them review comparing the remainder to the divisor. If the remainder is greater than or equal to the divisor, the quotient should be increased.

Skill 109

Objective Divide money.

Answers
1. $2.86 2. $1.32 3. $1.10
4. $0.86 5. $1.18 6. $1.49
7. $2.26 8. $9.44

Divide Money

Prerequisite Skill from Grade 4

Common Error Students may forget to write a dollar sign and decimal point in the quotient.

• Use Skill 109 for scaffolded review of the concept.

Teaching Tip Before students use the worksheet, you may wish to have them use a bill set to model dividing $6.75 by 3. ($2.25) Have them record the quotient using a dollar sign and decimal point.

Skill 110

Objective Estimate quotients.

Answers
1. 20 2. 90; 90 3. 4; 40; 40;
40 4. 4; 40; 40 5. 7 × 7;
49; 70 6. 6 × 8; 48; 80
7. 8 × 9; 72; 90 8. 8 × 4;
32; 40

Estimate More Quotients

Prerequisite Skill from Grade 4

Common Error Students may not recall basic multiplication facts.

• Use Skill 110 for scaffolded review of the concept.
• For more practice, use *Ways to Success* 14b.

Teaching Tip Before students use the worksheet, you may wish to have them review basic multiplication facts.

Skill 111

Objective Relate division of fractions to division of decimals.

Answers
1. 10 2. 12 3. 32 4. 20
5. 5 6. 10

Relate Fraction and Decimal Division

Skill from Chapter 14

Common Error Students may incorrectly count the number of fractional parts.

• Use Skill 111 for scaffolded review of the concept.
• For more practice, use *Ways to Success* 14.1 or blackline masters Practice 14.1 or Homework 14.1.
• For small group intervention use the Intervention Activity, *Teacher Edition*, p. 353.

Teaching Tip Before students use the worksheet, you may wish to have them draw models to find 2 ÷ 0.5. (4)

Skill 112

Objective Estimate decimal quotients.

Answers
1. 2; 120; 120 2. 4; 40; 40
3. 120 4. 100

Estimate Decimal Quotients

Skill from Chapter 14

Common Error Students may choose numbers that are not compatible.

- Use Skill 112 for scaffolded review of the concept.
- For more practice use *Ways to Success* 14.2 or blackline masters Practice 14.2 or Homework 14.2.
- For small group intervention use the Intervention Activity, *Teacher Edition*, p. 355.

Teaching Tip Before students use the worksheet, you may wish to have them use unit fractions and compatible numbers to find $64 \div 0.35$. (64 is close to 66 and 0.35 is close to $\frac{1}{3}$; $66 \div \frac{1}{3} = 66 \times 3 = 198$.)

Skill 113

Objective Divide with decimals and whole numbers.

Answers
1. 0.85 2. 1.24 3. 0.54
4. 1.41 5. 0.89 6. 0.63

Divide With Decimals and Whole Numbers

Skill from Chapter 14

Common Error Students may incorrectly place the decimal point in the quotient.

- Use Skill 113 for scaffolded review of the concept.
- For more practice use *Ways to Success* 14.4, 14.5 or blackline masters Practice 14.4, 14.5 or Homework 14.4, 14.5.
- For small group instruction, use the Intervention Activity *Teacher Edition*, pp. 360 and 364.

Teaching Tip As students use the worksheet, you may wish to have them highlight the decimal point in the dividend and immediately place a decimal point in the quotient above it.

Skill 114

Objective Divide a decimal by a decimal.

Answers
1. 320 2. 235.7 3. 603;
260.5 4. 132; 531.5 5. 61
6. 60.7 7. 2.1

Divide Decimals

Skill from Chapter 14

Common Error Students may incorrectly align digits when dividing.

- Use Skill 114 for scaffolded review of the concept.
- For more practice use *Ways to Success* 14.7 or blackline masters Practice 14.7 or Homework 14.7.
- For small group instruction, use the Intervention Activity, *Teacher Edition*, p. 369.

Teaching Tip Before students use the worksheet, you may wish to have them use lined paper turned sideways to use long division to find $3.76 \div 0.2$. (18.8)

Skill 115

Objective Use division to find repeating decimals.

Answers
1. $0.\overline{7}$ 2. $0.8\overline{3}$ 3. $0.\overline{3}$ 4. $0.\overline{6}$
5. $0.\overline{18}$

Repeating Decimals

Skill from Chapter 14

Common Error Students may forget to place the bar above the digits that repeat in the decimal.

- Use Skill 115 for scaffolded review of the concept.
- For more practice use *Ways to Success* 14.6 or blackline masters Practice 14.6 or Homework 14.6.
- For small group instruction, use the Intervention Activity, *Teacher Edition,* p. 367.

Teaching Tip Before students use the worksheet, you may wish to have them write $\frac{4}{9}$ as a repeating decimal. $(0.\overline{4})$

Skill 116

Objective Solve problems by deciding how to express the quotient.

Answers
1. 350 2. 40 3. *See student page.* 4. 8 5. No; Yes 6. 9
7. 8 8. *Check students' work.*

Problem Solving:
Express the Quotient

Skill from Chapter 14

Common Error Students may incorrectly express the quotient.

- Use Skill 116 for scaffolded review of the concept.
- For more practice use *Ways to Success* 14.8 or blackline masters Problem Solving 14.8, Practice 14.8, or Homework 14.8.
- For small group instruction, use the Intervention Activity, *Teacher Edition,* p. 372.

Teaching Tip Before students use the worksheet, you may wish to have them write and refer to the following questions: "What does the question ask me to find?" "What does the remainder represent?" "Does it make sense to write the remainder as a fraction or a decimal?"

Chapter 15: Plane Figures and Geometric Concepts

Skill 117

Objective Name points, lines, line segments, rays, and angles.

Answers
1. a. line *AB* 2. b. ray *YX*
3. a. angle *STU*
4. a. line *CD*
5. line *TP* or *PT*
6. ray *QP* 7. point *R*
8. angle *FGH* or *HGF* or *G.*

Points, Lines and Angles

Prerequisite Skill from Grade 4

Common Error Students may not write the endpoint first when they name a ray.

- Use Skill 117 for scaffolded review of the concept.
- For more practice use *Ways to Success* 15a.

Teaching Tip As students use the worksheet, you may wish to have them circle the endpoints of rays and line segments.

Skill 118

Objective Identify and classify plane geometric figures.

Answers
1. 4; 4; quadrilateral 2. 3; 3; triangle 3. 5; 5; pentagon
4. 4; 4; quadrilateral
5. scalene 6. equilateral
7. isosceles 8. equilateral

Identify Plane Figures *Prerequisite Skill from Grade 4*

Common Error Students may think that figures can only be classified in one way.

• Use Skill 118 for scaffolded review of the concept.

Teaching Tip Before students use the worksheet, you may wish to have them review the definitions of quadrilaterals (4-sided figures); Parallelograms: quadrilateral with opposite sides parallel and same length. Rectangle: parallelogram with 4 right angles, Square: rectangle with 4 sides of the same length. Rhombus: parallelogram with 4 sides of the same length. Trapezoid: quadrilateral with only 1 pair of parallel sides.

Skill 119

Objective Identify and describe basic geometric lines.

Answers
1. E 2. No; Yes 3. Yes; *Check students' work.*
4. parallel 5. intersects
6. parallel 7. perpendicular

Identify and Describe Lines *Skill from Chapter 15*

Common Error Students may confuse perpendicular and parallel lines.

• Use Skill 119 for scaffolded review of the concept.
• For more practice use *Ways to Success* 15.1 or blackline masters Practice 15.5 or Homework 15.1.
• For small group instruction use the Intervention Activity, *Teacher Edition*, p. 391.

Teaching Tip Before students use the worksheet, you may wish to draw and label pictures of perpendicular lines, parallel lines and intersecting lines. Then students can use these pictures as a reference.

Skill 120

Objective Name and classify angles.

Answers
1. acute angle; *TSR*
2. right angle; *NML*
3. straight angle; *GFE*
4. obtuse angle; *CBA*
5. acute angle; *JKL; LKJ*
6. obtuse angle; *QRS; SRQ*

Name and Classify Angles *Skill from Chapter 15*

Common Error Students may confuse obtuse and acute angles.

• Use Skill 120 for scaffolded review of the concept.
• For more practice use *Ways to Success* 15.2, blackline masters Practice 15.2 or Homework 15.2.
• For small group instruction use the Intervention Activity, *Teacher Edition*, p. 394.

Teaching Tip Before students use the worksheet, you may wish to draw a 45°, a 90°, and a 135° angle. Then have students classify and name each angle.

Skill 121

Objective Classify triangles and find missing angle measures.

Answers
1. 2; isosceles
2. 3; equilateral
3. 90°; acute 4. 90°; obtuse
5. 40° 6. 100°; 40°; 140°; 40°; 40°

Triangles

Common Error Students may use an incorrect order of operations when finding the measure of the missing angle.

- Use Skill 121 for scaffolded review of the concept.
- For more practice use *Ways to Success* 15.3 or blackline masters Practice 15.3 or Homework 15.3.
- For small group instruction use the Intervention Activity, *Teacher Edition*, p. 397.

Teaching Tip As students use the worksheet, you may wish to have them begin by subtracting one angle measure from 180° and then subtracting the other angle's measure from the difference to find the third angle's measure.

Skill 122

Objective Identify parts of a circle.

Answers
1. radius 2. chord 3. radius
4. chord 5. diameter 6. $\overline{KL}$
7. $\overline{KN}$ 8. *Answers may vary. Possible Answers:* $\overline{MJ}$, $\overline{KJ}$ or $\overline{JL}$

Circles

Common Error Students may confuse the diameter of a circle with the radius.

- Use Skill 122 for scaffolded review of the concept.
- For more practice use *Ways to Success* 15.8 or blackline masters Practice 15.8 or Homework 15.8.
- For small group instruction use the Intervention Activity, *Teacher Edition*, p. 413.

Teaching Tip Before students use the worksheet, you may wish to have them review that the diameter of a circle is always twice the length of the radius.

Skill 123

Objective Identify congruent figures.

Answers
1. No; Yes; No 2. Yes; Yes; Yes 3. Yes; Yes 4. Yes; Yes
5. No 6. Yes

Congruence

Common Error Students may have difficulty identifying congruent figures.

- Use Skill 123 for scaffolded review of the concept.
- For more practice use *Ways to Success* 15.4 or blackline masters Practice 15.4 or Homework 15.4.
- For small group instruction use the Intervention Activity, *Teacher Edition*, p. 399.

Teaching Tip Before students use the worksheet, you may wish to have them identify figures that are congruent and figures that are not congruent.

Skill 124

Objective Identify line symmetry.

Answers
1. No; No 2. Yes; Yes
3. Yes; Yes 4. 2 5. 1 6. 2

Symmetry

Common Error Students may find one line of symmetry but neglect to notice additional lines of symmetry.

- Use Skill 124 for scaffolded review of the concept.
- For more practice use *Ways to Success* 15.9 or blackline masters Practice 15.9 or Homework 15.9.
- For small group intervention use the Intervention Activity, *Teacher Edition,* p. 416.

Teaching Tip Before students use the worksheet, you may wish to model folding a figure to show more than one line of symmetry.

Skill 125

Objective Identify reflections, translations, or rotations.

Answers
1. translation 2. rotation
3. reflection 4. rotation
5. translation 6. reflection

Transformations

Common Error Students may confuse reflections, translations, and rotations.

- Use Skill 125 for scaffolded review of the concept.
- For more practice use *Ways to Success* 15.6 or blackline masters Practice 15.6 or Homework 15.6.
- For small group intervention use the Intervention Activity, *Teacher Edition,* p. 406.

Teaching Tip Before students use the worksheet, you may wish to have them use graph paper and cut out various figures to practice showing a reflection, rotation, and translation of each figure.

Skill 126

Objective Solve problems by making a model.

Answers
1. a triangle 2. a tessellation
3. Yes 4. Yes 5. *Check students' tessellations;* Model 6. Yes

Problem Solving:
Make a Model

Common Error Students may not understand the definition of a tessellation.

- Use Skill 126 for scaffolded review of the concept.
- For more practice use *Ways to Success* 15.7 or blackline masters Problem Solving 15.7, Practice 15.7 or Homework 15.7.
- For small group intervention use the Intervention Activity, *Teacher Edition,* p. 410.

Teaching Tip Before students use the worksheet, you may wish to have them use pattern blocks to build different tessellation patterns.

Chapter 16: Perimeter, Area, and Circumference

Skill 127

Objective Identify, classify, and describe plane geometric figures.

Answers
1. 5; 5; pentagon 2. 8; 8; octagon 3. 9; 9; nonagon 4. hexagon 5. quadrilateral 6. decagon

Plane Figures
Prerequisite Skill from Chapter 1$

Common Error Students may miscount the number of sides and angles.

- Use Skill 127 for scaffolded review of the concept.
- For more practice use *Ways to Success* 15.5, or blackline masters Practice 15.5 or Homework 15.5.
- For small group intervention use the Intervention Activity, *Teacher Edition*, p. 402.

Teaching Tip Before students use the worksheet, you may wish to have them draw an arrow on the side they start with and a dot on the angle they start with to avoid counting the side or angle twice.

Skill 128

Objective Find perimeter and area.

Answers
1. 6, 4, 20; 20; 24; 24
2. 3, 2, 3, 2, 10; 10; 6; 6
3. 4, 2, 4, 2, 12; 12; 8; 8
4. 12; 9 5. 18; 20

Perimeter and Area
Prerequisite Skill from Grade $

Common Error Students may confuse the operations for finding perimeter and area.

- Use Skill 128 for scaffolded review of the concept.
- For more practice use *Ways to Success* 15a, 15c.

Teaching Tip Before students use the worksheet, you may wish to have them review the array model of multiplication, which resembles a space covered by squares. This may help them remember to multiply when finding area.

Skill 129

Objective Find the perimeter of rectangles.

Answers
1. 18 in 2. (2 × 5) + (2 × 2); 10 + 4; 14; 14
3. (2 × 8) + (2 × 1); 16 + 2; 18; 18 cm 4. 14
5. 8

Perimeter of Rectangles
Skill from Chapter 1$

Common Error Students may neglect to label the perimeter.

- Use Skill 129 for scaffolded review of the concept.
- For more practice use *Ways to Success* 16.1 or blackline masters Practice 16.1 or Homework 16.1.
- For small group intervention use the Intervention Activity, *Teacher Edition*, p. 423.

Teaching Tip Before students use the worksheet, you may wish to have them find the perimeter of a rectangle that has a length of 6 feet and a width of 4 feet. (20 ft)

Skill 130

Objective Use a formula for the areas of parallelograms.

Answers
1. 9 in.; 4 in.; 9×4; 36
2. 18 ft; 10 ft; 18×10; 180
3. 30 **4.** 240 **5.** 20 yd^2
6. 36 in.^{2}

Area of Parallelograms *Skill from Chapter 16*

Common Error Students may forget that in a parallelogram the lengths of two adjacent sides might not be the base and the height.

- Use Skill 130 for scaffolded review of the concept.
- For more practice use *Ways to Success* 16.3 or blackline masters Practice 16.3 or Homework 16.3.
- For small group intervention use the Intervention Activity, *Teacher Edition*, p. 430.

Teaching Tip Before students use the worksheet, you may wish to have them use graph paper to draw parallelograms with varying bases and heights and then have them find their areas.

Skill 131

Objective Use a formula for the area of a triangle.

Answers
1. 6 in.; 4 in.; $\frac{1}{2} \times 6 \times 4$ $= \frac{1}{2} \times 24$; 12 **2.** 12 ft; 5 ft; $\frac{1}{2} \times 12 \times 5 = \frac{1}{2} \times 60$; 30
3. 49 cm^2 **4.** 80 m^2
5. 300 m^2 **6.** 30 ft^2
7. 132 in.^{2} **8.** 225 cm^2

Area of Triangles *Skill from Chapter 16*

Common Error Students may mistake the length of a side of a triangle for the height of the triangle.

- Use Skill 131 for scaffolded review of the concept.
- For more practice use *Ways to Success* 16.4 or blackline masters Practice 16.4 or Homework 16.4.
- For small group intervention use the Intervention Activity, *Teacher Edition*, p. 433.

Teaching Tip Before students use the worksheet, you may wish to have them use graph paper to draw several triangles. Have students find the height of their triangles by drawing lines from the vertex that are perpendicular to the base.

Skill 132

Objective Find perimeters and areas of irregular figures.

Answers
1. 28 **2.** 16 + 20; 36; 36
3. 32; $(8 \times 5) + (3 \times 5)$; 40 + 15; 55 **4.** 22 m; $3 \times 5 + \frac{1}{2} \times 4 \times 3$; 15 + 6; 21 m^2

Perimeter and Area of Irregular Figures *Skill from Chapter 16*

Common Error Students may incorrectly use formulas to find the areas of irregular figures.

- Use Skill 132 for scaffolded review of the concept.
- For more practice use *Ways to Success* 16.5 or blackline masters Practice 16.5 or Homework 16.5.
- For small group intervention use the Intervention Activity, *Teacher Edition*, p. 434.

Teaching Tip Before students use the worksheet, you may wish to have them use graph paper to draw several irregular figures and find their areas.

Skill 133

Objective Find the circumference of a circle.

Answers
1. 6.28; 6.28 2. 3; 9.42; 9.42 3. 5; 15.7; 15.7
4. 88; 88 5–6. *Check students' work.* 5. 22 6. 44
7. 31.4 8. 4.71 9. 11

Circumference of a Circle
Skill from Chapter 16

Common Error Students may not understand the difference between the formulas for the circumference of a circle.

- Use Skill 133 for scaffolded review of the concept.
- For more practice use *Ways to Success* 16.6 or blackline masters Practice 16.6 or Homework 16.6.
- For small group intervention use the Intervention Activity, *Teacher Edition,* p. 440.

Teaching Tip Before students use the worksheet, you may wish to have them review the formulas for the circumference of a circle. ($C = \pi d$; $C = 2\pi r$) Guide students to recognize that the diameter is twice as long as the radius.

Skill 134

Objective Solve problems by finding a pattern.

Answers
1. squares 2. 4 3. sixth
4. 15 5. 21 6. *Check students' work.* 7. 11

Problem Solving:
Find Patterns
Skill from Chapter 16

Common Error Students may confuse additive patterns with multiplicative patterns.

- Use Skill 134 for scaffolded review of the concept.
- For more practice use *Ways to Success* 16.2 or blackline masters Practice 16.2 or Homework 16.2.
- For small group intervention use the Intervention Activity, *Teacher Edition,* p. 426.

Teaching Tip As students use the worksheet, you may wish to have them draw the next figures in each pattern to check their work.

Chapter 17: Solid Figures, Surface Area, and Volume

Skill 135

Objective Identify and classify solid geometric figures.

Answers
1. 6; 12; 8 2. 5; 8; 5 3. 5; 9; 6 4. cylinder 5. cube
6. triangular pyramid

Solid Figures
Prerequisite Skill from Grade 4

Common Error Students may have difficulty counting faces, edges, and vertices without a physical model to manipulate.

- Use Skill 135 for scaffolded review of the concept.
- For more practice use *Ways to Success* 17a.

Teaching Tip As students use the worksheet, you may wish to have them use models of solid figures as references to help them find their answers.

Skill 136

Objective   Find area.

Answers
1. 6; 72 ft^2 2. 5; 9; 45 cm^2
3. 112 yd^2 4. 40 m^2
5. 12 ft^2 6. 240 m^2

Area of Figures
Prerequisite Skill from Grade 4

Common Error   Students may not write their answers in square units.

- Use Skill 136 for scaffolded review of the concept.
- For more practice use *Ways to Success* 17b.

Teaching Tip   As students use the worksheet, you may wish to have them write the measurement labels in their answer before they find the area. Remind students that area is measured in square units.

Skill 137

Objective   Determine the volume of solid figures.

Answers
1. 7; 105   2. 4; 4; 4; 64
3. 36 ft^3 4. 32 cm^3
5. 120 cm^3 6. 96 yd^3

Volume of Solid Figures
Prerequisite Skill from Grade 4

Common Error   Students may not include all the factors when multiplying.

- Use Skill 137 for scaffolded review of the concept.
- For more practice use *Ways to Success* 17d.

Teaching Tip   As students use the worksheet, you may wish to have them highlight the labeled parts of each solid figure to remind them to multiply all the factors.

Skill 138

Objective   Identify solid figures.

Answers
1. triangular   2. rectangle; rectangular prism   3. rectangular   4. pentagon; pentagonal pyramid   5. cylinder
6. curved; sphere

Identify Solid Figures
Skill from Chapter 17

Common Error   Students may have difficulty identifying the shapes of bases in solid figures.

- Use Skill 138 for scaffolded review of the concept.
- For more practice use *Ways to Success* 17.1 or blackline masters Practice 17.1 or Homework 17.1.
- For small group intervention use the Intervention Activity, *Teacher Edition,* p. 447.

Teaching Tip   As students use the worksheet, you may wish to have them shade the bases of the solid figures to help them identify their shapes.

Skill 139

Objective Identify the nets of solid figures.

Answers

1. square; square
2. rectangles; rectangles; rectangular prism
3. triangles; triangle; triangular pyramid
4. rectangular pyramid
5. cube or square prism

Nets

Skill from Chapter 17

Common Error Students may have trouble identifying and visualizing solid figures.

- Use Skill 139 for scaffolded review of the concept.
- For more practice use *Ways to Success* 17.3 or blackline masters Practice 17.3 or Homework 17.3.
- For small group intervention use the Intervention Activity, *Teacher Edition,* p. 451.

Teaching Tip Before students use the worksheet, you may wish to pass out solid figure models that they can manipulate.

Skill 140

Objective Find the surface area of solid figures.

Answers

1. 36; 48; 24; 36 + 48 + 24 = 108 in.^{2} **2.** 40; 3, 60; 3, 12; 40 + 60 + 12 = 112 in.^{2} **3.** 9, 3, 54; 9, 5, 90; 3, 5, 30; 54 + 90 + 30 = 174 cm^2 **4.** 146 ft^2
5. 184 cm^2

Surface Area of Solid Figures

Skill from Chapter 17

Common Error Students may write the units incorrectly when they write their answers.

- Use Skill 140 for scaffolded review of the concept.
- For more practice use *Ways to Success* 17.4 or blackline masters Practice 17.4 or Homework 17.4.
- For small group intervention use the Intervention Activity, *Teacher Edition,* p. 454.

Teaching Tip Before students use the worksheet, you may wish to remind them that area is written in units squared, or units^2.

Skill 141

Objective Find the volume of a rectangular prism, a cube, and a triangular prism.

Answers

1. 270 **2.** 4 × 2 × 6; 48
3. 42 **4.** 64 **5.** 5 × 5 × 5; 125 **6.** 216 **7.** 12 **8.** 8 × 8 × 2; 64 **9.** 60

Volume

Skill from Chapter 17

Common Error Students may multiply incorrectly when multiplying by $\frac{1}{2}$.

- Use Skill 141 for scaffolded review of the concept.
- For more practice use *Ways to Success* 17.6 or blackline masters Practice 17.6 or Homework 17.6.
- For small group intervention use the Intervention Activity, *Teacher Edition,* p. 463.

Teaching Tip Before students use the worksheet, you may wish to review how to multiply by $\frac{1}{2}$, using the example $\frac{1}{2} \times 182$. (91)

Skill 142

Objective Solve problems by solving a simpler problem first.

Answers
1. 5 cubes, 2 cubes, 2 cubes
2. front, back, top, and sides
3–6. *Check students' work.*
7. $6 + 6 + 4 + 6 + 4 = 26$

Problem Solving:
Solve a Simpler Problem
Skill from Chapter 17

Common Error Students may have difficulty identifying a simpler problem.

- Use Skill 142 for scaffolded review of the concept.
- For more practice use *Ways to Success* 17.7 or blackline masters Problem Solving, Practice 17.5 or Homework 17.5.
- For small group intervention use the Intervention Activity, *Teacher Edition*, p. 466.

Teaching Tip Before students use the worksheet, you may wish to have them begin with a simple problem and think of more complex problems that can be created from it.

Chapter 18: Ratio and Proportion

Skill 143

Objective Find equivalent fractions.

Answers

1. 6, $\frac{6}{16}$ 2. 15, $\frac{15}{18}$ 3. 5, $\frac{5}{6}$
4. 3, $\frac{3}{4}$ 5. $\frac{15}{20}$ 6. $\frac{4}{14}$ 7. $\frac{2}{5}$
8. $\frac{2}{3}$

Find Equivalent Fractions
Prerequisite Skill from Chapter 9

Common Error Students may write a fraction in a simpler form but not the simplest form.

- Use Skill 143 for scaffolded review of the concept.
- For more practice use *Ways to Success* 9.6 or blackline masters Practice 9.6 or Homework 9.6.
- For small group intervention use the Intervention Activity, *Teacher Edition*, p. 241.

Teaching Tip As students use the worksheet, you may wish to have them write the prime factorization of the numerator and denominator and use this to simplify the fraction.

Skill 144

Objective Write fractions as decimals.

Answers

1. $\frac{2}{2} = \frac{2}{10} = 0.2$
2. $\frac{2}{2} = \frac{6}{10} = 0.6$
3. $\frac{2}{2} = \frac{8}{10} = 0.8$
4. $\frac{2}{2} = \frac{14}{100} = 0.14$
5. $\frac{5}{5} = \frac{65}{100} = 0.65$
6. $\frac{4}{4} = \frac{24}{100} = 0.24$

Write Fractions as Decimals
Prerequisite Skill from Chapter 9

Common Error Students may multiply incorrectly.

- Use Skill 144 for scaffolded review of the concept.
- For more practice use *Ways to Success* 9.8 or blackline masters Practice 9.8 or Homework 9.8.
- For small group intervention use the Intervention Activity, *Teacher Edition*, p. 247.

Teaching Tip Before students use the worksheet, you may wish to have them use a place-value chart to write the following fractions as decimals: $\frac{7}{20}$; $\frac{3}{25}$; $\frac{8}{50}$. (0.35; 0.12; 0.16)

Skill 145

Objective Read and write ratios.

Answers
1. 2; 1 2. 1; 2 3. 1; 5 4. 5;
1 5. 3; 5 6. 5; 3 7. 6:7; $\frac{6}{7}$
8. 7:6, $\frac{7}{6}$ 9. 7:13; $\frac{7}{13}$

Ratios
Skill from Chapter 18

Common Error Students write the numbers in the wrong order when expressing a ratio as a fraction.

- Use Skill 145 for scaffolded review of the concept.
- For more practice use *Ways to Success* 18.1 or blackline masters Practice 18.1 or Homework 18.1.
- For small group instruction use the Intervention Activity, *Teacher Edition,* p. 485.

Teaching Tip As students use the worksheet, you may wish to point out that the first property represents the numerator, and the second property represents the denominator. Suggest that students write an *N* and a *D* above the pictures or words to remind them.

Skill 146

Objective Use multiplication and division to find equivalent ratios.

Answers
1. 6 2. $\frac{6}{10}$ 3. 2 4. 6 5. $\frac{3}{4}$
6. $\frac{2}{5}$ 7. 3; 3; $\frac{3}{8}$ 8. 8; 8; $\frac{1}{4}$
9. 2; $\frac{3}{5}$ 10. 5; $\frac{3}{4}$

Find Equivalent Ratios
Skill from Chapter 18

Common Error Students incorrectly multiply or divide to find equivalent ratios.

- Use Skill 146 for scaffolded review of the concept.
- For more practice use *Ways to Success* 18.2 or blackline masters Practice 18.2 or Homework 18.2.
- For small group intervention use the Intervention Activity, *Teacher Edition,* p. 487.

Teaching Tip As students use the worksheet, you may wish to have them draw models of each ratio to check their answers.

Skill 147

Objective Compare two quantities with different units.

Answers
1. 540 2. 600 3. 60 4. 7
5. 5 6. 24

Rates
Skill from Chapter 18

Common Error Students set up ratios incorrectly.

- Use Skill 147 for scaffolded review of the concept.
- For more practice use *Ways to Success* 18.3 or blackline masters Practice 18.3 or Homework 18.3.
- For small group intervention use the Intervention Activity, *Teacher Edition,* p. 490.

Teaching Tip Before students use the worksheet, you may wish to have them review the concept that if the first ratio represents hours\game, the second ratio must also be hours\game.

Skill 148

Objective Identify cross products and use them to solve problems.

Answers
1–4. *Check students' work.*
1. 15 **2.** 10 **3.** 16 **4.** 6

Proportions

Common Error Students may multiply cross products but forget to divide.

- Use Skill 148 for scaffolded review of the concept.
- For more practice use *Ways to Success* 18.4 or blackline masters Practice 18.4 or Homework 18.4.
- For small group intervention use the Intervention Activity, *Teacher Edition,* p. 494.

Teaching Tip Before students use the worksheet, you may wish to have them use cross products to solve the following proportions. $\frac{3}{4} = \frac{9}{n}; \frac{7}{8} = \frac{x}{32}.$ ($n = 12; x = 28$)

Skill 149

Objective Use proportions to interpret similar figures and scale drawings.

Answers
1. 40 m **2.** 180 yd **3.** 125 m
4. 1; 20; 8; 160; 160 km
5. $\frac{3}{4}$ ft **6.** 450 mi

Proportions and Scale Drawings

Common Error Students may write the incorrect unit in the answer.

- Use Skill 149 for scaffolded review of the concept.
- For more practice use *Ways to Success* 18.5 or blackline masters Practice 18.5 or Homework 18.5.
- For small group intervention use the Intervention Activity, *Teacher Edition,* p. 498.

Teaching Tip As students use the worksheet, before they solve each problem, you may wish to have them highlight the unit that will go with the answer. For example, in $\frac{1m}{5cm} = \frac{25m}{\square}$, students would highlight "cm."

Skill 150

Objective Decide if the answer to a problem should be an exact or estimated amount.

Answers
1. 6 **2.** $3.18 **3.** 8 **4.** $3.84
5. $0.50; 8; $0.50 **6.** $0.53; $3.84; 8; $0.48 **7.** $0.48; $0.53 **8.** Nutty **9.** Movie Master; estimate
10. Supplies Central; exact amount

Problem Solving:
Choose Exact or Estimated Amounts

Common Error Students may estimate incorrectly.

- Use Skill 150 for scaffolded review of the concept.
- For more practice use *Ways to Success* 18.6 or blackline masters Problem Solving 18.6, Practice 18.6, or Homework 18.6.

Teaching Tip Before students use the worksheet, you may wish to have them review rounding rules. Then estimate as a class the quotient of $485 ÷ 50 and $10.69 ÷ 6. ($10; $2)

Chapter 19: Percent

Skill 151

Objective Understand place value of decimals through thousandths.

Answers

1. 0.02 2. 0.9 3. 0.007
4. 0.005 5. 0.05 6. 0.009
7. 2 8. 0.9 9. 80 10. 0.07
11. 0.06 12. 0.5 13. 50
14. 50 15. 0.002 16. 1 and
43 hundredths 17. 7 and
699 thousandths 18. 65 and
27 hundredths 19. 12 and
385 thousandths 20. 355
and 4 tenths 21. 2 tenths
22. 30 and 9 hundredths
23. 99 and 508 thousandths

Place Value Through Thousandths *Prerequisite Skill from Chapter 1*

Common Error Students may not write the short word form of the number correctly.

- Use Skill 151 for scaffolded review of the concept.
- For more practice use *Ways to Success* 1.5 or blackline masters Practice 1.5 or Homework 1.5.
- For small group intervention use the Intervention Activity, *Teacher Edition*, p. 15.

Teaching Tip Before students use the worksheet, you may wish to have them write 2.063 in short word form. (two and 63 thousandths)

Skill 152

Objective Convert fractions, mixed numbers, and decimals.

Answers

1. $\frac{1}{5}$ 2. $1\frac{3}{4}$ 3. $\frac{2}{5}$ 4. $\frac{4}{5}$ 5. $\frac{4}{25}$
6. $1\frac{1}{4}$ 7. $2\frac{9}{25}$ 8. 0.6
9. 1.05 10. 0.8 11. 0.25
12. 0.15 13. 2.75 14. 3.4

Change Fractions and Decimals *Prerequisite Skill from Chapter 9*

Common Error Students may incorrectly write decimals as fractions.

- Use Skill 152 for scaffolded review of the concept.
- For more practice use *Ways to Success* 9.8 or blackline masters Practice 9.8 or Homework 9.8.
- For small group intervention use the Intervention Activity, *Teacher Edition*, p. 247.

Teaching Tip Before students use the worksheet, you may wish to have them write the following decimals as fractions in simplest form: 0.5; 0.36; 0.008. ($\frac{1}{2}$; $\frac{9}{25}$; $\frac{1}{125}$)

Skill 153

Objective Relate fractions, decimals, and percents.

Answers

1. 40%; 0.4; $\frac{2}{5}$ 2. 10%; 0.1;
$\frac{1}{10}$ 3. 70%; 0.7; $\frac{7}{10}$ 4. 0.15
5. 30% 6. $\frac{9}{50}$

Relate Fractions, Decimals, and Percents *Skill from Chapter 19*

Common Error Students may not write the percent symbol.

- Use Skill 153 for scaffolded review of the concept.
- For more practice use *Ways to Success* 19.2 or blackline masters Practice 19.2 or Homework 19.2.
- For small group intervention use the Intervention Activity, *Teacher Edition*, p. 509.

Teaching Tip Before students use the worksheet, you may wish to have them write the fractions $\frac{10}{100}$, $\frac{45}{100}$, and $\frac{86}{100}$ as percents. (10%; 45%; 86%)

Skill 154

Objective Compare and order percents, decimals, fractions, and mixed numbers.

Answers

1a. *Check students' work.*
1b. 34 hundredths **1c.** $\frac{34}{100}$; 0.34 **2.** 0.11, 0.25, 0.48
3. 0.08, 0.63, 0.8 **4.** 0.12, 0.51, 0.75 **5.** 0.40, 0.88, 0.96

Order Fractions, Decimals, and Percents

Skill from Chapter 19

Common Error Students may incorrectly write one-digit percents such as 9% as the decimal 0.9.

- Use Skill 154 for scaffolded review of the concept.
- For more practice use *Ways to Success* 19.3 or blackline masters Practice 19.3 or Homework 19.3.
- For small group intervention use the Intervention Activity, *Teacher Edition*, p. 512.

Teaching Tip Before students use the worksheet, you may wish to have them use a place-value chart to write the following percents as decimals: 8%, 53%, 5%. (0.08; 0.53; 0.05))

Skill 155

Objective Find a percent of a number.

Answers

1. 100; $\frac{300}{100}$; 3; 3 **2.** 30; 30; $\frac{50}{1}$, $\frac{1500}{100}$; 15; 15 **3.** 6 **4.** 5
5. 3 **6.** 15; 9 **7.** 0.58; 29
8. 12 **9.** 3 **10.** 52

Percent of a Number

Skill from Chapter 19

Common Error Students may find products that are too large when finding percents of a number.

- Use Skill 155 for scaffolded review of the concept.
- For more practice use *Ways to Success* 19.5 or blackline masters Practice 19.5 or Homework 19.5.
- For small group intervention use the Intervention Activity, *Teacher Edition*, p. 518.

Teaching Tip Before students use the worksheet, you may wish to have them review that if they are asked to find less than 100% of a number, the answer will be less than the original number. Remind students to count the number of places they need to move the decimal.

Skill 156

Objective Solve problems using circle graphs.

Answers

1. 80 **2.** 16 **3.** 6 **4.** 20
5. 30%; 40%; 10% **6.** *Check students' work.* **7.** 100%
8. 90

Problem Solving:
Use Circle Graphs

Skill from Chapter 19

Common Error Students may have difficulty converting the data from the frequency table into the circle graph.

- Use Skill 156 for scaffolded review of the concept.
- For more practice use *Ways to Success* 19.6 or blackline masters Problem Solving 19.6, Practice 19.6 or Homework 19.6.
- For small group intervention use the Intervention Activity, *Teacher Edition*, p. 522.

Teaching Tip Before students use the worksheet, you may wish to have them review reading a frequency table and changing a fraction into a percent.

Chapter 20: Probability

Skill 157

Objective Add and subtract fractions and mixed numbers with like denominators.

Answers

1. $\frac{12}{10}$; $1\frac{2}{10}$; $1\frac{1}{5}$ 2. $\frac{10}{6}$; $1\frac{4}{6}$; $1\frac{2}{3}$
3. $\frac{4}{8}$; $\frac{1}{2}$ 4. $\frac{10}{12}$; $\frac{5}{6}$ 5. $1\frac{2}{5}$ 6. 1
7. $\frac{3}{4}$ 8. $\frac{1}{9}$ 9. $\frac{1}{3}$ 10. $\frac{2}{5}$ 11. $\frac{1}{6}$
12. 1 13. $1\frac{3}{4}$ 14. $\frac{2}{9}$ 15. $1\frac{1}{13}$
16. $\frac{3}{5}$

Add and Subtract Fractions   *Prerequisite Skill from Grade 4*

Common Error Students may add or subtract denominators.

- Use Skill 157 for scaffolded review of the concept.
- For more practice use *Ways to Success* 20a.

Teaching Tip As students use the worksheet, you may wish to have them review the concept that $\frac{3}{4}$ is the same as 3 fourths, $\frac{2}{5}$ is the same as 2 fifths, and $\frac{5}{6}$ is the same as 5 sixths.

Skill 158

Objective Describe the probability of an event and determine the number of possible outcomes in an experiment.

Answers

1. 1; 4; $\frac{1}{4}$ 2. 2; 4; $\frac{1}{2}$ 3. I, T, X; 1; 3; $\frac{1}{3}$ 4. 1, 2, 3, 4, 5; 3;
5; $\frac{3}{5}$ 5. 8; $\frac{1}{4}$ 6. 4; 8; $\frac{1}{2}$ 7. 6;
8; $\frac{3}{4}$

Outcomes and Probability   *Prerequisite Skill from Grade 4*

Common Error Students may mix up the terms of the fraction when trying to describe a probability.

- Use Skill 158 for scaffolded review of the concept.
- For more practice use *Ways to Success* 20a.

Teaching Tip As students use the worksheet, you may wish to remind them that the denominator is always the total number of possible outcomes. You can tell students that the bar in a fraction expressing probability means "out of".

Skill 159

Objective Determine combinations.

Answers
1. 6 2. $5 \times 3 = 15$; 15 3. 6
4. 6 5. 16

Combinations   *Skill from Chapter 20*

Common Error Students may simply count all of the individual items rather than using multiplication to find the number of possible choice combinations.

- Use Skill 159 for scaffolded review of the concept.
- For more practice use *Ways to Success* 20.1 or blackline masters Practice 20.1 or Homework 20.1.
- For small group intervention use the Intervention Activity, *Teacher Edition*, p. 529.

Teaching Tip Before students use the worksheet, you may wish to make an organized list with the class of all the possible bread and filling combinations in Exercise 1. Point out that the total number of sandwich choices (6) is different than the number of individual bread and filling items (5).

Skill 160

Objective Describe the probability of an event.

Answers
1. 0 2. No 3. 1; 2 4. 2; 1
5. 1; 1 6. impossible
7. certain 8. more likely
9. less likely 10. equally likely

Probability

Skill from Chapter 20

Common Error Students may confuse probability terms.

- Use Skill 160 for scaffolded review of the concept.
- For more practice use *Ways to Success* 20.2 or blackline masters Practice 20.2 or Homework 20.2.
- For small group intervention use the Intervention Activity, *Teacher Edition*, p. 531.

Teaching Tip Before students use the worksheet, you may wish to help them connect the terms *certain, likely, equally likely, unlikely,* and *impossible* to everyday events in their lives.

Skill 161

Objective Use fractions to find probability.

Answers
1. 4 2. 8 3. $\frac{1}{2}$; $\frac{1}{2}$ 4. $\frac{2}{10}$; $\frac{1}{5}$
5. $\frac{4}{10}$; $\frac{2}{5}$ 6. $\frac{1}{10}$ 7. $\frac{3}{10}$

Fractions and Probability

Skill from Chapter 20

Common Error Students may miscount the number of possible outcomes when counting on a spinner.

- Use Skill 161 for scaffolded review of the concept.
- For more practice use *Ways to Success* 20.3 or blackline masters Practice 20.3 or Homework 20.3.
- For small group intervention use the Intervention Activity, *Teacher Edition*, p. 534.

Teaching Tip As students use the worksheet, you may wish to suggest that they mark the place where they start counting on the spinner so that they do not count an outcome twice.

Skill 162

Objective Find the probability of compound events.

Answers
1. *Check students' diagrams.*
2. 1; 6 3. $\frac{1}{6}$ 4. *Check students' diagrams.* 5. $\frac{1}{3}$
6. $\frac{1}{6}$

Compound Events

Skill from Chapter 20

Common Error Students may miscount the number of possible outcomes when using a tree diagram.

- Use Skill 162 for scaffolded review of the concept.
- For more practice use *Ways to Success* 20.6 or blackline masters Practice 20.6 or Homework 20.6.
- For small group intervention use the Intervention Activity, *Teacher Edition*, p. 545.

Teaching Tip As students use the worksheet, you may guide students to number the ends of the branches on their tree diagrams.

Skill 163

Objective Solve problems by making an organized list.

Answers
1. 2 2. blue; pink; green
3. *See student page.* 4. BP; BG 5. PG; PB 6. GB; GP
7. BP, PB; BG, GB; PG, GP
8. 3 9. 3 10. 6

Make an Organized List
Skill from Chapter 20

Common Error Students may repeat possible outcomes in their list.

- Use Skill 163 for scaffolded review of the concept.
- For more practice use *Ways to Success* 20.4 or blackline masters Practice 20.4 or Homework 20.4.
- For small group intervention use the Intervention Activity, *Teacher Edition*, p. 538.

Teaching Tip As students use the worksheet, you may wish to have them check for duplicate outcomes.

Chapter 21: Equations and Functions

Skill 164

Objective Solve addition and subtraction equations.

Answers
1. 7 2. 9 3. 13 4. 9 5. 9
6. 11 7. 8 8. 5 9. 7 10. 13
11. 8 12. 4 13. 6 14. 8
15. 12 16. 7 17. 13

Solve Equations
Prerequisite Skill from Grade 4

Common Error Students may use the wrong operation.

- Use Skill 167 for scaffolded review of the concept.
- For more practice use *Ways to Success* 21a.

Teaching Tip Before students use the worksheet, you may wish to have them review that addition and subtraction are inverse operations.

Skill 165

Objective Solve multiplication and division equations.

Answers
1. 5 2. 3 3. 24 4. 6 5. 9
6. 40 7. 4 8. 9 9. 5 10. 18
11. 6 12. 4 13. 7 14. 48
15. 6 16. 7 17. 18

Solve More Equations
Prerequisite Skill from Grade 4

Common Error Students may use the wrong operation.

- Use Skill 165 for scaffolded review of the concept.

Teaching Tip Before students use the worksheet, you may wish to have them review that multiplication and division are inverse operations.

Skill 166

Objective Write and solve equations using equality properties.

Answers

1. 8; 8; 31; $m = 31$ **2.** 9;
$k = 9$ **3.** 8; 8; 22; $w = 22$
4. 37; $c = 37$ **5.** 8; 7; $x = 7$
6. 14; $y = 14$ **7.** 5; $y = 100$;
$d = 100$ **8.** 210; $y = 210$

Use Inverse Operations   *Skill from Chapter 21*

Common Error Students may forget to "balance the equation" by applying the inverse operation to both sides of the equation.

- Use Skill 166 for scaffolded review of the concept.
- For more practice use *Ways to Success* 21.2 or blackline masters Practice 21.2 or Homework 21.2.
- For small group intervention use the Intervention Activity, *Teacher Edition,* p. 570.

Teaching Tip Before students use the worksheet, you may wish to have them review the concept that whatever they do to one side of the equation they should also do to the other side.

Skill 167

Objective Use a function table to solve equations.

Answers

1. 2; 4; 6; $14 - 6$; 8
2. 5 (0); 0; 5 (1); 5; 5 (4);
20; 5 (5); 25; 5 (7); 35
3. $0 \div 3$; 0; $6 \div 3$; 2; $12 \div 3$;
4; $15 \div 3$; 5; $21 \div 3$; 7

Use a Function Table   *Skill from Chapter 21*

Common Error Students may substitute from the wrong row when working with a function table.

- Use Skill 167 for scaffolded review of the concept.
- For more practice use *Ways to Success* 21.4 or blackline masters Practice 21.4 or Homework 21.4.
- For small group intervention use the Intervention Activity, *Teacher Edition,* p. 577.

Teaching Tip Before students use the worksheet, you may wish to have them review reading straight across the row to avoid picking up an incorrect x-value.

Skill 168

Objective Use a function table and equations to describe and extend patterns.

Answers

1. 12 **2.** 19 **3.** 17; 20
4. 4; $14 + 4$; 18 **5.** $10 + 3$;
$13 + 3$; 16 **6.** 2; 22 **7.** 30

Describe and Extend Patterns   *Skill from Chapter 21*

Common Error Students may try to find a formula to solve rather than look for patterns.

- Use Skill 168 for scaffolded review of the concept.
- For more practice use *Ways to Success* 21.5 or blackline masters Practice 21.5 or Homework 21.5.
- For small group intervention use the Intervention Activity, *Teacher Edition,* p. 580.

Teaching Tip As students use the worksheet, remind them to look for patterns in the y-column of the table.

Skill 169

Objective Solve problems by writing an equation.

Answers
1. 28 2. 168 3. *See student page.* 4. *Answers may vary.*
5. $28 \times s = 168$ 6. 6
7. $6 \times m = 72$; 12

Problem Solving:

Write an Equation
Skill from Chapter 21

Common Error Students may solve their equation incorrectly.

- Use Skill 169 for scaffolded review of the concept.
- For more practice use *Ways to Success* 21.3 or blackline masters Problem Solving 21.3, Practice 21.3, or Homework 21.3.
- For small group intervention use the Intervention Activity, *Teacher Edition,* p. 574.

Teaching Tip Before students use the worksheet, you may wish to review how to use inverse operations for solving equations.

Chapter 22: Integers

Skill 170

Objective Find missing numbers on a number line.

Answers
1. 8; 20 2. 22; 32 3. 9; 13
4. 4; 16 5. 22; 40 6. 9; 27

Use a Number Line
Prerequisite Skill from Grade 4

Common Error Students may confuse the meanings of the *greater than* (>) and *less than* (<) symbols.

- Use Skill 170 for scaffolded review of the concept.

Teaching Tip Before students use the worksheet, you may wish to have them create three different number lines using intervals of 3, 5, and 10.

Skill 171

Objective Compare whole numbers.

Answers
1. < 2. > 3. <; < 4. <;
< 5. 6 tens > 2 tens; >
6. 9 hundreds > 0 hundreds;
>

Compare Whole Numbers
Prerequisite Skill from Chapter 1

Common Error Students may confuse the meanings of the *greater than* (>) and *less than* (<) symbols.

- Use Skill 171 for scaffolded review of the concept.
- For more practice use *Ways to Success* 1.4 or blackline masters Practice 1.4 or Homework 1.4.
- For small group intervention use the Intervention Activity, *Teacher Edition,* p. 12.

Teaching Tip As students use the worksheet, you may wish to tell them that the symbol is like the open mouth of a hungry bird that always goes after the bigger bug.

Skill 172

Objective Add and subtract whole numbers.

Answers
1. 749 **2.** 201 **3.** 984
4. 701 **5.** 612 **6.** 561
7. 309 **8.** 73 **9.** 917 **10.** 672
11. 493

Addition and Subtraction · *Prerequisite Skill from Chapter 2*

Common Error Students may regroup when it is not necessary.

- Use Skill 172 for scaffolded review of the concept.
- For more practice use *Ways to Success* 2.3 or blackline masters Practice 2.3 or Homework 2.3.
- For small group intervention use the Intervention Activity, *Teacher Edition*, p. 36.

Teaching Tip As students use the worksheet, you may wish to remind them that regrouping is needed only if the number they are subtracting is greater than the number they are subtracting from.

Skill 173

Objective Locate integers and their opposites on a number line and find absolute value.

Answers
1. $^+5$ **2.** $^-8$ **3.** $^-6$ **4.** $^+1$
5. $^-15$ **6.** $^+30$ **7.** $^+27$
8. $^-95$ **9.** 4; 4 **10.** 2; 2
11. 6; 6 **12.** 10; 10 **13.** 85
14. 46 **15.** 27 **16.** 100

Locate Integers · *Skill from Chapter 22*

Common Error Students may forget to write the sign of an integer.

- Use Skill 173 for scaffolded review of the concept.
- For more practice use *Ways to Success* 22.1 or blackline masters Practice 22.1 or Homework 22.1.
- For small group intervention use the Intervention Activity, *Teacher Edition*, p. 587.

Teaching Tip As students use the worksheet, you may wish to have them check their answers to make sure each integer has a sign, but each absolute value does not.

Skill 174

Objective Compare and order integers.

Answers
1. left; less; $<$ **2.** right; greater; $>$
3. $^-2$; $^+4$; $^-2 < ^+3 < ^+4$
4. -3; $^+3$; $^-3 < ^-1 < ^+3$

Compare and Order Integers · *Skill from Chapter 22*

Common Error When students order a set of negative integers, they often forget that a negative integer with the greatest absolute value will be less than others in the set.

- Use Skill 174 for scaffolded review of the concept.
- For more practice use *Ways to Success* 22.2 or blackline masters Practice 22.2 or Homework 22.2.
- For small group intervention use the Intervention Activity, *Teacher Edition*, p. 590.

Teaching Tip Before students use the worksheet, you may wish to remind them that a number is less than all the integers to its right on a number line.

Skill 175
Objective Add integers.

Answers
1. $^+7$ 2. $^-7$ 3. $^+3$ 4. $^-3$
5. negative; $^-7$ 6. negative;
$^-4$ 7. $^+3$ 8. $^-1$

Add Integers
Skill from Chapter 22

Common Error Students may use the wrong sign when finding the sum of a negative and a positive integer.

- Use Skill 175 for scaffolded review of the concept.
- For more practice use *Ways to Success* 22.3, 22.5 or blackline masters Practice 22.3, 22.5 or Homework 22.3, 22.5.
- For small group intervention use the Intervention Activity, *Teacher Edition,* pp. 594 and 600.

Teaching Tip As students use the worksheet, you may wish to have them highlight the integer with the greater absolute value when finding the sum of a negative and a positive integer.

Skill 176
Objective Subtract integers.

Answers
1. $^+1$; $^+4 + {}^+1 = {}^+5$
2. $^+2$; $^-8 + {}^+2 = {}^-6$
3. $^-5$; $^-4 + {}^-5 = {}^-9$
4. $^-2 + {}^-3$; $^-2 + {}^-3 = {}^-5$ 5. $^-1 + {}^+7$; $^-1 + {}^+7 = {}^+6$ 6. $^+8 + {}^+3$; $^+8 + {}^+3 = {}^+11$ 7. $^+6 + {}^+2$; $^+8$
8. $^-4 + {}^+3$; $^-1$ 9. $^-7 + {}^-8$; $^-15$ 10. $^-3 + {}^-5$; $^-8$

Subtract Integers
Skill from Chapter 22

Common Error When students rewrite a subtraction expression as an addition expression, they may change the sign of the operation but forget to change the sign of the second integer.

- Use Skill 176 for scaffolded review of the concept.
- For more practice use *Ways to Success* 22.4, 22.5 or blackline masters Practice 22.4, 22.5 or Homework 22.4, 22.5.
- For small group intervention use the Intervention Activity, *Teacher Edition,* pp. 597 and 600.

Teaching Tip As students use the worksheet, you may wish to remind them to change both signs.

Skill 177
Objective Analyze and solve problems using integers.

Answers
1. $^-3$ 2. 8; 6 3. $^-6$
4. *Check students' number lines.* 5. $^-1$ 6. 2; *Check students' number lines.*

Problem Solving:
Use Integers to Solve
Skill from Chapter 22

Common Error Students may interchange positive and negative integers.

- Use Skill 177 for scaffolded review of the concept.
- For more practice use *Ways to Success* 22.6 or blackline masters Problem Solving 22.6, Practice 22.6, or Homework 22.6.
- For small group intervention use the Intervention Activity, *Teacher Edition,* p. 604.

Teaching Tip As students use the worksheet, you may wish to have them underline or highlight words that indicate positive and negative integers and then write the signs above the words.

Chapter 23: Coordinate Graphing

Skill 178

Objective Identify points on a coordinate plane.

Answers
1. 4; 4 2. 2; 2 3. 4; 3; (4, 3)
4. 5; 1; (5, 1) 5. 5 6. (3, 3)
7. (4, 1) 8. (5, 2)

Points on a Grid
Prerequisite Skill from Grade 4

Common Error Students may forget the order in which they should read the lines on a coordinate grid.

- Use Skill 178 for scaffolded review of the concept.
- For more practice use *Ways to Success* 23a.

Teaching Tip Before students use the worksheet, you may wish to have them review that they should read across the lines on the bottom of the grid first. Then they should read *up* the lines on the side of the grid.

Skill 179

Objective Write integers.

Answers
1. $^-2$ 2. $^+4$ 3. $^-5$ 4. $^+7$
5. $^+16$ 6. $^-104$ 7. 3 8. 1
9. 8 10. 9 11. 82 12. 121

Write Integers
Prerequisite Skill from Grade 4

Common Error Students may use positive or negative signs with absolute value.

- Use Skill 179 for scaffolded review of the concept.
- For more practice use *Ways to Success* 23b.

Teaching Tip While students use the worksheet, you may wish to remind them that because absolute value shows distance from zero, absolute value is *not* written with positive or negative signs.

Skill 180

Objective Graph ordered pairs in the four quadrants of the coordinate plane.

Answers
1. 4; 2 2. right; down 3. 0;
2; left; 1; down 4. 0; 1; left;
4; up 5–8. *Check students' work.*

Graph Ordered Pairs
Skill from Chapter 23

Common Error Sometimes students mistake x-coordinates for y-coordinates.

- Use Skill 180 for scaffolded review of the concept.
- For more practice use *Ways to Success* 23.1 or Practice 23.1 or Homework 23.1.
- For small group intervention use the Intervention Activity, *Teacher Edition*, p. 612.

Teaching Tip Before students use the worksheet, you may wish to have them review that the x-coordinate is always given first and the y-coordinate is always given second.

Skill 181

Objective Use a function rule to find the value of ordered pairs.

Answers
1. *Check students' answers;* table: 4, 7, 10, 13; ordered pairs: (1, 4); (2, 7); (3, 10); (4, 13) **2.** *Check students' answers;* table: 3, 4, 5, 6; ordered pairs: ($^-$2, 3); ($^-$1, 4); (0, 5); (1, 6)
3. table: 7; 14; 21; 28; ordered pairs: (1, 7); (2, 14); (3, 21); (4, 28) **4.** table: 2; 12; 22; 32; ordered pairs: (0, 2); (2, 12); (4, 22); (6, 32)

Functions and Ordered Pairs *Skill from Chapter 23*

Common Error Sometimes students write the *y*-value in the wrong place in the table.

- Use Skill 181 for scaffolded review of the concept.
- For more practice use *Ways to Success* 23.2 or blackline masters Practice 23.2 or Homework 23.2.
- For small group intervention use the Intervention Activity, *Teacher Edition*, p. 615.

Teaching Tip As students use the worksheet, you may wish to have them check that they are placing the *y*-value in the table next to the *x*-value they used to solve.

Skill 182

Objective Graph an equation in the coordinate plane.

Answers
1. 2 + 3; 5; (2, 5); 1 + 3; 4; (1, 4); 0 + 3; 3; (0, 3) **2.** *Check students' graphs.*
3. table: $^-$4; $^-$3; 0; 2; ordered pairs: ($^-$1, 4); (0, $^-$3); (3, 0); (5, 2)
4. *Check students' graphs.*

Graph Equations *Skill from Chapter 23*

Common Error When graphing ordered pairs, students sometimes forget to count left or down for negative integers.

- Use Skill 182 for scaffolded review of the concept.
- For more practice use *Ways to Success* 23.3 or blackline masters Practice 23.3 or Homework 23.3.
- For small group intervention use the Intervention Activity, *Teacher Edition*, p. 618.

Teaching Tip As students use the worksheet, you may wish to have them circle or highlight negative signs in the ordered pairs.

Skill 183

Objective Identify and describe transformations on the coordinate plane.

Answers
1. $^-$3 **2.** $^-$1 **3.** ($^-$1, $^-$3)
4. 2; $^+$7 **5.** 1; $^+$4 **6.** $^-$2
7. *x;* ($^-$5, $^+$2) **8.** ($^-$5, $^-$2)
9. 3; *y;* ($^+$5, $^+$5)

Coordinate Plane Transformations *Skill from Chapter 23*

Common Error Students sometimes reflect across the wrong axis.

- Use Skill 183 for scaffolded review of the concept.
- For more practice use *Ways to Success* 23.5 or blackline masters Practice 23.5 or Homework 23.6.
- For small group intervention use the Intervention Activity, *Teacher Edition*, p. 624.

Teaching Tip As students use the worksheet, you may wish to have them highlight the axis of reflection in color.

Skill 184

Objective Solve problems using a graph.

Answers

1. $12; $15; $21
2. *See student page.*
3–4. *Check students' graphs.*
5. $30 6. 12; *Check students' graphs.*

Use a Graph

Common Error   Students may graph coordinates incorrectly.

- Use Skill 184 for scaffolded review of the concept.
- For more practice use *Ways to Success* 23.4 or blackline masters Problem Solving 23.4, Practice 23.4, or Homework 23.4.
- For small group intervention use the Intervention Activity, *Teacher Edition,* p. 621.

Teaching Tip   As students use the worksheet, you may wish to have them identify the coordinates before plotting the points.

Student Skill Pages

Place Value

The number 746,321,589 is in the place-value chart.
Each digit in the number has a different value.

The chart shows 3 periods:
Millions, Thousands, Ones.

Millions			Thousands			Ones		
hundreds	tens	ones	hundreds	tens	ones	hundreds	tens	ones
7	4	6	3	2	1	5	8	9

The value of the digit **7** is 700,000,000.

The short word form of 746,321,589 is 746 *million,* 321 *thousand,* 589.

Use the chart above to write the value of the digit.

	Digit	Value
1.	4	4 0 , 0 0 0 , __ __ __
2.	6	6 , __ __ __ , __ __ __
3.	3	__ __ __ , __ __ __
4.	2	__ __ , __ __ __

	Digit	Value
5.	1	__ , __ __ __
6.	5	__ __ __
7.	8	__ __
8.	9	__

Write the value of the underlined digit. Then write the short word form.

| thousands place ↓

 42**1**, 376

 The value of the underlined digit is **1,000.**

 The short word form of the number is:
 421 thousand, 376 | **9.** 5**6**,098

 _____

 Short word form:
 _____ | **10.** **3**92,655,835

 _____

 Short word form:
 _____

 _____ |

Name _____ Date _____

Compare, Order, and Round

> means "is greater than"
< means "is less than"
= means "is equal to"

You can use place value to compare.

Compare.

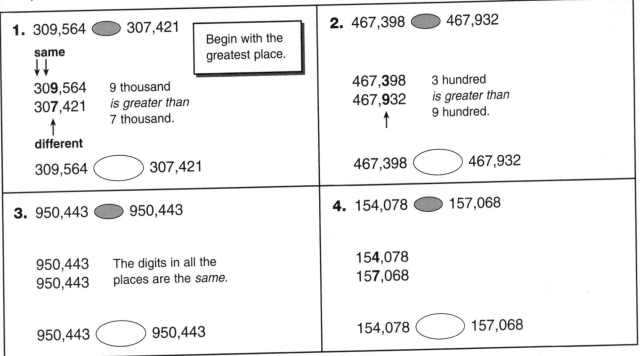

1. 309,564 ⬤ 307,421

Begin with the greatest place.

same
↓↓
30**9**,564   9 thousand
30**7**,421   *is greater than*
 ↑   7 thousand.

different

309,564 ◯ 307,421

2. 467,398 ⬤ 467,932

467,**3**98   3 hundred
467,**9**32   *is greater than*
    ↑   9 hundred.

467,398 ◯ 467,932

3. 950,443 ⬤ 950,443

950,443   The digits in all the
950,443   places are the *same*.

950,443 ◯ 950,443

4. 154,078 ⬤ 157,068

154,078
157,068

154,078 ◯ 157,068

Use place value to order the numbers from greatest to least.

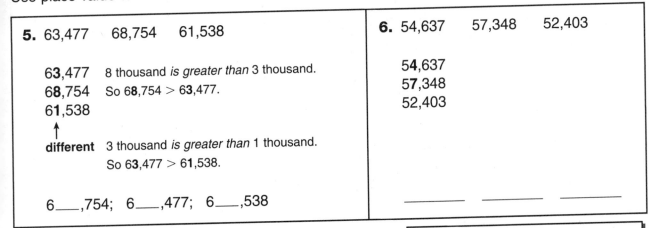

5. 63,477   68,754   61,538

6**3**,477   8 thousand *is greater than* 3 thousand.
6**8**,754   So 68,754 > 63,477.
6**1**,538
  ↑
different   3 thousand *is greater than* 1 thousand.
              So 63,477 > 61,538.

6___,754; 6___,477; 6___,538

6. 54,637   57,348   52,403

54,637
57,348
52,403

_____   _____   _____

Round to the nearest **thousand**.

- If the digit to the right of the rounding place is 5 or more, round up.
- If the digit is less than 5, round down.

rounding place
↓
1,432 Round down to 1,000.

rounding place
↓
2,859 Round up to 3,000.

7. ↓
3,258

___,000

8. ↓
4,753

___,000

9. ↓
8,537

___,000

Objective: Compare, order, and round whole numbers.
Chapter Intervention

Use with Chapter 1.
Grade 5

Name _____ Date _____

Round Decimals

You can use rounding rules to round decimals.

Round to the nearest **whole number.**

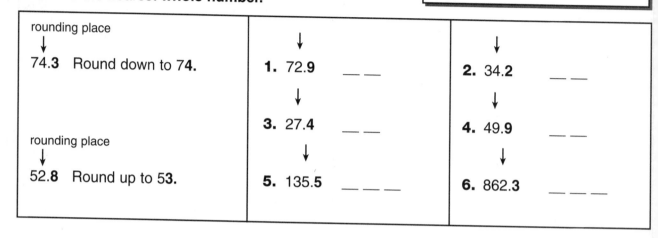

rounding place
↓
74.**3**   Round down to 7**4**.

rounding place
↓
52.**8**   Round up to 5**3**.

1. 72.9   _ _

2. 34.2   _ _

3. 27.4   _ _

4. 49.9   _ _

5. 135.5   _ _ _

6. 862.3   _ _ _

Round to the nearest **tenth.**

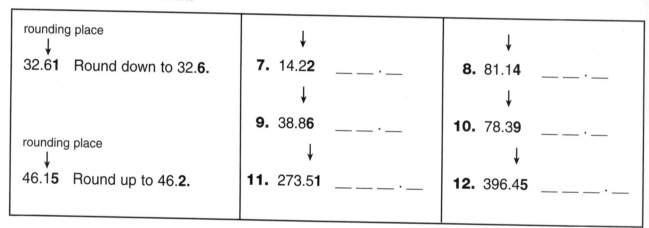

rounding place
↓
32.**6**1   Round down to 32.**6**.

rounding place
↓
46.**1**5   Round up to 46.**2**.

7. 14.22   _ _ . _

8. 81.14   _ _ . _

9. 38.86   _ _ . _

10. 78.39   _ _ . _

11. 273.51   _ _ _ . _

12. 396.45   _ _ _ . _

Round to the nearest whole number.

13. 12.4   _ _

14. 503.9   _ _ _

15. 707.5   _ _ _

16. 89.47   _ _

Round to the nearest tenth.

17. 36.81   _ _ . _

18. 249.76   _ _ _ . _

19. 89.47   _ _ . _

20. 154.25   _ _ _ . _

Name _____ Date _____

Compare and Order Decimals

You can use place value to compare decimals.

> means "is greater than"
< means "is less than"
= means "is equal to"

Compare.

0.31 ⬤ 0.37

same
↓ ↓
0.31
0.37
↑
different

- Align the decimal points.
- Start at the left.
- Compare the digits until they are different.

1 < 7

Since 1 < 7, then 0.31 < 0.37.

---

1. 0.15 ⬤ 0.13

Align. 0.1__

0.1__

0.15 ◯ 0.13

---

2. 0.02 ⬤ 0.21

Align. __ . __ __ __

__ . __ __ __

0.02 ◯ 0.21

---

3. 13.65 ⬤ 13.65

13.65
13.65

The digits in all the places are the *same*.

13.65 ◯ 13.65

---

4. 3.6 ⬤ 3.62

3.60 ← Write a zero in the hundredths place.
3.62

3.6 ◯ 3.62

Use place value to order the decimals from least to greatest.

0.35   0.3   0.21

Align   0.35
and   0.30 ← Write a zero.
compare. 0.21

2 < 3   So, 0.21 is the least number.

Continue   0.30
comparing. 0.35

0 < 5   So, 0.3 < 0.35.

Order from least to greatest.
0.21   0.3   0.35

---

5. 0.31   0.29   0.28

Align. 0.____

0.____

0.____

_____ is the greatest number.

---

6. 5.4   3.92   5.01

_____ _____ _____

7.   6.73   6.84   6.7

_____ _____ _____

Objective: Compare and order decimals.
Chapter Intervention

Use with Chapter 1.
Grade 5

Read and Write Whole Numbers

You can read and write the number in the place-value chart in different ways.

> Each place in the chart is ten times as great as the place to its right.

billions			millions			thousands			ones		
hundreds	tens	ones	hundreds	tens	ones	hundreds	tens	ones	hundreds	tens	ones
5	6	8	2	0	7	4	5	9	2	8	7
hundred billions 10^{11}	ten billions 10^{10}	billions 10^9	hundred millions 10^8	ten millions 10^7	millions 10^6	hundred thousands 10^5	ten thousands 10^4	thousands 10^3	hundreds 10^2	tens 10^1	ones 10^0

Different Forms of the Number in the Chart

Standard Form: 568,207,459,287

Short-Word Form: 568 billion, 207 million, 459 thousand, 287

Expanded Form with Exponents:

$$(5 \times 10^{11}) + (6 \times 10^{10}) + (8 \times 10^9) + (2 \times 10^8) + (7 \times 10^6) +$$
$$(4 \times 10^5) + (5 \times 10^4) + (9 \times 10^3) + (2 \times 10^2) + (8 \times 10^1) + (7 \times 10^0)$$

Use the number in the place-value chart. Write the value of the digit.

1. 6 ___6___ ___0___, ___0___ ___0___ ___0___, ____ ____ ____, ____ ____ ____

2. 8 ____, ____ ____ ____, ____ ____ ____, ____ ____ ____

3. 4 ____ ____ ____, ____ ____ ____

4. 9 ____, ____ ____ ____

Write each number in standard form.

5. 15 thousand, 281 ____, 281	**6.** 9 billion, 618 million, 27 thousand, 978 ____, ____, 027, ____	**7.** 15 billion, 528 thousand 15, ____, ____, ____
8. 12 million ____, ____, ____	**9.** 20 billion, 900 million ____, ____, 000, 000	**10.** 700 billion ____, ____, ____, ____

Objective: Read and write numbers in standard and expanded form.

Chapter Intervention

— 78 —

Use with Chapter 1.
Grade 5

Name _____ Date _____

Read and Write Decimals

> The value of each digit to the **right** of the decimal point is less than 1.

The number 27.468 is in the place-value chart.

decimal point

Whole Numbers				Decimals		
hundreds	tens	ones		tenths	hundredths	thousandths
	2	7	.	4	6	8

names the decimal parts

The value of the digit 8 is eight thousandths.
The word form of 27.468 is twenty-seven **and** four hundred sixty-eight *thousandths.*

shows the decimal point

Use place value to write each in standard form.

1. nine tenths 0.___	**2.** sixteen thousandths 0.__0__ ___ ___	**3.** one hundred twenty-five thousandths 0.___ ___ ___
4. twelve hundredths 0.___ ___	**5.** eighty-four thousandths 0.___ ___ ___	**6.** four hundred six thousandths 0.___ ___ ___
7. one and two tenths ___ . ___	**8.** thirty-one and two hundred seventy-nine thousandths ___ ___ . ___ ___ ___	

Use place value to write each decimal in word form.

9. 0.53 _____ hundredths	**10.** 0.249 _____
11. 4.27 four and _____	**12.** 9.002 _____

Compare and Round Whole Numbers

You can use place value to **compare** numbers.
Compare.

> means "is greater than"   < means "is less than"
= means "is equal to"

3,456,118 ⬭ 3,412,896

same
↓ ↓
- Align digits from the right.   3,456,118
- Starting from the left,   3,412,896
  compare the digits   ↑
  until they are different.   different

| 5 > 1 |

Since 5 > 1, then 3,456,118 > 3,412,896.

1. 3,126,403 ⬭ 3,142,128

Align.   3,126,403
          3,142,128

Compare.   3,126,403 ◯ 3,126,128

2. 8,537,268 ⬭ 8,537,901

Align.   _____

          _____

Compare.   8,537,268 ◯ 8,537,901

Use place value to **order** the numbers from least to greatest.

3. 428,900   456,212   410,562

Align.   428,900
           456,212 ← the greatest number
Compare.   410,562 ← the least number

____   ____   ____

4. 936,100   976,405   924,963

           936,100
           976,405
           924,963

____   ____   ____

Round to the nearest ten thousand.

rounding place
↓
☐2,349
2 < 5 | Do not change the rounding place digit. |

12,349 rounds to 10,000.

rounding place
↓
1,5☐7,152
7 > 5 | Change the rounding place digit. |

1,587,152 rounds
to 1,590,000.

- If the digit to the right of the rounding place is
  5 or more, increase the rounding place digit by **1**.
- If the digit is **less than 5**, do not change the
  rounding place digit. Write **zeros** to the right.

5. ☐2,415

____ 0,000

6. 8☐5,643

8 ____ 0,000

7. 128,543

____ ____ 0,000

8. 9,159,612

____, ____ ____ 0,000

Name _____ Date _____

Compare and Round Decimals

You can use place value to **compare** decimals.

Compare.

> means "is greater than"   < means "is less than"
= means "is equal to"

1. 0.78 ⬭ 0.63

- Align the decimal points.
- Starting from the left, compare the digits until they are different.

same
↓
0.**7**8
0.**6**3
↑
different

7 > 6

0.78 ◯ 0.63

2. 0.149 ⬭ 0.17

| Write zeros if needed. |

Align. 0.149
        0.170

Compare.
0.149 ◯ 0.170

3. 1.659 ⬭ 1.682

Align. _____

Compare.

_____   1.659 ◯ 1.682

Use place value to **order** the decimals from least to greatest.

4. 0.33   0.48   0.29

Align.   0.33
            0.48 ← the greatest number
Compare. 0.29 ← the least number
            ↑
        different

0.29 0._____ 0._____

5. 0.671   0.685   0.642

0.671

0.685

0.642

_____ _____ _____

Round to the nearest hundredth.

rounding place
↓
0.5⬚14
4 < 5

| Do not change the rounding place digit. |

0.514 rounds to 0.51.

rounding place
↓
0.0⬚47
7 > 5

| Change the rounding place digit. |

0.047 rounds to 0.05.

- If the digit to the right of the rounding place is **5 or more**, increase the rounding place digit by **1**.
- If the digit is **less than 5**, do not change the rounding place digit.

6. 0.2⬚61

0._____ _____

7. 0.128

0._____ _____

8. 6.025

6._____ _____

9. 32.986

_____ _____._____ _____

Objective: Round, compare, and order decimals.
Chapter Intervention

Use with Chapter 1.
Grade 5

Name _____ Date _____

Place Value and Exponents

The place-value chart shows each place as a power of ten.

10^5 ←— exponent

Thousands				Ones		
hundreds	tens	ones		hundreds	tens	ones
100,000	10,000	1,000		100	10	1
10×10×10×10×10	10×10×10×10	10×10×10		10×10	10	1
10^5	10^4	10^3		10^2	10^1	10^0

Write the number in expanded form and in expanded form with exponents.

1. 834,292

$800,000 \ + \ 30,000 \ + \ 4,000 \ + \ 200 \ + \ 90 \ + \ 2$ ←— Expanded form

$(8 \times 100,000) + (3 \times 10,000) + (4 \times 1,000) + (2 \times 100) + (9 \times 10) + (2 \times 1)$ — Expanded form with exponents

$(8 \times 10^5) \ + \ (3 \times 10^4) \ + \ (4 \times 10-) + (2 \times 10-) + (9 \times \underline{\ \ }) + (2 \times \underline{\ \ })$

2. 268,755

$(2 \times 100,000) + (6 \times 10,000) + (8 \times 1,000) + (\underline{\ \ } \times 100) + (\underline{\ \ } \times 10) + (\underline{\ \ } \times 1)$

$(2 \times 10^5) \ + \ (6 \times 10^4) \ + \ (8 \times 10-) + (\underline{\ \ } \times 10-) + (\underline{\ \ } \times 10-) + (\underline{\ \ } \times 1)$

Write the number in expanded form with exponents.

3. 6,489

$(6 \times 10^3) + (4 \times 10-) + (\underline{\ \ } \times 10-) + (\underline{\ \ } \times \underline{\ \ })$

4. 10,567

$(1 \times 10^4) + (5 \times 10^2) + (\underline{\ \ } \times \underline{\ \ }) + (\underline{\ \ } \times \underline{\ \ })$

5. 437,203

$(\underline{\ \ } \times \underline{\ \ }) + (\underline{\ \ } \times \underline{\ \ }) + (\underline{\ \ } \times \underline{\ \ }) + (\underline{\ \ } \times \underline{\ \ }) + (\underline{\ \ } \times \underline{\ \ })$

Name _____ Date _____

Find a Pattern

Problem   Kate is starting an exercise program.
She walks 5 minutes on Day 1. She walks 10 minutes
on Day 2. She walks 15 minutes on Day 3.
How many minutes is Kate likely to walk on Day 4?

Read to Understand

1. How many minutes does Kate walk on Day 1?   _____ minutes

2. How many minutes does Kate walk on Day 2?   _____ minutes

3. How many minutes does Kate walk on Day 3?   _____ minutes

4. Restate the problem another way. _I know how many minutes Kate_
walks on Days 1, 2, and 3. I am looking for the number of minutes
Kate is likely to walk on Day 4.

Choose a Way to Solve the Problem

You can begin by organizing the data in a table.

- Study the table to find a pattern.

- Describe the pattern.

- Then use the pattern to complete the table.

Day	1	2	3	4
Time (min)	5	10	15	?

+ 5   + 5   + 5

Show the Solution

5. Kate walks _____ minutes more each day.

6. Kate is likely to walk _____ minutes on Day 4.

Try This   Find a pattern to solve.

Jamal plants tulips each year. He plants
24 tulips in Year 1. He plants 36 tulips in
Year 2. He plants 48 tulips in Year 3. How
many tulips is he likely to plant in Year 4?

Year	1	2	3	4
Tulips	24	36	48	?

7. The number of tulips increases by _____ each year.

8. Solution   Jamal is likely to plant _____ tulips in Year 4.

Objective: Solve problems by finding patterns.
Chapter Intervention

Use with Chapter 1.
Grade 5

Name _____ Date _____

Use Addition Properties

You can use **addition properties** to add.
Use addition properties to find the sums.

Commutative Property If you change the **order** of the addends, the sum stays the same.

1. $7 + 8 = 15$

$8 + 7 =$ ___

So, $7 + 8 = 8 + 7$

2. $9 + 2 = 11$

___ + ___ = 11

3. $23 + 4 = 27$

___ + ___ = 27

4. $16 + 10 = 26$

___ + ___ = 26

Associative Property If you change the way addends are **grouped,** the sum stays the same. Remember: *Parentheses tell you what to do first.*

5. $(3 + 4) + 6 = 3 + (4 + 6)$

$7 + 6 = 3 +$ ___

___ = ___

6. $26 + (3 + 5) = (26 + 3) + 5$

$26 +$ ___ $=$ ___ $+ 5$

___ = ___

7. $(11 + 8) + 20 = 11 + ($ ___ $+$ ___ $)$

___ $+$ ___ $=$ ___ $+$ ___

___ = ___

8. $125 + (15 + 10) = ($ ___ $+$ ___ $) +$ ___

___ $+$ ___ $=$ ___ $+$ ___

___ = ___

Identity Property If you add zero to a number, the sum is that number.

9. $5 + 0 =$ ___

10. $0 + 10 =$ ___

11. $89 + 0 =$ ___

12. $0 + 276 =$ ___

Complete each number sentence. Tell which property you used.

13. $6 + (19 + 8) = ($ ___ $+ 19) + 8$

_____

14. $26 + 14 =$ ___ $+ 26$

_____

15. $156 + 0 =$ ___

_____

16. $12 + (3 + 0) = 12 +$ ___

_____

Name _____ Date _____

Add and Subtract Greater Numbers

Sometimes you must regroup before you can add or subtract.

Add. Regroup if necessary.

1.

Th	H	T	O
1		**1**	
2,	7	2	6
+ 1,	5	2	5
4,	2	5	1

Add the ones. Then regroup.
Add the tens.
Add the hundreds. Then regroup.
Add the thousands.

TT	Th	H	T	O
	☐	☐		
4	4,	8	9	1
+ 5	1,	5	2	3

Subtract. Regroup if necessary.

2.

Th	H	T	O
	6	**15**	
4,	~~7~~	~~5~~	6
− 1,	5	8	4
3,	4	7	2

Subtract the ones.
Subtract the tens.
Regroup 1 hundred as 10 tens.
Subtract the hundreds.
Subtract the thousands.

TT	Th	H	T	O
			☐	☐
8	9,	5	5	2
− 5	3,	4	2	3

Add or subtract.

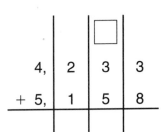

3.

		☐	
4,	2	3	3
+ 5,	1	5	8

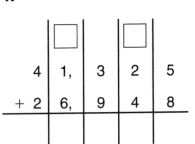

4.

	☐		☐	
4	1,	3	2	5
+ 2	6,	9	4	8

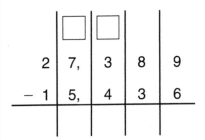

5.

	☐	☐		
2	7,	3	8	9
− 1	5,	4	3	6

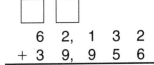

6.

☐ ☐

	6	2,	1	3	2
+	3	9,	9	5	6

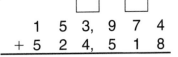

7.

☐ ☐

	1	5	3,	9	7	4
+	5	2	4,	5	1	8

8.

☐ ☐

	7	9,	3	5	0
−	1	8,	1	3	5

Objective: Add and subtract up to 6-digit whole numbers.
Chapter Intervention

Use with Chapter 2.
Grade 5

Name _____ Date _____

Estimate Sums and Differences

Use rounding rules to estimate.

Round to the nearest **thousand.** Then estimate the *sum.*

rounding place
↓
2,**1**35 **down** →   2,000
+ 3,**6**10 **up**   → + 4,000
                        6,000

1.
↓
4,**3**29   ___,000
+ 4,**8**42
          + ___,000
          _____

2.
↓
9,**5**12   ___ ___,___ ___ ___
+ 2,**0**31
          +   ___,___ ___ ___
          _____

Round to the nearest **hundred.** Then estimate the *difference.*

rounding place
↓
6,3**4**9 **down** →   6,300
− 3,2**8**2 **up**   → − 3,300
                        3,000

3.
↓
5,**2**61   ___,___ 00
− 4,**7**35
          − ___,___ 00
          _____

4.
↓
8,**9**24   ___,___ ___ ___
− 5,**5**48
          −   ___,___ ___ ___
          _____

Round to the nearest **ten.** Then estimate the *sum* or *difference.*

rounding place
↓
2,14**5** **up**   →   2,150
+ 3,15**2** **down** → + 3,150
                        5,300

5.
↓
9,32**9**   ___,___ ___ 0
− 6,33**1**
          − ___,___ ___ 0
          _____

6.
↓
3,49**7**   3 , 5 ___ ___
+ 2,**3**03
          + ___,___ ___ ___
          _____

Round to the place shown. Then estimate the *sum* or *difference.*

7.
thousands
↓
7,490
− 2,681

8.
hundreds
↓
1,528
+ 3,765

9.
hundreds
↓
9,354
− 8,206

10.
tens
↓
4,492
+ 7,003

Solve Equations

You can use models and mental math to solve equations.

Solve.

1. $n + 9 = 16$

Look at the model of the equation.

16	
n	9

Use mental math.
Think What number plus 9 equals 16?
Try 7.

$7 + 9 = 16$, so $n =$ ___

2. $3 + x = 12$

Look at the model of the equation.

12	
3	x

Use mental math.
Think 3 plus what number equals 12?

$x =$ ___

3. $c + 5 = 8$

8	
c	5

Use mental math.

$c =$ ___

4. $15 - n = 9$

Look at the model of the equation.

15	
n	9

Use mental math.
Think 15 minus what number equals 9?

$15 - 6 = 9$, so $n =$ ___

5. $9 - y = 7$

Look at the model of the equation.

9	
7	y

Use mental math.
Think 9 minus what number equals 7?

$y =$ ___

6. $11 - a = 6$

11	
6	a

Use mental math.

$a =$ ___

Solve each addition or subtraction equation. Draw models if needed.

7. $d + 4 = 12$	**8.** $4 - n = 1$	**9.** $12 = 4 + p$	**10.** $n - 3 = 4$
$d =$ ___	$n =$ ___	$p =$ ___	$n =$ ___

Addition Properties and Expressions

When you **evaluate** an expression, you can use addition properties.

Evaluate each expression when $n = 7$.

1.

$(4 + 3) + n$

$(4 + 3) + 7$ Substitute 7 for n.

$4 + (3 + 7)$ Use the **Associative Property** to change the grouping of the addends.

$4 + 10$

_____

2.

$n + (3 + 2)$

___ $+ (3 + 2)$ Substitute 7 for n.

$(\_\_ + 3) + 2$ Use the Associative Property.

_____ $+ 2$

_____

3.

$43 + (n + 5)$

$43 + (\_\_ + 5)$

$(\_\_ + \_\_) + 5$

_____ $+ 5$

_____

4.

$(n + 41) + 13$

$(7 + 41) + 13$ Use the **Commutative Property** to change the order of the addends.

$(41 + 7) + 13$

$41 + (7 + 13)$

$41 + $ _____

_____

5.

$n + (25 + 53)$

$7 + (25 + 53)$ Use the Commutative Property.

$7 + (53 + \_\_)$

$(7 + \_\_) + 25$

_____ $+$ _____

_____

6.

$93 + (21 + n)$

$93 + (21 + \_\_)$

$93 + (\_\_ + 21)$

$(93 + \_\_) + 21$

_____ $+$ _____

_____

Evaluate each expression when $n = 15$.

7.

$56 + (n - 15)$

$56 + (15 - 15)$ Substitute 15 for n. **Identity Property**

$56 + $ _____

_____

8.

$(8 + 15) - n$

$(8 + 15) - \_\_$

$8 + (\_\_ - \_\_)$

$8 + $ _____

_____

9.

$(10 + 5) - n$

_____

Objective: Use addition properties to evaluate algebraic expressions.
Chapter Intervention

Use with Chapter 2.
Grade 5

Name _____ Date _____

Estimate Differences and Sums

Sometimes you do not need an exact answer when you add or subtract.
You can *estimate* the sum or difference.

Round to the greatest place. Then estimate the sum or difference.

rounding place
↓
  2,328 down →   2,000
+ 4,685 up → + 5,000
                        7,000
 	
The sum is about 7,000.
	1. 6,703 + 1,424
	
	  6,703 → ____,000
	+ 1,424 → + ____,000
	
	          ____ , ____
		2. 8,560 + 5,863
		
		  8,560 → ____,000
		+ 5,863 → + ____,000
		
		          ____ , ____

3. 7,391 − 5,921
 	
  7,391 →   7,000
− 5,921 → − 6,000
 	
        ____ , ____
 	
The difference is about
 	
_____ .
	4.
	
	  9,105 →
	− 2,687 →
	
	The difference is about
	
	_____ .
		5.
		
		  3,857 →
		+ 5,258 →
		
		The sum is about
		
		_____ .

Round up and down to find an estimated range for the sum.

7,143 + 2,861
 	
Round down   Round up
 	
  7,000   8,000
+ 2,000   + 3,000
  9,000   11,000
 	
The sum is between 9,000
and 11,000.
	6. 5,149 + 2,611
	
	Round down Round up
	
	  5,000 ___,000
	+ 2,000 + ___,000
	  ___,____ ___,____
	
	The sum is between _____
	
	and _____ .
		7. 9,512 + 6,513
		
		Round down Round up
		
		The sum is between _____
		
		and _____ .

Name _____ Date _____

Subtract and Add Greater Numbers

Sometimes you may need to regroup when you add or subtract.

Add.

Start at the right. Add in each place.
Regroup as needed.

HT	TT	Th	H	T	O
			1	1	
1	3	8,	6	4	3
+ 1	1	0,	2	6	7
2	4	8,	9	1	0

Think 3 + 7 = 10
Regroup 10 ones as
1 ten 0 ones.

1.

HT	TT	Th	H	T	O
			□	□	
3	2	6,	0	2	8
+ 2	7	2,	5	8	3

Subtract.

Start at the right. Subtract in each place.
Regroup as needed.

HT	TT	Th	H	T	O
				15	
			8	5̸	13
4	2	8,	9̸	6̸	3̸
− 1	1	2,	6	9	5
3	1	6,	2	6	8

Think Not enough ones to subtract.
Regroup 6 tens as 5 tens 10 ones.
10 + 3 = 13

2.

HT	TT	Th	H	T	O
				□	
			□	□	□
7	4	6,	8	2	5
− 1	2	5,	7	3	6

Add or Subtract.

3.	**4.**	**5.**	**6.**
299,865 +238,457	278,622 + 58,358	499,815 −361,326	549,284 −237,095

Objective: Add and subtract up to 6-digit whole numbers.
Chapter Intervention

Use with Chapter 2.
Grade 5

Name _____ Date _____

Use Mental Math

In an **equation** the quantities on both sides
of the equal sign have the same value.

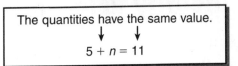
You can use mental math to solve addition and subtraction equations.

Write an addition equation for the model. Use mental math to solve.	**1.**	**2.**

1.

20	
n	9

$n + 9 = 20$

Think
What number plus 9 equals 20?

$n + 9 = 20$
$n = 11$

2.

12	
3	m

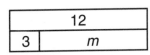

___ $+ m =$ ___

$m =$ _____

25	
x	23

$x +$ ___ $=$ ___

$x =$ _____

Write a subtraction equation for the model. Use mental math to solve.

3.

34	
w	10

$34 - w = 10$

Think
What number subtracted from 34 equals 10?

$34 - w = 10$
$w = 24$

17	
m	9

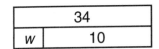

___ $- m = 9$

$m =$ _____

4.

47	
k	17

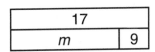

___ $- k = 17$

$k =$ _____

Use mental math to solve these equations.

5. $25 + c = 100$	**6.** $x - 24 = 10$	**7.** $a + 35 = 70$	**8.** $75 - d = 25$
$c =$ _____	$x =$ _____	$a =$ _____	$d =$ _____

Objective: Solve addition and subtraction equations using mental math.
Chapter Intervention

Use with Chapter 2.
Grade 5

Name _____ Date _____

Identify Relevant Information

Problem The Railroad Museum had 5,212 visitors last week. The museum sold 2,125 adult tickets. The other tickets sold were children's tickets. Special programs cost $9 each. How many children visited the museum?

Read to Understand

1. How many visitors were there in all? _____

2. How many visitors were adults? _____

3. Who were the rest of the visitors? _____

Choose a Way to Solve the Problem

Sometimes a problem has too much information. Other times it has too little information.

- Draw a model to identify which information is necessary for solving the problem.

- Write an equation and solve it.

Total number of tickets	
_____	
Number of adult tickets	Number of children's tickets
_____	n

Show the Solution

4. Write the missing information in the model.

5. Use the model to write an equation.

$2{,}125 + n =$ _____

6. Solution _____ children visited the museum.

Try This Use a model to solve.

7. Max has some gold coins and some silver coins. He has 241 coins in all. The silver coins are worth $0.25 each. He has 37 gold coins. How many silver coins does Max have?

Total number of coins	
_____	
Number of gold coins	Number of silver coins
_____	n

Solution Max has _____ silver coins.

Name _____ Date _____

Use Multiplication Properties

You can use **multiplication properties** when you multiply.
Complete each number sentence.

Commutative Property   When you change the **order** of the factors,
the product stays the same.

1. $3 \times 9 = 27$ **2.** $4 \times 2 = 8$ **3.** $5 \times 3 = 15$ **4.** $8 \times 10 = 80$

$9 \times 3 =$ ____   ____ $\times$ ____ $= 8$ ____ $\times$ ____ $= 15$ ____ $\times$ ____ $= 80$

So, $3 \times 9 = 9 \times 3$

Associative Property   When you change the way
factors are **grouped,** the product stays the same.

| Parentheses tell you what to do first. |

5. $(3 \times 2) \times 4 = 3 \times (2 \times 4)$

$6 \quad \times 4 = 3 \times$ ____

____ $=$ ____

6. $9 \times (1 \times 5) = (9 \times 1) \times 5$

$9 \times$ ____ $=$ ____ $\times 5$

____ $=$ ____

7. $(2 \times 2) \times 4 = 2 \times ($ ____ $\times$ ____ $)$

____ $\times$ ____ $=$ ____ $\times$ ____

____ $=$ ____

8. $7 \times (5 \times 1) = ($ ____ $\times$ ____ $) \times$ ____

____ $\times$ ____ $=$ ____ $\times$ ____

____ $=$ ____

Identity Property   The product of any
number and 1 is that number.

9. $64 \times 1 =$ ____   **10.** $1 \times 48 =$ ____

Zero Property   The product of any
number and 0 is 0.

11. $12 \times 0 =$ ____   **12.** $0 \times 72 =$ ____

Complete each number sentence. Tell which property or properties you used.

13. $4 \times (2 \times 6) = (4 \times 2) \times$ ____	**14.** $26 \times 1 =$ ____
_____	_____
15. $0 \times 158 =$ ____	**16.** $6 \times (0 \times 12) = 0 \times$ ____
_____	_____

Objective: Use multiplication properties.
Chapter Intervention

Use with Chapter 3.
Grade 5

Multiply by 1-Digit Numbers

Sometimes you need to regroup when you multiply.

1. Find 3 × 245.

Multiply the ones.
3 × 5 ones = 15 ones

Regroup 15 ones as 1 ten 5 ones.

H	T	**O**
	☐	
2	4	**5**
×		**3**
		5

Multiply the tens.
3 × 4 tens = 12 ones
Add the 1 ten.
12 + 1 = 13 tens

Regroup 13 tens as 1 hundred 3 tens.

H	**T**	O
☐	1	
2	**4**	5
×		**3**
	3	5

Multiply the hundreds.
3 × 4 hundreds = 6 hundreds
Add the 1 hundred.
6 + 1 = 7 hundreds

H	T	O
1	1	
2	4	5
×		3
7	3	5

3 × 245 = _____

Multiply. Regroup when necessary.

2. 3 × 215

H	T	O
2	1	5
×		**3**

3. 2 × 463

H	T	O
4	6	3
×		2

4. 4 × 205

H	T	O
2	0	5
×		4

5. 6 × 136

H	T	O
1	3	6
×		6

6. 3 × 3,259

Th	H	T	O
3,	2	5	9
×			3

7. 4 × 1,631

Th	H	T	O
1,	6	3	1
×			4

8. 2 × 4,409

Th	H	T	O
4,	4	0	9
×			2

9. 4 × 1,915

Th	H	T	O
1,	9	1	5
×			4

Name _____ Date _____

Estimate Products

You can use rounding to estimate products.
Round to the greatest place. Estimate each product.

> • If the digit to the right of the rounding place is 5 or more, round up.
> • If the digit is less than 5, round down.

The greatest place value is **hundreds**, so round to the nearest **hundred**.
 	
226 **round down** ⟶ 200
$\times$ 4 $\times$ 4
            800
	1.
	
	242 ⟶ 200
	$\times$ 3 $\times$ 3
	_____
	     __00
		2.
		
		163 ⟶ 200
		$\times$ 4 $\times$ 4
		_____
		     __00

The greatest place value is **thousands**, so round to the nearest **thousand**.
 	
1,569 **round up** ⟶ 2,000
$\times$ 2 $\times$ 2
       4,000
	3.
	
	1,269 ⟶ 1,000
	$\times$ 9 $\times$ 9
	_____
	     __,000
		4.
		
		5,620 ⟶ 6,000
		$\times$ 5 $\times$ 5
		_____
		    __ __,000

Round to the greatest place. Estimate each product.

5. 123 ⟶
    $\times$ 7

6. 344 ⟶
    $\times$ 2

7. 490 ⟶
    $\times$ 6

8. 620 ⟶
    $\times$ 9

9. 2,620
    $\times$ 2

10. 8,053
    $\times$ 5

11. 2,850
    $\times$ 2

12. 5,537
    $\times$ 8

Name _____ Date _____

Evaluate Expressions

You can use properties to evaluate multiplication expressions.

Commutative Property: $a \times b = b \times a$	Associative Property: $a \times (b \times c) = (a \times b) \times c$
Identity Property: $a \times 1 = a$	Zero Property: $a \times 0 = 0$

Distributive Property: $a(b + c) = (a \times b) + (a \times c)$

Use multiplication properties to evaluate the expressions.

1. Use the **Distributive Property.**
Find $6n$ when $n = 24$.

$$6 + 24 = 6 \times (20 + 4)$$

$$= (6 \times 20) + (6 \times 4)$$

Multiply. = _____ + _____

Add. = _____

2. Use the **Associative Property.**
Find $5 \times (4 \times n)$ when $n = 7$.

$$5 \times (4 \times n) = 5 \times (4 \times 7)$$

$$= (\underline{} \times 4) \times 7$$

Multiply. = _____ × _____

= _____

3. $5n$ when $n = 35$.

$$5n = 5 \times (30 + \underline{})$$

$$= (5 \times 30) + (5 \times \underline{})$$

= _____ + _____

= _____

4. $8 \times (n \times 10)$ when $n = 2$.

$$8 \times (n \times 10) = 8 \times (\underline{} \times 10)$$

$$= (8 \times \underline{}) \times 10$$

= _____ × _____

= _____

Evaluate each expression when $n = 9$.

5. $3 \times (10 + n)$	**6.** $8 \times (5 \times n)$	**7.** $56 \times (0 \times n)$	**8.** $12 \times (n \times 10)$	**9.** $(7 \times n) \times 1$
_____	_____	_____	_____	_____

Name _____ Date _____

Multiply by 2-Digit Numbers

Sometimes you need to regroup when you multiply.
Find 53 × 216.

Multiply the ones.	Multiply the tens.	Add the partial products.

Multiply the ones.

```
    1
  2 1 6
×   5 3
  6 4 8  ← 3 × 216
```

Multiply the tens.

```
      3
      1
    2 1 6
  ×   5 3
    6 4 8
1 0, 8 0 0  ← 50 × 216
```

Add the partial products.

```
      3
      1
    2 1 6
  ×   5 3
    6 4 8
+ 1 0, 8 0 0
  1 1, 4 4 8
```

Multiply.

1.

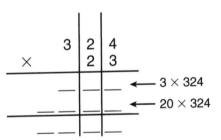

```
    3 2 4
  ×   2 3
  _____
  _ _ _   ← 3 × 324
  _ _ _   ← 20 × 324
  _____
  _ _ _ _
```

23 × 324 = _____

2.

```
    2 3 5
  ×   3 4
  _____
  _ _ _   ← 4 × 235
  _ _ _   ← 30 × 235
  _____
  _ _ _ _
```

34 × 235 = _____

3.

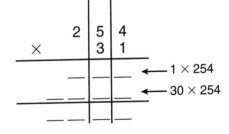

```
    2 5 4
  ×   3 1
  _____
  _ _ _   ← 1 × 254
  _ _ _   ← 30 × 254
  _____
  _ _ _ _
```

31 × 254 = _____

4.

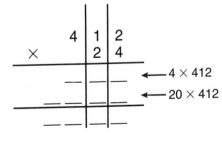

```
    4 1 2
  ×   2 4
  _____
  _ _ _   ← 4 × 412
  _ _ _   ← 20 × 412
  _____
  _ _ _ _
```

24 × 412 = _____

Product Estimation

You can estimate products using **front-end estimation** or **rounding**.

Estimate.

Front-end Estimation	1.	2.
Use front digits only. ↓ $28 \rightarrow 20$ $\times 43 \rightarrow \times 40$ $\overline{}$ $\qquad 800$	$77 \rightarrow \underline{}0$ $\times 31 \rightarrow \times \underline{}0$ $\overline{}$ $\underline{},\underline{}$	$47 \rightarrow \underline{}0$ $\times 52 \rightarrow \times \underline{}0$ $\overline{}$ $\underline{},\underline{}$

Find a Range by Rounding	3.	4.
Round both factors down. | Round both factors up. $14 \rightarrow 10$ | $14 \rightarrow 20$ $\times 37 \rightarrow \times 30$ | $\times 37 \rightarrow \times 40$ $\overline{300}$ | $\overline{800}$ The actual product is *between* 300 and 800.	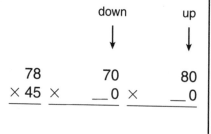 The actual product is between _____ and _____.	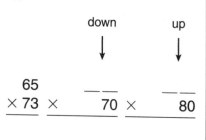 The actual product is between _____ and _____.

5.	6.	7.
down up ↓ ↓ 41 $\times 53 \quad \times \underline{} \quad \times \underline{}$ $\underline{} \quad \underline{}$ The actual product is between _____ and _____.	down up ↓ ↓ 88 $\times 24 \quad \times \underline{} \quad \times \underline{}$ $\underline{} \quad \underline{}$ The actual product is between _____ and _____.	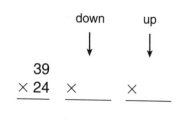 The actual product is between _____ and _____.

Use Logical Reasoning

Problem   Connor, Tina, Brad, and Jolie each play a different instrument. The instruments are drums, guitar, piano, and bass. Connor plays drums. Tina does <u>not</u> play the guitar or the piano. Jolie does <u>not</u> play the guitar. Brad does <u>not</u> play the piano. What do Tina, Brad, and Jolie play?

Read to Understand

1. What are the friends' names? _____   _____   _____   _____

2. What are the instruments?   _____   _____   _____   _____

Choose a Way to Solve the Problem
You can use logical reasoning to solve the problem.
Make a chart to organize the information.

Show the Solution

	drums	guitar	piano	bass
Connor				
Tina				
Brad				
Jolie				

3. Connor plays the drums. Write YES in the column for drums in Connor's row. Write NO in the other columns in Connor's row.

4. If you write YES in Connor's row for drums, what can you write in that column for the other names? _____

5. Where can you write NO in Tina's row? _____

Where can you write YES? _____

6. Where can you write NO in Brad's row? _____

Where can you write YES? _____

7. Solution   Tina plays the _____. Brad plays the _____.

Jolie plays the _____.

Try This   Use logical reasoning. Make a chart to help you.

	blue	red	yellow
Jon			
Kyle			
Lila			

8. Jon, Kyle, and Lila each have a book. Kyle has the blue book. Jon does *not* have the red book. The other book is yellow. Use the chart to organize the data.

9. Solution   Jon has the _____ book.

Lila has the _____ book.

Estimate Quotients

You can use basic facts and multiples of 10 to estimate quotients.

Estimate.

$128 \div 4$

- Use a basic fact and a multiple of 10 to find a new dividend.

Think	basic fact
	$\nearrow$
	$3 \times 4 = 12$
	$10 \times 12 = 120$
	$\uparrow$
	multiple of 10

$4\overline{)128} \longrightarrow 4\overline{)120}$

$\uparrow$
120 is close to 128

- Divide to estimate.

$\overset{30}{4\overline{)120}}$

$128 \div 4$ is about 30.

---

1. $294 \div 7$

Basic Fact: $4 \times 7 = 28$ Choose $4 \times 7 = 28$ because 28 is close to 29.

$7\overline{)294} \longrightarrow 7\overline{)280}$

Think	$4 \times 7 = 28$
	$10 \times 28 = 280$

$294 \div 7$ is about _____.

---

2. $171 \div 8$

Basic Fact: _____

$8\overline{)171} \longrightarrow$ _____

$171 \div 8$ is about _____.

Estimate. Write the basic fact you used.

3. $326 \div 6$ Basic Fact: _____ Estimate: _____	**4.** $278 \div 7$ Basic Fact: _____ Estimate: _____	**5.** $137 \div 7$ Basic Fact: _____ Estimate: _____
6. $412 \div 8$ Basic Fact: _____ Estimate: _____	**7.** $147 \div 5$ Basic Fact: _____ Estimate: _____	**8.** $278 \div 3$ Basic Fact: _____ Estimate: _____

Name _____ Date _____

Divide Whole Numbers

When you divide, start by estimating where to place
the first digit of the quotient.

Divide.

$3,020 \div 5$ Estimate. Think of a basic fact. $\quad\quad\quad\dfrac{600}{5)3,000}$ $30 \div 5 = 6$ $\begin{array}{r} 604 \\ 5)\overline{3,020} \\ -30 \\ \hline 020 \\ -20 \\ \hline 0 \end{array}$ ← The first digit is in the **hundreds** place.	**1.** $5,635 \div 6$ Estimate. $6)\overline{5,\ 4\ 0\ 0}$ $6)\overline{5,\ 6\ 3\ 5}$ R__	**2.** $1,784 \div 4$ Estimate. $4)\overline{1,\ 6\ 0\ 0}$ $4)\overline{1,\ 7\ 8\ 4}$ R__
3. $3,341 \div 5$ Estimate. _____ $5)\overline{3,\ 3\ 4\ 1}$ R__	**4.** $4,226 \div 7$ Estimate. _____ $7)\overline{4,\ 2\ 2\ 6}$ R__	**5.** $7,326 \div 9$ Estimate. _____ $9)\overline{7,\ 3\ 2\ 6}$ R__
6. $2,504 \div 8$ Estimate. _____ $8)\overline{2,\ 5\ 0\ 4}$	**7.** $5,504 \div 9$ Estimate. _____ $9)\overline{5,\ 5\ 0\ 4}$	**8.** $6,283 \div 7$ Estimate. _____ $7)\overline{6,\ 2\ 8\ 3}$

Objective: Divide 4-digit dividends by 1-digit divisors.
Chapter Intervention

Use with Chapter 4.
Grade 5

Name _____ Date _____

Factors and Multiples

The table to the right shows
that $3 \times 6 = 18$.

So, 3 and 6 are **factors** of 18.

Look at the row that starts with 3.
The first four **multiples** of 3 are
3, 6, 9, and 12.

x	1	2	3	4	5	6	7	8	9	10	11	12
1	1	2	3	4	5	6	7	8	9	10	11	12
2	2	4	6	8	10	12	14	16	18	20	22	24
3	3	6	9	12	15	18	21	24	27	30	33	36
4	4	8	12	16	20	24	28	32	36	40	44	48
5	5	10	15	20	25	30	35	40	45	50	55	60
6	6	12	18	24	30	36	42	48	54	60	66	72
7	7	14	21	28	35	42	49	56	63	70	77	84
8	8	16	24	32	40	48	56	64	72	80	88	96
9	9	18	27	36	45	54	63	72	81	90	99	108
10	10	20	30	40	50	60	70	80	90	100	110	120
11	11	22	33	44	55	66	77	88	99	110	121	132
12	12	24	36	48	60	72	84	96	108	120	132	144

- Find the factors of 18.

  $1 \times \mathbf{18} = 18$
  $2 \times \mathbf{9} = 18$
  $3 \times \mathbf{6} = 18$

- List the factors from least to greatest.

  Factors of 18: 1, 2, 3, 6, 9, 18

List the factors of each number from least to greatest.

1. 12

$1 \times \underline{\quad} = 12$

$2 \times \underline{\quad} = 12$

$3 \times \underline{\quad} = 12$

The factors are:

1, 2, 3, _____, _____, _____.

2. 20

$1 \times \underline{\quad} = 20$

$2 \times \underline{\quad} = 20$

$4 \times \underline{\quad} = 20$

The factors are:

1, 2, 4, _____, _____, _____.

3. 24

$1 \times \underline{\quad} = 24$

$2 \times \underline{\quad} = 24$

$3 \times \underline{\quad} = 24$

$4 \times \underline{\quad} = 24$

The factors are:

1, 2, __, __, __, __, __, __.

List the first 4 multiples of each number.

4. 8

$1 \times 8 = \underline{\quad}$

$2 \times 8 = \underline{\quad}$

$3 \times 8 = \underline{\quad}$

$4 \times 8 = \underline{\quad}$

The multiples are:

8, 16, 24, _____.

5. 10

$1 \times 10 = \underline{\quad}$

$2 \times 10 = \underline{\quad}$

$3 \times 10 = \underline{\quad}$

$4 \times 10 = \underline{\quad}$

The multiples are:

_____, _____, _____, _____.

6. 4

The multiples are:

_____, _____, _____, _____.

Objective: Find factors and multiples of a number.
Chapter Intervention

Use with Chapter 4.
Grade 5

Name _____ Date _____

Use Mental Math to Divide

You can use patterns and basic facts to help you divide mentally.

Use basic facts and patterns to find each quotient.

$150 \div 3 = $ 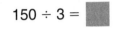	**1.** $4{,}500 \div 5 = $ ▨	**2.** $56{,}000 \div 7 = $ ▨

$15 \div 3 = 5$
$150 \div 3 = 50$
$1{,}500 \div 3 = 500$
$15{,}000 \div 3 = 5000$

↑ 3 zeros   ↑ 3 zeros

$150 \div 3 = 50$

1.
$45 \div 5 = 9$
$450 \div 5 = 9\_\_$
$4{,}500 \div 5 = \_\_\ \_\_\ \_\_$
$45{,}000 \div 5 = \_\_,\ \_\_\ \_\_\ \_\_$

$4{,}500 \div 5 = $ _____

2.
$56 \div 7 = \_\_$
$560 \div 7 = \_\_\ \_\_$
$5{,}600 \div 7 = \_\_\ \_\_\ \_\_$
$56{,}000 \div 7 = \_\_,\ \_\_\ \_\_\ \_\_$

$56{,}000 \div 7 = $ _____

---

3. $240 \div 8 = $ ▨

$24 \div 8 = $ _____
$240 \div 8 = $ _____
$2{,}400 \div 8 = $ _____
$24{,}000 \div 8 = $ _____

$240 \div 8 = $ _____

4. $9{,}000 \div 9 = $ ▨

$9 \div 9 = $ _____
$90 \div 9 = $ _____
$900 \div 9 = $ _____
$9{,}000 \div 9 = $ _____

$9{,}000 \div 9 = $ _____

5. $24{,}000 \div 6 = $ ▨

$24 \div 6 = $ _____
$240 \div 6 = $ _____
$2{,}400 \div 6 = $ _____
$24{,}000 \div 6 = $ _____

$24{,}000 \div 6 = $ _____

Use mental math to find each quotient.

6. $120 \div 2 = $ _____	**7.** $1{,}800 \div 6 = $ _____	**8.** $81{,}000 \div 9 = $ _____	**9.** $2{,}000 \div 4 = $ _____
10. $3{,}500 \div 5 = $ _____	**11.** $360 \div 9 = $ _____	**12.** $6{,}000 \div 3 = $ _____	**13.** $40{,}000 \div 8 = $ _____

Name _____ Date _____

Use Compatible Numbers

Compatible numbers are numbers that divide easily.
You can use compatible numbers to make a new **dividend**
to estimate the **quotient**.

$$\begin{array}{r} 811 \leftarrow \textbf{quotient} \\ 8\overline{)6,488} \leftarrow \textbf{dividend} \end{array}$$

Estimate.

1,387 ÷ 4

- Use a compatible number to make
a new dividend.

> **Think** What number is compatible with 4
> and close to 13?
>
> $4\overline{)13} \longrightarrow 4\overline{)12}$
>
> 12 is compatible with 4.

$4\overline{)1,387} \longrightarrow 4\overline{)1,200}$

- Divide to estimate.

$\begin{array}{r} 300 \\ 4\overline{)1,200} \end{array}$

1,387 ÷ 4 is about **300**.

---

1. 2,892 ÷ 7

Compatible numbers: 2,800 ÷ 7

$7\overline{)2,892} \longrightarrow 7\overline{)2,800}$

2,892 ÷ 7 is about _____.

2. 2,176 ÷ 3

Compatible numbers: _____

$3\overline{)2,176} \longrightarrow$ _____

2,176 ÷ 3 is about _____.

Write compatible numbers and estimate.

---

3. 2,578 ÷ 5

Compatible numbers: _____

$5\overline{)2,578} \longrightarrow$ _____

2,578 ÷ 5 is about _____.

4. 2,477 ÷ 6

Compatible numbers: _____

$6\overline{)2,477} \longrightarrow$ _____

2,477 ÷ 6 is about _____.

---

5. 4,169 ÷ 8

Compatible numbers: _____

$8\overline{)4,169} \longrightarrow$ _____

4,169 ÷ 8 is about _____.

6. 2,899 ÷ 9

Compatible numbers: _____

$9\overline{)2,899} \longrightarrow$ _____

2,899 ÷ 9 is about _____.

Objective: Use compatible numbers to estimate quotients.
Chapter Intervention

Use with Chapter 4.
Grade 5

Name _____ Date _____

Divide by 1-Digit Divisors

As you divide in each place, think of basic facts
to help you estimate the quotient.

Find 328 ÷ 5.

• Decide where to place the first digit of the quotient.	• Divide the tens.	• Bring down 8 ones. Divide the ones. Write the remainder.

Panel 1:

Think

$$5\overline{)328} \rightarrow \begin{array}{r} 60 \\ 5\overline{)300} \end{array}$$

Place the first digit
of the quotient in
the tens place.

↓

H	T	O

5) 3 | 2 | 8

Panel 2:

H	T	O
	6	
5) 3	2	8
− 3	0	
	2	

Multiply. 6 × 5 = 30

Subtract. 32 − 30 = 2

Compare. 2 < 5

Panel 3:

H	T	O
	6	5	R 3
5) 3	2	8
− 3	0	
	2	8
−	2	5
		3

Multiply. 5 × 5 = 25

Subtract. 28 − 25 = 3

Compare. 3 < 5
The remainder is 3.

Divide.

1.

H	T	O
	7	__
4) 2	9	2
− 2	8	
	1	__
−	__	__
		__

2.

H	T	O
	1	__	__ R__
3) 5 | 2 | 7

3.

Th	H	T	O
	2	__	__
7) 1, | 5 | 1 | 2

4.

$$2\overline{)3\ 7\ 9} \quad \underline{\ \underline{}\ \underline{}}\ R\underline{}$$

5.

$$7\overline{)4,\ 5\ 8\ 5} \quad \underline{\ \underline{}\ \underline{}}$$

6.

$$4\overline{)2,\ 5\ 1\ 7} \quad \underline{\ \underline{}\ \underline{}}\ R\underline{}$$

Name _____ Date _____

Zeros in the Quotient

You may need to write zeros in the quotient when there are not enough hundreds, tens, or ones to divide.

Find $3,223 \div 4$.

• Decide where to place the first digit of the quotient. Then divide.	• Bring down the tens. There are not enough tens to divide by 4. So write 0 in the tens place.	• Bring down the ones. Divide the ones. Write the remainder.
$\begin{array}{r} 8 \\ 4\overline{)3,223} \\ -32 \\ \hline 0 \end{array}$ Multiply. $8 \times 4 = 32$ Subtract. $32 - 32 = 0$ Compare. $0 < 5$	$\begin{array}{r} 80 \\ 4\overline{)3,223} \\ -32\downarrow \\ \hline 02 \end{array}$ **Think** Can I divide the tens?	$\begin{array}{r} 805 \text{ R3} \\ 4\overline{)3,223} \\ -32\downarrow \\ \hline 023 \\ -20 \\ \hline 3 \end{array}$ Subtract. $23 - 20 = 3$ Compare. $3 < 5$ The remainder is 3.

Divide.

1. $850 \div 8$	2. $3,632 \div 6$	3. $9,232 \div 3$	4. $4,153 \div 5$
$\begin{array}{r} 1\ 0\rule{1em}{0.4pt}\ \text{R}\rule{1em}{0.4pt} \\ 8\overline{)8\ 5\ 0} \end{array}$	$\begin{array}{r} 6\ \rule{1em}{0.4pt}\ \rule{1em}{0.4pt}\ \text{R}\rule{1em}{0.4pt} \\ 6\overline{)3,\ 6\ 3\ 2} \end{array}$	$\begin{array}{r} 3\ \rule{1em}{0.4pt}\ \rule{1em}{0.4pt}\ \rule{1em}{0.4pt}\ \text{R}\rule{1em}{0.4pt} \\ 3\overline{)9,\ 2\ 3\ 2} \end{array}$	$\begin{array}{r} \rule{1em}{0.4pt}\ \rule{1em}{0.4pt}\ \rule{1em}{0.4pt}\ \text{R}\rule{1em}{0.4pt} \\ 5\overline{)4,\ 1\ 5\ 3} \end{array}$
5. $3\overline{)1,\ 2\ 2\ 8}$	**6.** $2\overline{)8,\ 1\ 2\ 5}$	**7.** $5\overline{)3,\ 7\ 5\ 3}$	**8.** $6\overline{)4,\ 2\ 2\ 5}$

Objective: Determine when to put zeros in the quotient.
Chapter Intervention

Use with Chapter 4.
Grade 5

Name _____ Date _____

Use Divisibility Rules

A number is **divisible** by another number when the quotient is a whole number with no remainder.

Give another example for each divisibility rule.

	Divisibility Rules	Examples
1.	Even numbers are **divisible by 2.** Even numbers have 0, 2, 4, 6, or 8 in the ones place.	34, ___36___
2.	If a number is **divisible by 3,** the sum of the digits is divisible by 3. $627 \rightarrow 6 + 2 + 7 = 15 \rightarrow 15 \div 3 = 5$	627, _____
3.	A number is **divisible by 4** if its last two digits make a number that is divisible by 4. $312 \rightarrow 12 \div 4 = 3$	312, _____
4.	Numbers **divisible by 5** have 0 or 5 in the ones place.	265, _____
5.	Every number that is divisible by both 2 and 3 is **divisible by 6.** $42 \div 2 = 21 \quad 42 \div 3 = 14 \quad 42 \div 6 = 7$	42, _____
6.	If a number is **divisible by 9,** the sum of the digits is divisible by 9. $783 \rightarrow 7 + 8 + 3 = 18 \rightarrow 18 \div 9 = 2$	783, _____
7.	Numbers **divisible by 10** have zeros in the ones place.	930, _____

Write **yes** or **no** to tell if each number is divisible by 2, 3, 4, 5, 6, 9, and 10.

		2	3	4	5	6	9	10
8.	425							
9.	750							
10.	824							
11.	3,190							
12.	1,638							

Name _____ Date _____

Solve Equations

You can use mental math to solve
some multiplication and division equations.

Multiply.

$5n = 45$

$5 \times 9 = 45$

Think
$5 \times ? = 45$

So, $n = 9$.

1.

$3y = 15$

$3 \times \_\_ = 15$

Think
$3 \times ? = 15$

$y = \_\_$

2.

$5b = 35$

$5 \times \_\_ = 35$

Think
$5 \times ? = 35$

$b = \_\_$

3.

$6a = 60$

$6 \times \_\_ = 60$

$a = \_\_$

4.

$3k = 24$

$3 \times \_\_ = 24$

$k = \_\_$

5.

$8p = 56$

$8 \times \_\_ = 56$

$p = \_\_$

6.

$7t = 63$

$7 \times \_\_ = 63$

$t = \_\_$

Divide.

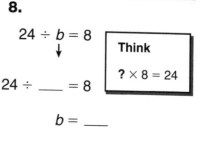

Remember
Division is the inverse of multiplication.

$n \div 4 = 8$

$32 \div 4 = 8$

Think
$4 \times 8 = ?$

So, $n = 32$.

7.

$y \div 4 = 3$

$\_\_ \div 4 = 3$

Think
$4 \times 3 = ?$

$y = \_\_$

8.

$24 \div b = 8$

$24 \div \_\_ = 8$

Think
$? \times 8 = 24$

$b = \_\_$

9.

$p \div 10 = 5$

$\_\_ \div 10 = 5$

$p = \_\_$

10.

$t \div 8 = 6$

$\_\_ \div 8 = 6$

$t = \_\_$

11.

$25 \div k = 5$

$25 \div \_\_ = 5$

$k = \_\_$

12.

$16 \div a = 4$

$16 \div \_\_ = 4$

$a = \_\_$

Objective: Solve multiplication and division equations using mental math.
Chapter Intervention

Use with Chapter 4.
Grade 5

Guess and Check

Problem   Alicia is sorting clothes for the school store.
There are **3 different kinds of tops.** She has 3 times as many
sweatshirts as vests. The number of T-shirts is divisible by
3 and 4. There are 20 tops altogether. How many of each top is there?

Read to Understand

1. How many tops are there in all? _____

2. The **number of sweatshirts** is _____ the **number of vests.**

3. The **number of T-shirts** is divisible by _____ and _____.

Choose a Way to Solve the Problem
Make a table and use the Guess and Check strategy.

Show the Solution

4. Start by guessing a number of vests,
for example, 1 vest. Record it in the table.

> **Think**
> For 1 vest there are 3 × 1 sweatshirts.
>
> The sum of the vests, sweatshirts,
> and T-shirts must equal 20.

5. How many sweatshirts are there? _____
Record the number in the table.

6. When there is 1 vest and
3 sweatshirts, how many
T-shirts are there?   _____
Record the number in the table.

Vests	Sweatshirts	T-Shirts	Divisible by 3 and 4?
1	3	16	no
2	—	—	—

7. Test whether the number of T-shirts is divisible
by both 3 and 4. Record *yes* or *no* in the table.

Continue guessing and checking until you find the correct answer.

8. Solution   Alicia has _____ vests, _____ sweatshirts, and _____ T-shirts.

Try This   Use a Guess and Check strategy.
9. Two numbers have a product of 32.
When the greater number is divided by
the lesser number, the quotient is 2.

What are the numbers? _____ and _____

Greater Number	Lesser Number	Product is 32?	Quotient is 2?
—	—	—	—
—	—	—	—
—	—	—	—

Divide 3-Digit Dividends

You can estimate to decide where to place the first digit
in the quotient.

Find $1,587 \div 31$.

• **Estimate** the quotient.	• **Decide** where to write the first digit. Then **divide**.	• **Check** your answer. Multiply. Then add the remainder.
$1,587 \div 31$ ↓ ↓ $1,500 \div 30 = 50$	First digit in the **tens place.** → $\underset{31)\overline{1,587}}{51\ \text{R6}}$	$\begin{array}{r} 51 \\ \times\ 31 \\ \hline 51 \\ +\ 153 \\ \hline 1,581 \end{array}$ $\begin{array}{r} 1,581 \\ +\ \ \ \ 6 \\ \hline 1,587 \end{array}$

Divide. Then check your answer.

1. $1,298 \div 21$

Estimate: $1,200 \div 20 =$ _____

Divide: | Check:

$21)\overline{1,\ 2\ 9\ 8}$ R __

2. $885 \div 42$

Estimate: $800 \div$ _____ $=$ _____

Divide: | Check:

$42\ )\overline{8\ 8\ 5}$ R __

3. $1,899 \div 31$

Estimate: _____

Divide: | Check:

$31)\overline{1,\ 8\ 9\ 9}$ R __

4. $1,685 \div 41$

Estimate: _____

Divide: | Check:

$41)\overline{1,\ 6\ 8\ 5}$ R __

Name _____ Date _____

Order of Operations

You can use the **order of operations** to simplify expressions.

Simplify. Use the order of operations.

$48 \div (3 \times 4) - 1$

Parentheses first $\longrightarrow$ $48 \div (3 \times 4) - 1$
$48 \div \quad 12 \quad - 1$

Divide $\longrightarrow$ $48 \div 12 - 1$
$4 \quad - 1$

Subtract $\longrightarrow$ $4 - 1$
3

---

1. $(2 + 6) \times (15 - 6) + 3$

Parentheses first $\longrightarrow$ $(2 + 6) \times (15 - 6) + 3$

Multiply $\longrightarrow$ _____ $\times$ _____ $+ 3$

Add $\longrightarrow$ _____

---

2. $20 \times (5 - 2) + 10$

Parentheses first _____

Multiply _____

Add

_____

---

3. $18 \div (3 \times 3) + (9 - 4)$

Parentheses first _____

Divide _____

Add _____

---

4. $90 \div 3 - (4 + 4) \times 2$

Parentheses first _____

Divide and multiply _____

Subtract _____

---

5. $10 - 6 \div 2 + (10 + 6) \times 2$

Parentheses first _____

Divide and multiply _____

Subtract and add _____

Objective: Use order of operations.
Chapter Intervention

Use with Chapter 5.
Grade 5

Divide by 2-Digit Divisors

When you divide, use an estimate to predict the quotient.

---

1. Find 338 ÷ 42.

Use **compatible numbers** to estimate the quotient.

$$42\overline{)338} \longrightarrow \overset{8}{40\overline{)320}}$$

An **estimate** for the quotient is **8.**

Write **8** in the **ones** place in the quotient. Then divide.

$$\begin{array}{r} 8\ \text{R}\_\_ \\ 42\overline{)338} \\ -336 \\ \hline 2 \end{array}$$

← Multiply. 8 × 42 = 336

← Subtract to find the remainder.
338 − 336 = 2

Check your answer.
Multiply the divisor by the quotient.
Then add the remainder.

$$\begin{array}{r} 42 \\ \times\ 8 \\ \hline 336 \\ +\ 2 \\ \hline \end{array}$$

← Divisor
← Quotient

← Remainder

Think Does the sum equal the dividend, 338?

Divide. Check your answer.

2.

Estimate.

$$32\overline{)98} \longrightarrow 30\overline{)90}$$

R__

$$-\rule{2em}{0.4pt}$$

Check:

3.

Estimate.

$$44\overline{)146} \longrightarrow 40\overline{)120}$$

R__

$$-\rule{2em}{0.4pt}$$

Check:

4.

$$85\overline{)496} \longrightarrow 80\overline{)400}$$

R__

Check:

5.

$$19\overline{)79} \longrightarrow 20\overline{)80}$$

R__

Check:

Name _____ Date _____

Adjust the Quotient

Use estimation to place the first digit of the quotient.
Remember to adjust the quotient, if necessary.

---

1. Find $557 \div 24$.

Estimate the quotient.

$557 \div 24$
↓   ↓

$600 \div 20 =$ ___

First try **3.**	$\begin{array}{r} 23\ R\underline{\ \ } \\ 24\overline{)557} \\ -48 \\ \hline 77 \\ -72 \\ \hline 5 \end{array}$
$3 \times 24 = 72$	
$72 > 55$	
3 is too **large.**	
Try **2.**	
$2 \times 24 = 48$	
$48 < 55$	
2 is **correct.**	
Continue to divide.	

---

2. Find $751 \div 23$.

Estimate the quotient.

$751 \div 23$
↓   ↓

$800 \div 20 =$ ___

$$\begin{array}{r} \underline{\ \ }\ R\underline{\ \ } \\ 23\overline{)751} \end{array}$$

---

3. Find $436 \div 14$.

Estimate the quotient.

$436 \div 14$
↓   ↓

$400 \div$ ___ $=$ ___

$$\begin{array}{r} \underline{\ \ }\ R\underline{\ \ } \\ 14\overline{)436} \end{array}$$

---

4. Find $768 \div 15$.

Estimate the quotient.

$768 \div 15$
↓   ↓

$800 \div 20 =$ ___

First try **4.**	$\begin{array}{r} 51\ R\underline{\ \ } \\ 15\overline{)768} \\ -75 \\ \hline 18 \\ -15 \\ \hline 3 \end{array}$
$4 \times 15 = 60$	
$76 - 60 = 16$	
$16 > 15$	
4 is too **small.**	
Try **5.**	
$5 \times 15 = 75$	
$75 < 76$	
5 is **correct.**	
Continue to divide.	

---

5. Find $622 \div 16$.

Estimate the quotient.

$622 \div 16$
↓   ↓

$600 \div 20 =$ ___

$$\begin{array}{r} \underline{\ \ }\ R\underline{\ \ } \\ 16\overline{)622} \end{array}$$

---

6. Find $818 \div 17$.

Estimate the quotient.

$818 \div 17$
↓   ↓

$800 \div$ ___ $=$ ___

$$\begin{array}{r} \underline{\ \ }\ R\underline{\ \ } \\ 17\overline{)818} \end{array}$$

Objective: Adjust the quotient.
Chapter Intervention

Use with Chapter 5.
Grade 5

Name _____ Date _____

Divide with Greater Numbers

You can estimate and adjust to place each digit of a quotient.

---

1. Find $1,782 \div 31$.

• Estimate to place the first digit of the quotient.

$$31\overline{)1,782} \longrightarrow \overset{60}{30\overline{)1,800}}$$

The quotient will be about _____.

• Divide the tens.

Th	H	T	O
		5	

$31\overline{)1,}$ | 7 | 8 | 2
-1 | 5 | 5 | ↓ ←——— $5 \times 31 = 155$
 | 2 | 3 | 2 ←——— $178 - 155 = 23$

> Place the first digit in the quotient. 6 is too large. Adjust. Try 5.

• Divide the ones. Estimate. $7 \times 30 = 210$

Th	H	T	O
		5	R __

$31\overline{)1,}$ | 7 | 8 | 2
-1 | 5 | 5 |
 | 2 | 3 | 2

> Remember to write the remainder next to the quotient.

Estimate the quotient. Then divide.

---

2. $3,816 \div 17$

$$17\overline{)3,816} \longrightarrow 20\overline{)4,\ \ \overline{\overline{0}}\ \ \overline{\overline{0}}\ \ \overline{\overline{0}}}$$

$17\overline{)3,}$ | 8 | 1 | 6   R __

---

3. $3,280 \div 39$

$$39\overline{)3,280} \longrightarrow \_\_\overline{)3,\ \ \overline{\overline{2}}\ \ \overline{\overline{0}}\ \ \overline{\overline{0}}}$$

$39\overline{)3,}$ | 2 | 8 | 0   R __

> **Think**
> $32 \div 4$

---

4. $4,478 \div 48$

$48\overline{)4,}$ | 4 | 7 | 8   R __

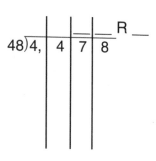

---

5. $8,495 \div 22$

$22\overline{)8,}$ | 4 | 9 | 5   R __

Name _____ Date _____

Order of Operations and Exponents

You can use the **order of operations** to simplify expressions.

Simplify. Use the order of operations.

$$(4 + 2)^2 \div (6 \div 2) - 2^2$$

Parentheses first → $(4 + 2)^2 \div (6 \div 2) - 2^2$

Exponents next → $6^2 \div 3 - 2^2$

Divide → $36 \div 3 - 4$

Subtract → $12 - 4$
$$8$$

---

1. $8^2 + 15 \times (12 - 10)$

Parentheses first $8^2 + 15 \times \underline{\qquad}$

Exponents next $\underline{\qquad} + 15 \times \underline{\qquad}$

Multiply $\underline{\qquad} + \underline{\qquad}$

Add $\underline{\qquad}$

---

2. $5 + (2 + 5)^2 \div (3 + 4)$

Parentheses first _____

Exponents next _____

Divide _____

Add _____

---

3. $(2 + 3)^2 - 12 \div 4 + (8 \div 2)$

Parentheses first _____

Exponents next _____

Divide _____

Subtract and add _____

---

4. $(1 + 2)^2 + (3 + 2)^2 \times 2$

Parentheses first _____

Exponents next _____

Multiply _____

Add _____

---

5. $12 \div 2^2 + (4 - 1)^2 - 6$

Parentheses first _____

Exponents next _____

Divide _____

Add and subtract _____

Objective: Use order of operations.
Chapter Intervention

Use with Chapter 5.
Grade 5

Interpret Remainders

Problem A library group is going to a book exhibit. There are 32 members who will travel in vans. Each van holds 7 passengers. How many vans will the group need?

Read to Understand

1. How many members will go to the exhibit? _____ members

2. How many passengers does each van hold? _____ passengers

3. Restate the problem another way. <u>32 members of a group are going to an exhibit.</u> <u>They are going in vans that hold 7 passengers. I have to find the number of vans</u> <u>they will use.</u>

Choose a Way to Solve the Problem

4. You can _____ to find how many groups of 7 are in 32.

```
    4 R4
7)32
  − 28
    4
```

Show the Solution

5. How many groups of 7 are in 32? _____ groups

The next step is to decide what to do with the remainder.

➤ **Increase the quotient when you must include the remainder.**

6. Are 4 vans enough? _____ Should you include the remainder? _____

➤ **Drop the remainder when you do not need to include it.**

7. For this problem, does it make sense to drop the remainder? _____

➤ **Use the remainder when you want to know how many are left over.**

8. Does the remainder answer the question in the problem? _____

Since everyone must have a seat in a van, you should *increase* the quotient. Then there will be enough vans.

9. $32 \div 7 = 4$ R4 Increase the quotient, 4 to _____. The group will need _____ vans.

Try This Solve. Tell what to do with the remainder.

10. The library group is holding a bake sale. They have 47 cookies. They place 3 cookies in each bag. How many full bags of cookies can they make?

11. The librarian ordered 58 new books. She shares the books equally among 6 classes and keeps the extra books. How many books does she keep?

_____

_____

Name _____ Date _____

Change Units of Measure

To change from one unit of measure to another, multiply or divide.

| 1 liter (L) = 1,000 milliliters (mL) |
| 1 kilogram (kg) = 1,000 grams (g) |

To change *larger* units to *smaller* units, **multiply.**

Larger to Smaller	1.	2.
4 liters = ▨ milliliters	6 kg = ▨ g	7 L = ▨ mL
Milliliters are **smaller** than liters.	____ × 1,000 = ____	____ × 1,000 = ____
4 × 1,000 = 4,000	6 kg = ____ g	7 L = ____ mL
4 liters = 4,000 milliliters		

To change *smaller* units to *larger* units, **divide.**

Smaller to Larger	3.	4.
3,000 grams = ▨ kilograms	8,000 mL = ▨ L	5,000 mL = ▨ L
Kilograms are **larger** than grams.	____ ÷ 1,000 = ____	____ ÷ 1,000 = ____
3,000 ÷ 1,000 = 3	8,000 mL = ____ L	5,000 mL = ____ L
3,000 grams = 3 kilograms		

Multiply or divide to change units.

5.	6.	7.
8 kg = ▨ g	2,000 g = ▨ kg	9,000 mL = ▨ L
____ × ____ = ____	____ ÷ ____ = ____	____ ÷ ____ = ____
8 kg = ____ g	2,000 g = ____ kg	9,000 mL = ____ L
8.	9.	10.
2 L = ____ mL	5 L = ____ mL	7,000 g = ____ kg

Objective: Convert units of capacity and mass.
Chapter Intervention

Use with Chapter 6.
Grade 5

Find Elapsed Time

Elapsed time is the number of hours and minutes that has passed from a starting time to an ending time.

1 hour (h) = 60 minutes (min)

Find the elapsed time.

1. Start Time: 11:45 A.M.
   End Time: 2:15 P.M.

Count the hours.	Count the minutes.
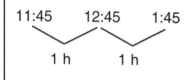	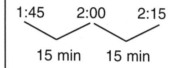
1 h + 1 h = _____ h	15 min + 15 min = _____ min

Add the hours and minutes
to find the elapsed time.   _____ h + _____ min = _____ h _____ min

Find the elapsed time.

2. Start time: 8:15 A.M.
   End time: 10:30 A.M.

   Number of Hours: _____ h

   Number of Minutes: _____ min

   Elapsed Time: _____ h _____ min

3. Start time: 7:15 P.M.
   End time: 9:05 A.M.

   Number of Hours: _____ h

   Number of Minutes: _____ min

   Elapsed Time: _____ h _____ min

4. Start time: 8:10 P.M.
   End time: 11:30 P.M.

   Elapsed Time: _____ h _____ min

5. Start time: 3:55 A.M.
   End time: 9:20 P.M.

   Elapsed Time: _____ h _____ min

6. Start time: 6:15 A.M.
   End time: 1:30 P.M.

   Elapsed Time: _____ h _____ min

7. Start time: 10:30 P.M.
   End time: 3:10 P.M.

   Elapsed Time: _____ h _____ min

Name _____ Date _____

Convert Customary Units

You can multiply or divide to change from one unit of measure to a larger or smaller unit of measure.

Length	Capacity	Weight
12 in. = 1ft	2 c = 1pt	16 oz = 1lb
3 ft = 1yd	2 pt = 1qt	2,000 lb = 1T
5,280 ft = 1mi	4 qt = 1gal	

To change *larger* units to *smaller* units, **multiply**.

Change units of length.	1. Change units of weight.	2. Change units of capacity.
3 ft = ▢ in. 1 foot = 12 inches Inches are **smaller** than feet. 3 × 12 = 36 3 ft = 36 in.	4 lb = ▢ oz 1 lb = _____ oz _____ × 16 = _____ 4 lb = _____ oz	5 gal = ▢ qt 1 gal = _____ qt _____ x 4 = _____ 5 gal = _____ qt

To change *smaller* units to *larger* units, **divide**.

Change units of capacity.	3. Change units of length.	4. Change units of weight.
16 pt = ▢ qt 2 pints = 1 quart Quarts are **larger** than pints. 16 ÷ 2 = 8 16 pt = 8 qt	18 ft = ▢ yd _____ ft = 1 yd _____ ÷ 3 = _____ 18 ft = _____ yd	6,000 lb = ▢ T _____ lb = 1 T _____ ÷ 2,000 = _____ 6,000 lb = _____ T

Multiply or divide to change units.

5. 2 mi = ▢ ft _____ × _____ = _____ 2 mi = _____ ft	6. 96 oz = ▢ lb _____ ÷ _____ = _____ 96 oz = _____ lb	7. 52 qt = ▢ gal _____ ÷ _____ = _____ 52 qt = _____ gal
8. 5 lb = _____ oz	9. 48 in. = _____ ft	10. 22 c = _____ pt

Name _____ Date _____

Change Metric Units

You can multiply or divide to change
to a larger or smaller unit of measure.

Length	Mass	Capacity
10 mm = 1 cm	1,000 mg = 1 g	1,000 mL = 1 L
100 cm = 1 m	1,000 g = 1 kg	10 dL = 1 L
1000 m = 1 km		

To change *larger* units to *smaller* units, **multiply.**

| Change units of length.

6 m = [ ] cm

1 m = 100 cm

Centimeters are **smaller** than meters.

6 × 100 = 600

6 m = 600 cm | **1.** Change units of mass.

12 g = [ ] mg

1 g = _____ mg

_____ × 1,000 = _____

12 g = _____ mg | **2.** Change units of capacity.

deciliter (dL)

15 L = [ ] dL

1 L = _____ dL

_____ × 10 = _____

15 L = _____ dL |

To change *smaller* units to *larger* units, **divide.**

| Change units of mass.

9,000 g = [ ] kg

1,000 g = 1 kg

Kilograms are **larger** than grams.

9,000 ÷ 1,000 = 9

9,000 g = 9 kg | **3.** Change units of length.

2,300 cm = [ ] m

_____ cm = 1 m

_____ ÷ 100 = _____

2,300 cm = _____ m | **4.** Change units of capacity.

7,000 mL = [ ] L

_____ mL = 1 L

_____ ÷ 1,000 = _____

7,000 mL = _____ L |

Multiply or divide to change units.

| **5.**　　4 cm = [ ] mm

_____ × _____ = _____

4 cm = _____ mm | **6.**　8,000 mg = [ ] g

_____ ÷ _____ = _____

8,000 mg = _____ g | **7.**　　500 dL = [ ] L

_____ ÷ _____ = _____

500 dL = _____ L |
| **8.**
　　20 kg = _____ g | **9.**
35,000 m = _____ km | **10.**
　　18 L = _____ mL |

Name _____ Date _____

Add and Subtract Measurements

When you add or subtract measurements, you may need to regroup.

Add.

---

1. 2 ft 10 in. + 3 ft 6 in. = ▢

Add inches.
Then add feet.

| Add the smaller units first. Then add the larger units. |

2 ft 10 in.

+ 3 ft   6 in.
_____

_____ ft 16 in.

Simplify the answer. | 12 in. = 1 ft |

5 ft 16 in. = 5 ft + _____ ft + _____ in.

= _____ ft _____ in.

---

2. 5 lb 14 oz + 7 lb 3 oz = ▢

5 lb   14 oz | 16 oz = 1 lb |

+   7 lb   3 oz
_____

_____ lb _____ oz

Simplify the answer. _____ lb _____ oz

3. 12 gal 3 qt + 2 gal 3 qt = ▢

_____ gal _____ qt | 4 qt = 1 gal |

+ _____ gal _____ qt
_____

_____ gal _____ qt

Simplify the answer. _____ gal _____ qt

Subtract.

---

4. 5 h 30 min − 2 h 55 min = ▢

Regroup to subtract.

 4   90
 5̸ h   3̸0 min | 1 h = 60 min
60 min + 30 min = 90 min |

− 2 h   55 min
_____

_____ h _____ min

5. 7 h 37 min − 4 h 46 min = ▢

_____ h _____ min

− _____ h _____ min
_____

_____ h _____ min

Add or subtract. Simplify.

---

6.   4 ft   9 in.
       + 2 ft   8 in.

7.   6 h   18 min
       − 1 h   45 min

Solve Multi-Step Problems

Problem It takes Pablo 15 minutes to walk to the school bus stop. The bus arrives at the bus stop at 7:40 A.M. It reaches the school at 8:05 A.M. About how long does it take Pablo to travel to school?

Read to Understand

1. How long does it take Pablo to walk to the bus stop? _____

2. What time does the bus arrive at the bus stop? _____

3. What time does the bus reach the school? _____

4. Restate the problem.
   Pablo walks 15 minutes to the bus stop. He gets on the bus at 7:40 A.M.
   He gets to school at 8:05 A.M. How long does it take Pablo to get to school?

Choose a Way to Solve the Problem
Use two steps to solve the problem.

   • First, subtract to find the elapsed time from 7:40 to 8:05.
   • Then add the elapsed time to the 15 minutes it takes Pablo to walk to the bus stop.

Show the Solution

| 1 hour = 60 minutes |

5.

Bus reaches school:	8:05	Elapsed time:	_____ minutes
Bus arrives at bus stop:	− 7:40	Time it takes Pablo to walk:	+ _____ minutes
Elapsed time:	:25	Total time:	_____ minutes

6. Solution It takes Pablo about _____ to reach school.

Try This Solve.

Problem It takes Ms. Fuller 10 minutes to walk to the train station. The train arrives at the station at 5:50 P.M. It reaches her stop at 6:45 P.M. About how long does it take Ms. Fuller to travel to her stop.

7. How long does it take the train to reach Ms. Fuller's stop from the train station?

_____

8. Solution It takes Ms. Fuller about _____ to reach her stop.

Name _____ Date _____

Bar Graphs

You can use a bar graph to compare data.
Use the bar graph to answer Questions 1–9.

The bar graph shows the favorite winter activities of Mr. Marley's class.
Find how many students chose snowboarding.

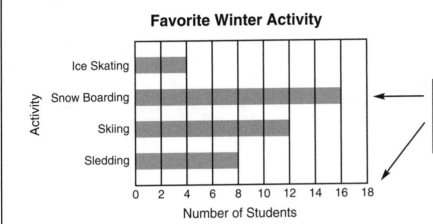

Favorite Winter Activity

• Find the snowboarding bar.

• Use the interval to find the number of students.

The **interval** is the difference between two numbers on the scale.

1. What is the title of the graph?	**2.** What is the interval used on the graph?

3. Which activity has the longest bar?

4. Which activity did most students choose?

5. Which activity did fewest students choose?

6. How many students chose skiing as their favorite activity?

7. Which activity did exactly 8 students choose?

8. How many more students chose skiing than sledding?

9. How many students are in Mr. Marley's class?

Line Graphs

You can use a **line graph** to show how data changes over time.
Use the line graph to answer Questions 1–8.

The line graph shows the temperature at noon for a five-day period.

- The **vertical scale** shows the temperature. The difference between two numbers on the scale is the **interval.** Intervals are always equal.

- To find the temperature for a day, find the day on the **horizontal axis.** Then use the interval to read the temperature.

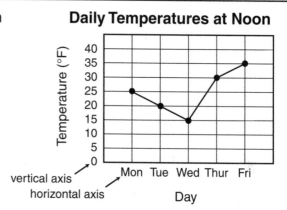

Daily Temperatures at Noon

1. What is the title of the graph? _____

2. What is the interval used on the graph? _____

3. What unit of temperature is used on the graph? _____

You can use the line connecting the points to decide whether the temperature at noon rose or fell between two days.

4. Did the temperature at noon rise or fall from Monday to Tuesday? _____

5. Did the temperature at noon rise or fall from Wednesday to Thursday? _____

6. Look at the line connecting the points for Monday, Tuesday, and Wednesday.

   Did the temperature at noon rise or fall from Monday to Wednesday? _____

7. Which day had the lowest temperature at noon? _____

   What was the temperature? _____

8. Which day had the highest temperature at noon? _____

   What was the temperature? _____

Analyze Graphs

You can use graphs to display different types of data.

Use the **bar graph** to answer Questions 1–4.

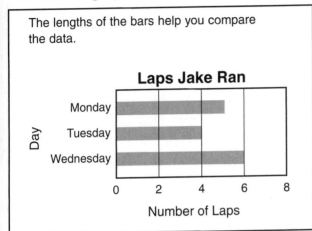

The lengths of the bars help you compare the data.

Laps Jake Ran

1. Which day has the longest bar? _____

2. Which day has the shortest bar? _____

3. Did Jake run more laps on Tuesday or Wednesday? _____

4. How many more laps did Jake run on Wednesday than on Tuesday? _____

Use the **line graph** to answer Questions 5–8.

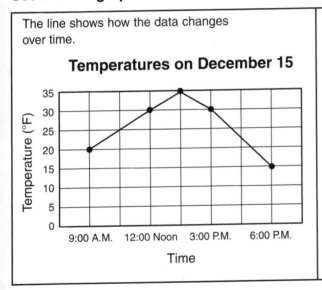

The line shows how the data changes over time.

Temperatures on December 15

5. The temperature at 12:00 noon was 30°F. At what other time was the temperature 30°F? _____

6. What was the temperature at 9:00 A.M.? _____

7. Did the temperature rise or fall between 9:00 A.M. and 12:00 noon? _____

8. Did the temperature rise or fall after 3:00 P.M.? _____

Use the **circle graph** to answer Questions 9–11.

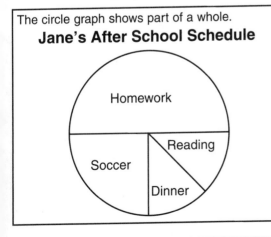

The circle graph shows part of a whole.

Jane's After School Schedule

9. Does Jane spend more time reading or playing soccer? _____

10. On which activity does Jane spend half her time? _____

11. About what part of Jane's schedule is spent reading? _____

Double Bar Graphs

You can use a double bar graph to compare data.

The graph shows the number of students
who take music lessons at Alta Elementary School.

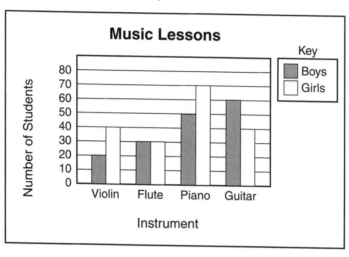

Use the double bar graph to answer Questions 1–10.

1. What is the title?

   _____

2. What does the vertical axis show?

   _____

3. What scale is used on the vertical axis?

   _____

4. What does the horizontal axis show?

   _____

5. Use the key. What do the

   shaded bars represent? _____

   the white bars? _____

6. How many girls take piano lessons?

   _____ how many boys? _____

7. Which instrument
   is played by
   the **same number**
   of girls and boys? _____

8. How many **more** girls
   than boys take
   piano lessons? _____

9. How many boys
   and girls take **piano**
   lessons altogether? _____

10. How many boys
    and girls take **violin**
    lessons altogether? _____

Name _____ Date _____

Histograms

A **histogram** shows how frequently data occurs within equal intervals.

Use the histogram to answer Questions 1–8.

Doctor Han weighed each cat at the animal clinic. The frequency table shows the number of cats in each range of weights.

Intervals	Tally Marks	Frequency
0–4	⊥⊥⊥⊤	5
5–9	| |	2
10–14	| |	2
15–19	|	1

1. How many cats did the doctor weigh? _____

2. What are the intervals on the horizontal axis? _____

3. Which interval had the greatest number of cats? _____

4. Which interval had the least number of cats? _____

5. How many cats are in the 5–9 weight group? _____

6. Do you think all the cats in the 10–14 weight group were the same weight? _____

Why or why not? _____

7. How many more cats are in the 0–14 weight group than in the 15–20 weight group? _____

8. Suppose there is a different histogram.

The first two intervals are $0–$9 and $10–$19.

What is the next interval? _____

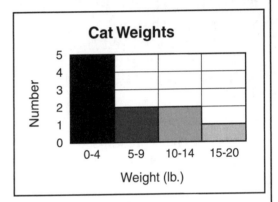

The intervals on the horizontal axis are all equal.

Objective: Make and use histograms.
Chapter Intervention

Use with Chapter 7.
Grade 5

Name _____ Date _____

Double Line Graphs

You can use a **double line graph**
to compare two sets of data.

The double line graph shows the distances
that Brett and Frank rode on their bikes.
Use the double line graph to answer Questions 1–6.

1. What is the title
of the graph? _____

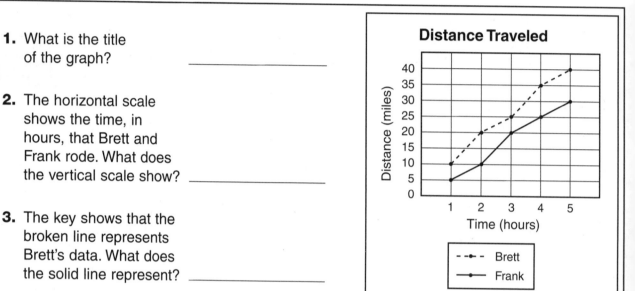

Distance Traveled

2. The horizontal scale
shows the time, in
hours, that Brett and
Frank rode. What does
the vertical scale show? _____

3. The key shows that the
broken line represents
Brett's data. What does
the solid line represent? _____

4. How many miles did Brett ride in 1 hour?

_____ miles

How many miles did Frank ride in 1 hour? _____ miles

Who rode a greater distance in 1 hour? _____

5. How many miles did Brett ride in 3 hours? _____

How many miles did Frank ride in 3 hours? _____

Use subtraction to find
how many *more* miles Brett
rode than Frank in 3 hours. _____

6. How many *more* miles did Brett
ride than Frank in 4 hours? _____

Name _____ Date _____

Choose Appropriate Graphs

Different types of graphs show different types of data.

Bar Graph	Line Graph	Pictograph	Circle Graph	Histogram
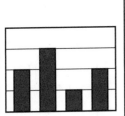	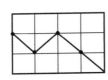	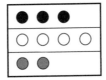		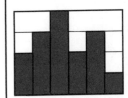
Compares *different* data using different lengths of bars.	Shows how the *same* data changes over time.	Shows data that are multiples of a number.	Compares data that are parts of a whole.	Shows *how often* data occur in equal intervals.

Write the appropriate type of graph for the data described.

1. Ryan wants to make a graph to show how many of each kind of coin he has in his collection.

Should he use a pictograph or a histogram to display the data? _____

2. Shelly wants to make a graph to show favorite lunches in her class.

Should she use a line graph or a bar graph to display the data? _____

3. Jordan wants to make a graph to show how his puppy's weight changes over 6 months.

Should he use a pictograph or a line graph to display the data? _____

4. Maria wants to make a graph to show the parts of her birthday money that she spends on clothes, books, and sports equipment.

Should she use a circle graph or a line graph to display the data? _____

5. Mr. Russo wants to make a graph showing students' test scores, organized in intervals.

What type of graph should he use? _____

Objective: Decide which type of graph is most appropriate.
Chapter Intervention

— 129 —

Use with Chapter 7.
Grade 5

Misleading Graphs

The **intervals** used for a scale can make a graph **misleading.**

Graphs A and B compare the same data.
They show the number of people who chose
Regular Toothpaste and the number of
people who chose Tooth Sparkle.

Remember

The zigzag
line shows
that some
numbers
are missing
from the
scale.

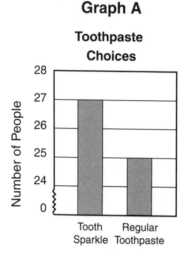

Graph A

Toothpaste Choices

Graph B

Toothpaste Choices

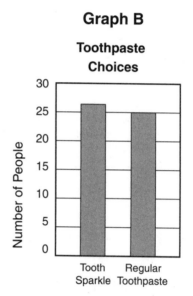

Think

The **vertical scale**
on these
graphs
shows the
number of
people.

The **interval**
is the
difference
between two
numbers on
the scale.

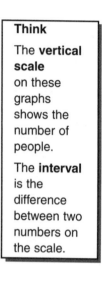

Use Graph A and Graph B to complete Exercises 1–6.

1. Look at Graph A.
   The scale jumps from
   0 to 24. Are **all** the intervals
   on Graph A equal? _____

2. Look at Graph B.
   Does the scale jump? _____
   Are **all** the intervals
   on Graph B equal? _____

3. According to **Graph A:**

   The number of people who
   chose Tooth Sparkle was **27.**

   The number of people
   who chose Regular
   Toothpaste was
   _____.

4. According to **Graph B:**

   The number of people who
   chose Tooth Sparkle was **27.**

   The number of
   people who chose
   Regular Toothpaste was _____.

5. On **Graph A,** the bar for Tooth
   Sparkle is about twice the
   height of the bar for Regular
   Toothpaste. But did twice
   as many people choose
   Tooth Sparkle? _____

6. Which graph is misleading,

   Graph A or Graph B? _____

Identify Information in a Graph

Problem Ms. Richmond asked her fifth and sixth graders to choose a favorite planet to study. The double bar graph shows their choices.

Which planet was selected by the greatest number of students in *both* grades? How many students chose the planet?

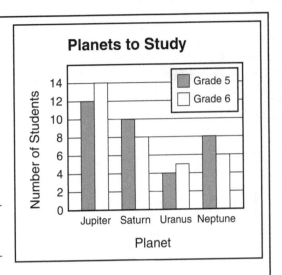

Planets to Study

Read to Understand

1. Which grades chose their planets? _____

2. What data does the bar graph show? _____

3. What question does the problem ask?

_____

Choose a Way to Solve the Problem

You need to find the planet selected by the greatest number of students in both grades. So, find the tallest bars and record the number for each grade. Then, find the total.

Show the Solution

4. Complete the chart.

	Grade 5	Grade 6	Total
Jupiter			

5. So, _____ students in both grades chose _____.

Try This The graph shows points scored by three basketball players in the first two games of the season. Who had the greatest number of total points? How many points did she score?

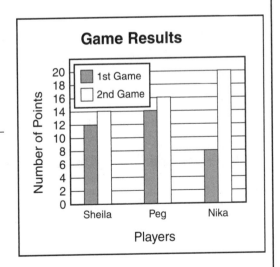

Game Results

6. Find the total for each player.

Sheila _____ Peg _____ Nika _____

7. Solution _____ scored the greatest number of points.

She scored _____ points.

Line Plots and Stem-and-Leaf Plots

A **line plot** is a way to show data using Xs.

The line plot shows the number of books that students in Ms. Carter's fifth grade class read last month. Each X stands for one student.

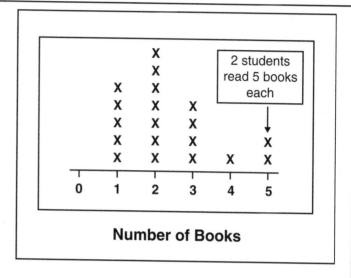

Number of Books

1. How many Xs are shown for 2? _____

2. How many students read 2 books? _____

3. How many Xs are shown for 3? _____

4. How many students read 3 books? _____

5. You can count the total number of Xs to find how many students are represented on the line plot.

   How many students are represented? _____

A **stem-and-leaf plot** is a way to show data arranged by place value.

The stem-and-leaf plot shows the number of points the Falcons scored in their basketball games last season. Each **stem** stands for the tens digit of a score. Each **leaf** stands for the ones digit of a score.

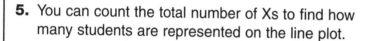

Number of Points Scored	
Stem (tens)	**Leaves (ones)**
1	8 9
2	3 5 6 6 7 8
3	0 1

1|8 means 18.

6. What does 3 | 1 mean? _____ points scored

7. What was the Falcons' highest score? _____

8. You can count the total number of leaves to find how many basketball game scores are represented on the stem-and-leaf plot.

   How many basketball game scores are represented? _____

Name _____ Date _____

Median, Mode, and Range

You can use the median, the mode, and the range to describe
a set of data. The list shows the number of minutes a group
of piano students spent practicing.
Use the list to answer Questions 1–6.

| 40, 35, 50, 35, 20, 25, 35, 35, 20, 30, 45 |

1. List the numbers in the chart from *least* to *greatest*.

20, 20, ___, ___, ___, ___, ___, ___, ___, ___, ___

Use the ordered list to find the **median,** the **mode,** and the
range of the data.

The **median** is the middle number in an ordered set of data.

2. How many numbers are on the list? _____

What is the middle number? _____

3. Record the median. _____

The **mode** is the number that occurs most often in a set of data.

4. What number occurs most often? Record the mode. _____

The **range** is the difference between the *greatest number* and
the *least number* in a set of data.

5. What is the greatest number on the list? _____ The least number? _____

6. Subtract to find the range.

What is the range? _____

The list shows the distances students rode their bikes.
Use the list to answer Questions 9–10.

| 15, 20, 15, 12, 18, 15, 23, 17, 18 |

7. List the numbers from *least* to *greatest.* ___, ___, ___, ___, ___, ___, ___, ___, ___

8. Find the median, the mode, and the range.

Median: _____ Mode: _____ Range: _____

Name _____ Date _____

Use Stem-and-Leaf Plots

The list at the right shows the scores from a board game Kyle and his friends are playing. Use the list to answer Questions 1–8.

| 23, 17, 35, 51, 28, 25, 30, 32, 19, 28, 25, 30, 28 |

1. List the numbers in the box from *least* to *greatest*.

17, 19, ___, ___, ___, ___, ___, ___, ___, ___, ___, ___, ___

2. Use the ordered list to complete the stem-and-leaf plot.

| Break apart each number into tens and ones. |

3. The key tells what the numbers in the stem-and-leaf plot mean. What does 5 | 1 mean? _____

4. What are the **stems,** or tens digits? _____

5. What are the **leaves,** or ones digits, for the second row in the stem-and-leaf plot? _____

6. What is the **mode,** or the number that occurs most often? _____

7. What is the **median,** or the middle number? _____

8. What is the **range,** or the difference between the greatest and least number? _____

Game Scores	
Stem	**Leaf**
1	7 9
2	— — — — — —
—	— — — —
—	
—	—

Key: 1 | 7 means 17.

The list at the right shows the temperatures recorded at noon for 11 days in one month. Use the list to answer Questions 9–11.

| 58°, 53°, 48°, 59°, 37°, 38°, 48°, 33°, 48°, 45°, 32° |

9. List the numbers from least to greatest.

___, ___, ___, ___, ___, ___, ___, ___, ___, ___, ___

10. Complete the stem-and-leaf plot.

11. Use the stem-and-leaf plot to find each value.

median: _____ mode: _____

range: _____

Temperatures at Noon	
Stem	**Leaf**
—	— — — — —
—	— — — —
—	— — —

Name _____ Date _____

Mean, Median, Mode, and Range

You can describe a set of data using the mean, median, mode, or range.

Each X on the line plot stands for one student. In the plot, 2 students have 1 pet.

The line plot to the right shows the number of pets owned by 5th-grade students.

Number of Pets

```
              X
              X
        X     X     X
  X     X     X     X     X
  ┬─────┬─────┬─────┬─────┬
  0     1     2     3     4
```

1. List the number of pets on the line plot from least to greatest.

   0, 1, 1, ___, ___, ___, ___, ___, ___, ___

   Mean: the sum of all the numbers divided by the number of addends.

2. Find the sum of the numbers on the list. _____

3. How many addends are there? _____

4. Divide to find the *mean* number of pets.

   What is the *mean?* _____

   Median: the middle number in an ordered set of numbers.

5. What are the two middle numbers on the list? _____ and _____

6. What is the *median?* _____

   Mode: the number that occurs most often in a data set.

   If there is an even number of data, find the mean of the two middle numbers.

7. What is the *mode* of the number of pets? _____

   Range: the difference between the greatest number and the least number in a data set.

8. What is the greatest number on the list? _____
   The least number? _____

9. What is the *range* of the number of pets? _____

Name _____ Date _____

Draw Conclusions

Sometimes you can use the mean, median, or mode to draw conclusions about a set of data.

The line plot shows ticket prices at different ballparks. Use the line plot to answer Questions 1–4.

1. What is the mean? _____ median? _____ mode? _____

2. What number are the three measures close to? _____

3. Circle all the measures that are **typical** of the data.

   mean   median   mode

4. Complete the sentence to describe the typical price.

   Since the _____, _____, and _____ are

   all about _____, the typical price is _____.

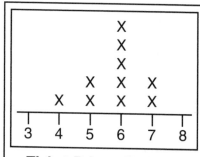

Ticket Prices (Dollars)

The line plot shows the runs scored in each of the Hawks' games. Use the line plot to answer Questions 5–7.

5. Use the line plot to find each value.

   mean: _____ median: _____ mode: _____

6. Do the data **cluster** around any score? _____

   Remember A cluster is an isolated group of data.

7. Complete the sentence to describe the typical score.

   Since the data do not cluster around any score,

   the _____ is the best measure of the data.

   So, the typical score is _____.

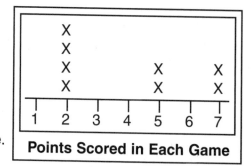

Points Scored in Each Game

Make a Table

Problem Students in Jared's class recorded the number of minutes it takes them to travel from home to school. The results are shown at the right. Do most of the students spend 0–9, 10–19, 20–29, or 30–35 minutes traveling to school?

35	15	5	30
15	10	20	8
25	26	35	20

Read to Understand

1. What intervals are stated in the problem? _____ _____ _____ _____

2. What does the list of data represent? _____

3. What must you decide about the data? _____

Choose a Way to Solve the Problem

You need to organize the data. Use the strategy *Make a Table.*

- Use the intervals you listed in Question 1.

- Write a tally mark next to the interval for each number in the list.

- Count the tally marks and write the frequencies.

Minutes	Tally	Frequency
0–9		
10–19		
20–29		
30–39		

Show the Solution

4. Complete the table.

5. How many students travel 0–9 minutes? _____ 10–19 minutes? _____

20–29 minutes? _____ 30–39 minutes? _____

6. Compare the frequencies. Which interval

has the greatest frequency? _____

Try This The frequency table at right shows the heights of the tropical plants in a greenhouse. Use the data for Questions 7–9.

Height (cm)	Tally	Frequency
150–154	I I	
155–159	⊦⊦⊦⊦	
160–164	I I I	
165–169	I I	

7. Write the frequencies to complete the table.

8. How many plants are between 160 and 164 cm tall? _____

9. Most of the plants are between _____ and _____ cm tall.

Prime and Composite Numbers

You can use arrays to tell if a number is prime or composite.

A **prime number** is a number greater than 1 that has **exactly two factors**, 1 and the number itself.	**1.** You can make *only* 1 array for 11. ■■■■■■■■■■■ ← 1 × 11 What are the factors of 11? 1 and _____ So, 11 is a prime number.

A **composite number** is a number greater than 1 that has **more than two factors**.	**2.** You can make *more than* 1 array for 12.
	
	■■■■■■■■■■■■ ← 1 × 12
	
	■■■■■■
	■■■■■■ ← 2 × 6 ■■■■
	                              ■■■■ ← 3 × 4
	                              ■■■■
	
	What are the factors of 12?
	
	_____ _____ _____ _____ _____ _____
	
	So, 12 is a composite number.

Draw arrays. Write the factors. Tell whether the number is **prime** or **composite**.

3. Number: 7 Factors: _____ 7 is a _____ number.	**4.** Number: 9 Factors: _____ 9 is a _____ number.
5. Number: 15 Factors: _____ 15 is a _____ number.	**6.** Number: 18 Factors: _____ 18 is a _____ number.

Name _____ Date _____

Factors and Multiples

You can use a multiplication table to find multiples and factors.

columns ↓

x	1	2	3	4	5	6	7	8	9	10	11	12
1	1	2	3	4	5	6	7	8	9	10	11	12
2	2	4	6	8	10	12	14	16	18	20	22	24
3	3	6	9	12	15	18	21	24	27	30	33	36
4	4	8	12	16	20	24	28	32	36	40	44	48
5	5	10	15	20	25	30	35	40	45	50	55	60
6	6	12	18	24	30	36	42	48	54	60	66	72
7	7	14	21	28	35	42	49	56	63	70	77	84
8	8	16	24	32	40	48	56	64	72	80	88	96
9	9	18	27	36	45	54	63	72	81	90	99	108
10	10	20	30	40	50	60	70	80	90	100	110	120
11	11	22	33	44	55	66	77	88	99	110	121	132
12	12	24	36	48	60	72	84	96	108	120	132	144

rows →

A **multiple** is the product of a given whole number and another whole number.

Look at the *column* or *row* for 4. All the numbers in that column or row are multiples of 4.

1. Find multiples of 4.

Some multiples of 4 are:

4, 8, 12, 16, 20, ___, ___, 32, ___.

Factors are numbers that are multiplied to give a product.

Look for the product 12 in the table. When you find 12, look at the column and row numbers to find the factors.

2. Find the factors of 12.

Factors of 12 are: 1, 2, 3, ___, ___, 12.

Use the multiplication table to write four **multiples** for each number.

3. 5

___, ___, ___, ___

4. 6

___, ___, ___, ___

5. 3

___, ___, ___, ___

Use the multiplication table to find **factors** for each product.

6. 18

___, ___, ___, ___

7. 20

___, ___, ___, ___

8. 48

___, ___, ___, ___

Objective: Find factors and multiples of a number.
Chapter Intervention

— 139 —

Name _____ Date _____

Represent Fractions

You can use a fraction to represent a part of a whole or a part of a group.

Write a fraction for the shaded part of a whole.

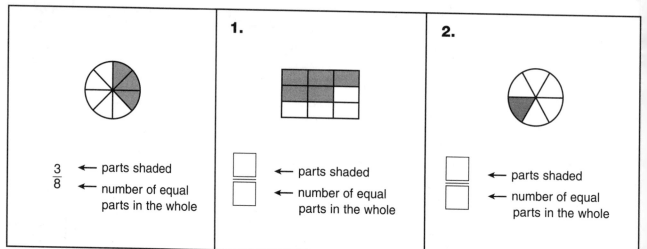

$\frac{3}{8}$ ← parts shaded
← number of equal parts in the whole

1.

☐/☐ ← parts shaded
← number of equal parts in the whole

2.

☐/☐ ← parts shaded
← number of equal parts in the whole

Write a fraction for the shaded part of the group.

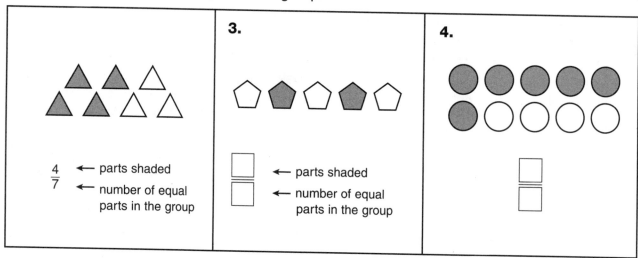

$\frac{4}{7}$ ← parts shaded
← number of equal parts in the group

3.

☐/☐ ← parts shaded
← number of equal parts in the group

4.

☐/☐

Write a fraction for the point on a number line.

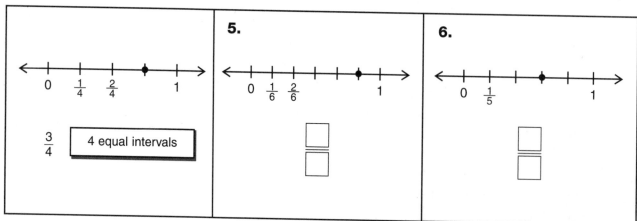

$\frac{3}{4}$ | 4 equal intervals |

5.

☐/☐

6.

☐/☐

Objective: Represent a fraction of a region, set, and a number.
Chapter Intervention

Use with Chapter 9.
Grade 5

Compare and Order Fractions

You can use fraction strips to compare fractions.

Compare. Write >, <, or = for each ◯.

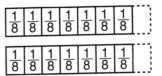
> is greater than   < is less than

$\frac{3}{4}$ ⬭ $\frac{1}{4}$
- The fractions have the *same* denominator.
- Compare the numerators.

| $\frac{1}{4}$ | $\frac{1}{4}$ | $\frac{1}{4}$ |

| $\frac{1}{4}$ |

$3 > 1$, so $\frac{3}{4} > \frac{1}{4}$.

1. $\frac{2}{5}$ ⬭ $\frac{4}{5}$

| $\frac{1}{5}$ | $\frac{1}{5}$ |

| $\frac{1}{5}$ | $\frac{1}{5}$ | $\frac{1}{5}$ | $\frac{1}{5}$ |

$\frac{2}{5}$ ◯ $\frac{4}{5}$

2. $\frac{7}{8}$ ⬭ $\frac{7}{8}$

| $\frac{1}{8}$ | $\frac{1}{8}$ | $\frac{1}{8}$ | $\frac{1}{8}$ | $\frac{1}{8}$ | $\frac{1}{8}$ | $\frac{1}{8}$ |

| $\frac{1}{8}$ | $\frac{1}{8}$ | $\frac{1}{8}$ | $\frac{1}{8}$ | $\frac{1}{8}$ | $\frac{1}{8}$ | $\frac{1}{8}$ |

$\frac{7}{8}$ ◯ $\frac{7}{8}$

Compare. Write >, <, or = for each ◯.

$\frac{4}{9}$ ⬭ $\frac{2}{3}$
- The fractions have *different* denominators.
- Find equivalent fractions.

$\frac{2}{3} = \frac{6}{9}$ (×3, ×3)

Think Equivalent fractions have the same denominator.

Compare $\frac{4}{9}$ and $\frac{6}{9}$.

$4 < 6$, so $\frac{4}{9} < \frac{2}{3}$.

3. $\frac{3}{5}$ ⬭ $\frac{7}{10}$

$\frac{3}{5} = \frac{6}{10}$ (×2, ×2)

$\frac{3}{5}$ ◯ $\frac{7}{10}$

4. $\frac{7}{12}$ ⬭ $\frac{2}{3}$

$\frac{2}{3} = \frac{\square}{12}$

$\frac{7}{12}$ ◯ $\frac{2}{3}$

Order from least to greatest.

$\frac{1}{2}$ $\frac{3}{8}$ $\frac{5}{8}$
- Find equivalent fractions.
- Compare the numerators.
- Order the fractions.

$\frac{1}{2} = \frac{4}{8}$ $3 < 4 < 5$, so $\frac{3}{8} < \frac{4}{8} < \frac{5}{8}$

and $\frac{3}{8}$ $\frac{1}{2}$ $\frac{5}{8}$.

5. $\frac{8}{9}$ $\frac{2}{3}$ $\frac{7}{9}$

$\frac{2}{3} = \frac{\square}{9}$

___ ___ ___

6. $\frac{3}{4}$ $\frac{11}{12}$ $\frac{5}{12}$

$\frac{3}{4} = \frac{\square}{12}$

___ ___ ___

Name _____ Date _____

Prime Factorization

You can write a composite number as a
product of prime numbers. This is called the
prime factorization of the number.

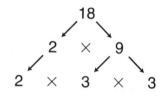

$$12 = 2 \times 2 \times 3$$

composite number — all prime numbers

Complete a factor tree for each number.
Then write the prime factorization.

A factor tree is complete when the factors at
the bottom of the tree are all prime numbers.

Number: 18

| Write 18 as the product of two numbers. | | 2 is a prime number, but 9 is not. Write 9 as the product of two prime numbers. | 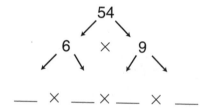 |

The prime factorization of 18 is $2 \times 3 \times 3$.

---

1. Number: 20

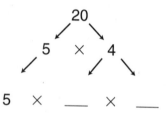

$5 \times \underline{\ \ } \times \underline{\ \ }$

The prime factorization of 20 is

$5 \times \underline{\ \ } \times \underline{\ \ }$.

---

2. Number: 54

54
6 × 9

$\underline{\ \ } \times \underline{\ \ } \times \underline{\ \ } \times \underline{\ \ }$

The prime factorization of 54 is

$\underline{\ \ } \times \underline{\ \ } \times \underline{\ \ } \times \underline{\ \ }$.

---

3. Number: 56

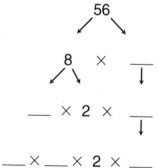

$\underline{\ \ } \times 2 \times \underline{\ \ }$

$\underline{\ \ } \times \underline{\ \ } \times 2 \times \underline{\ \ }$

$56 = \underline{\ \ } \times \underline{\ \ } \times 2 \times \underline{\ \ }$

---

4. Number: 50

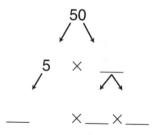

$\underline{\ \ } \times \underline{\ \ } \times \underline{\ \ }$

$50 = \underline{\ \ } \times \underline{\ \ } \times \underline{\ \ }$

Name _____ Date _____

Greatest Common Factor

Two or more numbers can have some factors that are the same. These factors are called **common factors**.

The greatest number that is a factor of two or more numbers is the **greatest common factor (GCF)** of the numbers.

Factors of 15: ①, 3, 5, ⑮

Factors of 20: ①, 2, 4, ⑤ 10, 20

Common factors of 15 and 20: 1, 5

GCF of 15 and 20: 5

Circle the **common factors** of each pair of numbers.
Then write the **greatest common factor** of the numbers.

1. 12 and 18	**2.** 16 and 40	**3.** 35 and 42
12: ①②③ 4, ⑥ 12	**16:** 1, 2, 4, 8, 16	**35:** 1, 5, 7, 35
18: ①②③⑥ 9, 18	**40:** 1, 2, 4, 5, 8, 10, 20, 40	**42:** 1, 2, 3, 6, 7, 14, 21, 42
GCF of 12 and 18: ___	GCF of 16 and 40: ___	GCF of 35 and 42: ___

List the **factors** of each number.
Circle the **common factors**.
Then write the **greatest common factor** of the numbers.

4. 24 and 30	**5.** 27 and 45
24: 1, 2, 3, 4, ___, ___, ___, 24	27: _1_, ___, ___, 27
30: 1, 2, 3, 5, ___, ___, ___, 30	45: _1_, ___, ___, ___, ___, 45
GCF of 24 and 30: ___	GCF of 27 and 45: ___
6. 21 and 56	**7.** 32 and 48
21: _____	32: _____
56: _____	48: _____
GCF of 21 and 56: ___	GCF of 32 and 48: ___

Least Common Multiple

Two or more numbers can have some multiples that are the same. These multiples are called **common multiples.**

The least number that is a multiple of two or more numbers is the **least common multiple (LCM)** of the numbers.

Multiples of 8:   8, 16, ㉔, 32, 40, ㊽, ...

Multiples of 12:   12, ㉔, 36, ㊽, 60, 72, ...

Some common multiples of 8 and 12:   24, 48

LCM of 8 and 12:   24

Circle the **common multiples** shown in the lists for each pair of numbers.
Then write the **least common multiple** of the numbers.

1. 2 and 4	**2.** 6 and 9	**3.** 4 and 8
2: 2, ④, 6, ⑧, 10, ⑫, ...	**6:** 6, 12, 18, 24, 30, 36, ...	**4:** 4, 8, 12, 16, 20, 24, ...
4: ④, ⑧, ⑫, 16, 20, 24, ...	**9:** 9, 18, 27, 36, 45, 54, ...	**8:** 8, 16, 24, 32, 40, 48, ...
LCM of 2 and 4: _____	LCM of 6 and 9: _____	LCM of 4 and 8: _____

List the **first six multiples** of each number.
Circle the **common multiples** for each pair of numbers.
Then write the **least common multiple** of the numbers.

4. 9 and 12	**5.** 5 and 10
9: 9, 18, 27, 36, 45, 54	**5:** 5, 10, 15, _____, _____, _____
12: 12, 24, 36, _____, _____, _____	**10:** 10, 20, 30, _____, _____, _____
LCM of 9 and 12: _____	LCM of 5 and 10: _____
6. 15 and 20	**7.** 16 and 24
15: _____	**16:** _____
20: _____	**24:** _____
LCM of 15 and 20: _____	LCM of 16 and 24: _____

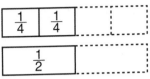

Name _____ Date _____

Equivalent Fractions and Simplest Form

Equivalent fractions name the same number.
You can find an equivalent fraction by multiplying or dividing
the numerator and the denominator by the same number.

| $\frac{1}{4}$ | $\frac{1}{4}$ | | |

| $\frac{1}{2}$ | |

$\frac{2}{4}$ and $\frac{1}{2}$
are equivalent fractions.

Multiply or divide to find equivalent fractions.

1. $\frac{2}{5} = \frac{6}{\square}$

$\frac{2 \times 3}{5 \times 3} = \frac{6}{\square}$

So $\frac{2}{5} = \frac{\square}{\square}$

2. $\frac{3}{7} = \frac{\square}{14}$

$\frac{3 \times 2}{7 \times 2} = \frac{\square}{14}$

So $\frac{3}{7} = \frac{\square}{\square}$

3. $\frac{5}{8} = \frac{\square}{24}$

Think
8 times what is 24?

4. $\frac{12}{18} = \frac{\square}{3}$

$\frac{12 \div 6}{18 \div 6} = \frac{\square}{3}$

So $\frac{12}{18} = \frac{\square}{\square}$

5. $\frac{18}{24} = \frac{6}{\square}$

$\frac{18 \div 3}{24 \div 3} = \frac{6}{\square}$

So $\frac{18}{24} = \frac{\square}{\square}$

6. $\frac{15}{21} = \frac{\square}{7}$

Think
21 divided by what is 7?

A fraction is in **simplest form** when the
Greatest Common Factor (GCF) of its
numerator and denominator is 1.

Complete. Write the fraction in simplest form.

$\frac{8}{12} = \frac{\square}{\square}$

Think
The GCF of
8 and 12 is 4.
Divide by
that number.

$\frac{8 \div 4}{12 \div 4} = \frac{2}{3}$

7.

$\frac{6}{10} = \frac{\square}{\square}$

Think
The GCF of
6 and 10 is __.
Divide by
that number.

8.

$\frac{24}{32} = \frac{\square}{\square}$

Think
The GCF of
24 and 32 is __.
Divide by
that number.

Objective: Find equivalent fractions and write fractions in simplest form.

Chapter Intervention

— 145 —

Use with Chapter 9.
Grade 5

Name _____ Date _____

Fractions, Mixed Numbers, and Decimals

You can use fractions and decimals to write numbers less than 1.

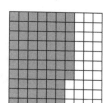

67 hundredths are shaded.

Fraction: $\frac{67}{100}$

Decimal: 0.67

Write a fraction and a decimal to describe the shaded part.

1. 	**2.** 	**3.** 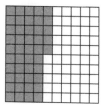
Fraction: $\frac{25}{100}$	Fraction: _____	Fraction: _____
Decimal: 0._____	Decimal: 0._____	Decimal: _____

Write a mixed number and a decimal to describe the shaded part.

4.

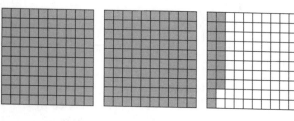

Mixed Number: $2\frac{33}{100}$ Decimal: 2._____

5.

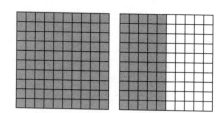

Mixed Number: _____ Decimal: _____

6.

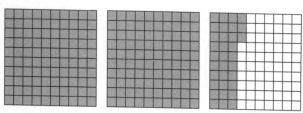

Mixed Number: _____ Decimal: _____

7.

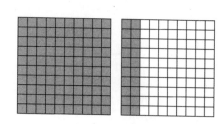

Mixed Number: _____ Decimal: _____

Objective: Relate fractions, mixed numbers, and decimals.
Chapter Intervention

Use with Chapter 9.
Grade 5

Name _____ Date _____

Change Decimals and Fractions

You can use place value ideas to write decimals as fractions and fractions as decimals.

> **Remember** To find simplest form, divide the numerator and denominator by their greatest common factor (GCF).

Write each decimal as a fraction or mixed number in **simplest form.**

Write 0.25 as a fraction.	**1.** $0.8 =$ ▨	**2.** $0.65 =$ ▨	**3.** $0.24 =$ ▨

Write 0.25 as a fraction.

ones	tenths	hundredths
0 .	2	5

25 **hundredths** $= \dfrac{25}{100} = \dfrac{1}{4}$

$0.25 = \dfrac{1}{4}$

1. $0.8 =$ ▨

8 tenths $= \dfrac{8}{10} = \dfrac{\square}{5}$

$0.8 =$ _____

2. $0.65 =$ ▨

$0.65 = \dfrac{\square}{\square}$

3. $0.24 =$ ▨

$0.24 = \dfrac{\square}{\square}$

Write 1.5 as a mixed number.

ones	tenths	hundredths
1 .	5	0

1 and 5 **tenths** $= 1\dfrac{5}{10} = 1\dfrac{1}{2}$

$1.5 = 1\dfrac{1}{2}$

4. $4.36 =$ ▨

4 and 36 hundredths $= 4\dfrac{36}{100} = 4\dfrac{\square}{25}$

$4.36 =$ _____

> The GCF of 36 and 100 is 4.

5. $6.4 =$ ▨

$6.4 = \dfrac{\square}{\square}$

Write each fraction as a decimal.

Write $\dfrac{3}{5}$ as a decimal.

Write an equivalent fraction with a denominator that is a power of 10.

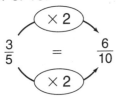

$\dfrac{3}{5} \;=\; \dfrac{6}{10}$ ($\times 2$)

$\dfrac{3}{5} = \dfrac{6}{10}$

6 tenths $= 0.6$

$\dfrac{3}{5} = 0.6$

6.

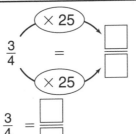

$\dfrac{3}{4} = \dfrac{\square}{\square}$ ($\times 25$)

$\dfrac{3}{4} = \dfrac{\square}{\square}$

$\dfrac{3}{4} = 0.$___

7.

$\dfrac{7}{20} = \dfrac{\square}{\square}$

$\dfrac{7}{20} = 0.$___

8.

$\dfrac{13}{50} = \dfrac{\square}{\square}$

$\dfrac{13}{50} =$ _____

9.

$\dfrac{12}{25} = \dfrac{\square}{\square}$

$\dfrac{12}{25} =$ _____

Objective: Change decimals to fractions, and change fractions to decimals.

Chapter Intervention

— 147 —

Use with Chapter 9.
Grade 5

Name _____ Date _____

Compare Decimals and Fractions

When you compare and order decimals and fractions,
write them in the same form.

Compare the fractions and decimals.
Write >, <, or = for each ◯.

---

1. $\frac{11}{20}$ ⬭ 0.67

   • Write the fraction as a decimal.

> Write an equivalent fraction
> with a denominator of 100.

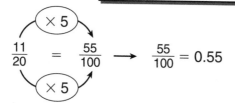

$$\frac{11}{20} = \frac{55}{100} \longrightarrow \frac{55}{100} = 0.55$$

   • Compare.

$$0.55 \bigcirc 0.67$$

$$\frac{11}{20} \bigcirc 0.67$$

---

2. $\frac{3}{5}$ ⬭ 0.51

   • Write the fraction as a decimal.

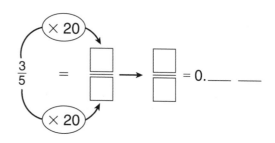

   • Compare.

$$0.\_\_\ \_\_ \bigcirc 0.51$$

$$\frac{3}{5} \bigcirc 0.51$$

Order the fractions and decimals from *least* to *greatest.*

---

3.   0.3 , $\frac{3}{5}$, 0.25

   • Write the fraction as a decimal.

$$\frac{3}{5} = \frac{60}{100} \longrightarrow 0.60$$

   • Compare to order.

> Write zeros if needed.

0.3**0**   0.60   0.25
               ↑   ↑
              greatest   least

$$0.25 < 0.30 < 0.60$$

$$\_\_\_ < \_\_\_ < \_\_\_$$

---

4.   0.2 , $\frac{7}{20}$, 0.33

   • Write the fraction as a decimal.

$$\frac{7}{20} = \frac{\square}{\square} \longrightarrow 0.\_\_\ \_\_$$

   • Compare to order.

$$\underline{\quad\quad} \quad\quad \underline{\quad\quad} \quad\quad \underline{\quad\quad}$$
     ↑   ↑
    least   greatest

$$\_\_\_ < \_\_\_ < \_\_\_$$

Use Logical Reasoning

Problem   The LCM of two numbers is 90.
The GCF of the two numbers is 6. The sum of
the two numbers is 48. What are the two numbers?

Read to Understand

1. What is the LCM of the two numbers? _____

2. What is the GCF of the two numbers? _____

> **Remember**
>
> LCM stands for *least common multiple*.
> GCF stands for *greatest common factor*.

3. Restate the problem another way. <u>I am looking for two numbers. Their GCF is 6 and</u>
<u>their LCM is 90, and their sum is 48.</u>

Choose a Way to Solve the Problem

Since you are looking for multiples and factors, you can use a step-by-step
approach. So, use logical reasoning to solve the problem.

4. The LCM of the two numbers is 90.
The two numbers must be **factors** of 90.
Write all of the factors of 90.   1, 2, ___, ___, ___, ___, ___, 15, 18, 30, 45, 90

5. The GCF of the two numbers is 6.
The two numbers must be **multiples** of 6.
Write the factors of 90 that are also multiples of 6.   6, ___, ___, 90

6. Find two numbers in the list that have a sum of 48.   ___, ___

Show the Solution

7. The two numbers are _____ and _____.

Try This   The LCM of the two numbers is 18.
The GCF of the two numbers is 3.
The sum of the two numbers is 15.
What are the two numbers?

> **Check:** Find the GCF and the LCM of your
> two numbers. Is the GCF equal to 6?
> Is the LCM equal to 90?

8. Write all the factors of 18.   1, ___, ___, ___, ___, ___

9. Write the factors of 18 that are also **multiples** of 3.   3, ___, ___, ___
Find the two numbers that have a sum of 15.

10. Solution   The numbers are _____ and _____.

Name _____ Date _____

Estimate Fraction Sums

To estimate the sum of two fractions, compare each fraction to $\frac{1}{2}$.

• If both addends are less than $\frac{1}{2}$, the sum is less than 1.
• If both addends are $\frac{1}{2}$ or greater, the sum is 1 or greater.

Find $\frac{5}{8} + \frac{2}{3}$. Compare each addend to $\frac{1}{2}$.

• Compare

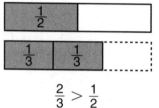

$\frac{5}{8} > \frac{1}{2}$

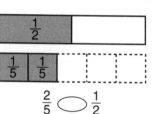

$\frac{2}{3} > \frac{1}{2}$

• Estimate

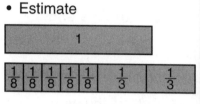

The sum is greater than 1.

Compare to $\frac{1}{2}$. Estimate the sum.

Write **greater than 1** or **less than 1.**

1. $\frac{1}{3} + \frac{2}{5}$

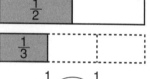

$\frac{1}{3} \bigcirc \frac{1}{2}$ $\frac{2}{5} \bigcirc \frac{1}{2}$

• Estimate

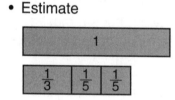

The sum is _____.

2. $\frac{4}{9} + \frac{3}{10}$

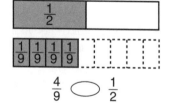

$\frac{4}{9} \bigcirc \frac{1}{2}$ $\frac{3}{10} \bigcirc \frac{1}{2}$

• Estimate

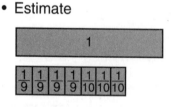

The sum is _____.

3. $\frac{3}{4} + \frac{4}{8}$

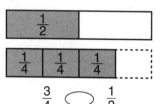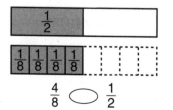

$\frac{3}{4} \bigcirc \frac{1}{2}$ $\frac{4}{8} \bigcirc \frac{1}{2}$

• Estimate

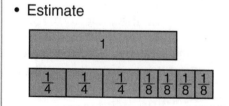

The sum is _____.

Objective: Estimate sums of fractions.
Chapter Intervention

Use with Chapter 10.
Grade 5

Name _____ Date _____

Fractions With Like Denominators

When you add or subtract fractions with like denominators,
add or subtract the numerators. The denominator stays the same.

Add. Write the sum in simplest form.

$\frac{2}{6} + \frac{2}{6} =$ ▢

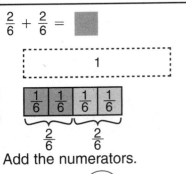

Add the numerators.

$\frac{2}{6} + \frac{2}{6} = \frac{4}{6} = \frac{2}{3}$ $\div 2$ $\div 2$

simplest form

1.

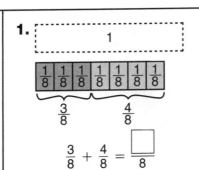

$\frac{3}{8}$ $\frac{4}{8}$

$\frac{3}{8} + \frac{4}{8} = \frac{\square}{8}$

2.

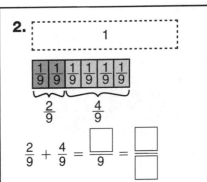

$\frac{2}{9}$ $\frac{4}{9}$

$\frac{2}{9} + \frac{4}{9} = \frac{\square}{9} = \frac{\square}{\square}$

3.

$\frac{1}{6} + \frac{4}{6} = \frac{\square}{6}$

4.

$\frac{3}{10} + \frac{2}{10} = \frac{\square}{10} = \frac{\square}{\square}$

Subtract. Write the difference in simplest form.

$\frac{7}{8} - \frac{3}{8} =$ ▢

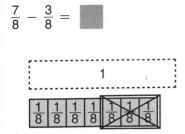

Subtract the numerators.

$\frac{7}{8} - \frac{3}{8} = \frac{4}{8} = \frac{1}{2}$ $\div 4$ $\div 4$

simplest form

5.

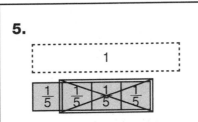

$\frac{4}{5} - \frac{3}{5} - \frac{\square}{5}$

6.

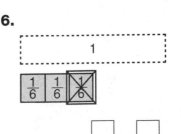

$\frac{3}{6} - \frac{1}{6} = \frac{\square}{6} = \frac{\square}{\square}$

7.

$\frac{7}{9} - \frac{3}{9} = \frac{\square}{9}$

8.

$\frac{7}{12} - \frac{4}{12} = \frac{\square}{12} = \frac{\square}{\square}$

Objective: Add and subtract fractions with like denominators.
Chapter Intervention

Use with Chapter 10.
Grade 5

Name _____ Date _____

Fractions With Unlike Denominators

When you add and subtract fractions with unlike denominators,
you can use fraction strips to find equivalent fractions that have
the same denominators.

Add.

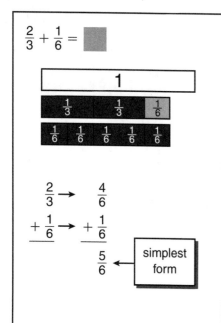

$\frac{2}{3} + \frac{1}{6} = $ ▢

1

| $\frac{1}{3}$ | $\frac{1}{3}$ | $\frac{1}{6}$ |

| $\frac{1}{6}$ | $\frac{1}{6}$ | $\frac{1}{6}$ | $\frac{1}{6}$ | $\frac{1}{6}$ |

$\frac{2}{3} \rightarrow \frac{4}{6}$

$+\frac{1}{6} \rightarrow +\frac{1}{6}$

$\frac{5}{6}$ ← simplest form

1. $\frac{1}{4} + \frac{1}{8} = $ ▢

1

| $\frac{1}{4}$ | $\frac{1}{8}$ |

| $\frac{1}{8}$ | $\frac{1}{8}$ | $\frac{1}{8}$ |

$\frac{1}{4} \rightarrow \frac{\square}{8}$

$+\frac{1}{8} \rightarrow +\frac{\square}{8}$

$\frac{\square}{8}$ ← simplest form

2. $\frac{1}{2} + \frac{3}{4} = $ ▢

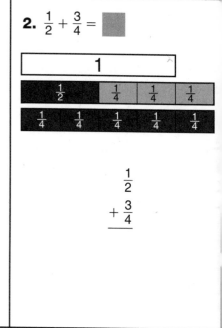

1

| $\frac{1}{2}$ | $\frac{1}{4}$ | $\frac{1}{4}$ | $\frac{1}{4}$ |

| $\frac{1}{4}$ | $\frac{1}{4}$ | $\frac{1}{4}$ | $\frac{1}{4}$ | $\frac{1}{4}$ |

$\frac{1}{2}$

$+\frac{3}{4}$

Subtract.

$\frac{8}{10} - \frac{1}{2} = $ ▢

1

| $\frac{1}{10}$ | $\frac{1}{10}$ | $\frac{1}{10}$ | $\frac{1}{10}$ | $\frac{1}{10}$ | $\frac{1}{10}$ | $\frac{1}{10}$ | $\frac{1}{10}$ |

| $\frac{1}{2}$ | ? |

$\frac{8}{10} \rightarrow \frac{8}{10}$

$-\frac{1}{2} \rightarrow -\frac{5}{10}$

$\frac{3}{10}$ ← simplest form

3. $\frac{4}{6} - \frac{4}{12} = $ ▢

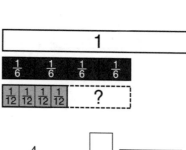

1

| $\frac{1}{6}$ | $\frac{1}{6}$ | $\frac{1}{6}$ | $\frac{1}{6}$ |

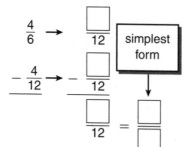

| $\frac{1}{12}$ | $\frac{1}{12}$ | $\frac{1}{12}$ | $\frac{1}{12}$ | ? |

$\frac{4}{6} \rightarrow \frac{\square}{12}$

$-\frac{4}{12} \rightarrow -\frac{\square}{12}$ 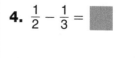 simplest form

$\frac{\square}{12} = \frac{\square}{\square}$

4. $\frac{1}{2} - \frac{1}{3} = $ ▢

1

| $\frac{1}{2}$ |

| $\frac{1}{3}$ | ? |

$\frac{1}{2}$

$-\frac{1}{3}$

Estimate with Fractions

You can round fractions to 0, $\frac{1}{2}$, or 1 to estimate sums and differences.

Estimate the sum.

1. $\frac{5}{6} + \frac{3}{8}$	• Round. 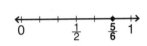 $\frac{5}{6}$ is close to 1.　　$\frac{3}{8}$ is close to $\frac{1}{2}$.	• Add. $1 + \frac{1}{2} = 1\frac{1}{2}$ So $\frac{5}{6} + \frac{3}{8}$ is about _____.

Compare to 0, $\frac{1}{2}$, or 1. Estimate the sum.

2. $\frac{3}{8} + \frac{2}{6}$ 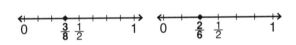 $\frac{1}{2} + \frac{1}{2} =$ _____ So $\frac{3}{8} + \frac{2}{6}$ is about _____.	**3.** $\frac{5}{6} + \frac{7}{8}$ 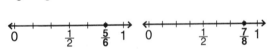 _____ + _____ = _____ So $\frac{5}{6} + \frac{7}{8}$ is about _____.

Compare to 0, $\frac{1}{2}$, or 1. Estimate the difference.

4. $\frac{1}{3} - \frac{1}{5}$ 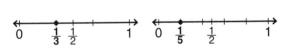 $\frac{1}{2} - 0 =$ _____ So $\frac{1}{3} - \frac{1}{5}$ is about _____.	**5.** $\frac{4}{5} - \frac{2}{3}$ 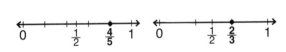 _____ − _____ = _____ So $\frac{4}{5} - \frac{2}{3}$ is about _____.

Name _____ Date _____

Add Fractions and Mixed Numbers

When you add fractions or mixed numbers with unlike denominators, find equivalent fractions first.

Add. Write the answer in simplest form.

1. Write equivalent fractions with like denominators.

$$\frac{2}{3} \quad \times 4 \quad \frac{\square}{12}$$

$$\frac{2}{3}$$

$$+ \frac{1}{4} \quad \frac{1}{4} \quad \times 3 \quad \frac{\square}{12}$$

Rewrite the addition.

$$\frac{2}{3} = \frac{\square}{12}$$

$$+ \frac{1}{4} = \frac{\square}{12}$$

Add the numerators.

$$\frac{\square}{12}$$

$$+ \frac{\square}{12}$$

$$\frac{\square}{12} \leftarrow \text{simplest form}$$

2.

$$\frac{2}{5} \quad \times 2 \quad = \frac{\square}{10}$$

$$+ \frac{1}{2} \quad = \quad + \frac{\square}{10}$$

$$\times 5$$

3.

$$\frac{2}{3}$$

$$+ \frac{1}{4}$$

4.

$$\frac{1}{6}$$

$$+ \frac{3}{4}$$

5.

$$2\frac{2}{5} \qquad \frac{2}{5} = \frac{\square}{15} \longrightarrow 2\frac{\square}{15}$$

$$+ 4\frac{1}{3} \qquad \frac{1}{3} = \frac{\square}{15} \longrightarrow + 4\frac{\square}{15}$$

$$\frac{\square}{15} \leftarrow \text{simplest form}$$

6.

$$3\frac{3}{5}$$

$$+ 4\frac{1}{4}$$

Subtract Fractions: Like Denominators

When you subtract fractions with like denominators, subtract
the numerators. Keep the denominators the same.

$\frac{4}{5} - \frac{1}{5} = \frac{3}{5}$
↑ ↑ ↑
like denominators

Subtract fractions. Write the difference in simplest form.

1.

$\frac{7}{8} - \frac{1}{8} = \frac{\square}{8} = \frac{\square}{4}$

↑
simplest
form

2.

$\frac{11}{12} - \frac{7}{12} = \frac{\square}{12} = \frac{\square}{3}$

↑
simplest
form

3.

$\frac{7}{10} - \frac{3}{10} = \frac{\square}{10} = \frac{\square}{5}$

↑
simplest
form

Subtract mixed numbers. Write the difference in simplest form.

4.

Cannot subtract.

$7\frac{1}{6}$ $\frac{1}{6} < \frac{5}{6}$

$-2\frac{5}{6}$

Rename $7\frac{1}{6}$.

$7\frac{1}{6} = 6 + 1 + \frac{1}{6}$

$\phantom{7\frac{1}{6}} = 6 + \frac{6}{6} + \frac{1}{6}$

$\phantom{7\frac{1}{6}} = 6\frac{7}{6}$

Subtract fractions.

$6\frac{7}{6}$

$-2\frac{5}{6}$

$\dfrac{\square}{6}$

Subtract the whole
numbers.

$6\frac{7}{6}$ simplest
form

$-2\frac{5}{6}$ ↓

$\square\frac{2}{6} = 4\frac{\square}{3}$

5.

$8\frac{2}{3}$

$-\ 2\frac{1}{3}$

$\dfrac{\square}{\square}$

6.

$9\frac{3}{8} \rightarrow 8\frac{\square}{8}$

$-3\frac{5}{8} \rightarrow -\ 3\ \frac{5}{8}$

$\dfrac{\square}{\square}$

7.

$4 \rightarrow 3\frac{\square}{5}$

$-1\frac{3}{5} \rightarrow -\ 1\ \frac{3}{5}$

$\dfrac{\square}{\square}$

Subtract With Unlike Denominators

When you subtract fractions or mixed numbers with unlike
denominators, write equivalent fractions with like denominators.

Subtract. Write the answer in simplest form.

1. Write equivalent fractions with like denominators.	Rewrite the subtraction.	Subtract the numerators.
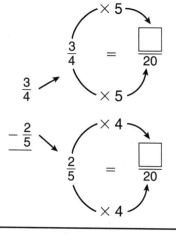	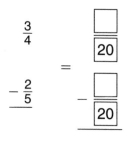	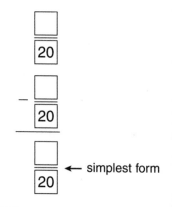 ← simplest form

2.

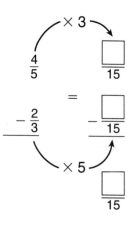

3.

$\dfrac{5}{6}$
$-\dfrac{1}{4}$

4.

$\dfrac{1}{2}$
$-\dfrac{2}{5}$

5.

$4\dfrac{2}{3}$ $\dfrac{2}{3}=\dfrac{\square}{24}$ → $4\dfrac{\square}{24}$

$-1\dfrac{5}{8}$ $\dfrac{5}{8}=\dfrac{\square}{24}$ → $-1\dfrac{\square}{24}$

$\dfrac{\square}{24}$ ← simplest form

6.

$5\dfrac{3}{5}$
$-2\dfrac{1}{6}$

Draw a Diagram

Problem Nina buys a $\frac{1}{2}$ pound bag of grapes. Jolene buys 4 times as much as Nina. How many pounds of grapes did they buy in all?

Read to Understand

1. How many pounds of grapes did Nina buy? _____ pound

2. How much did Jolene buy? _____ times as much

3. Restate the problem another way. <u>One bag of grapes weighs $\frac{1}{2}$ pound. Another bag weighs 4 times that amount. Find the total weight of the two bags of grapes.</u>

Choose a Way to Solve the Problem

You can draw a diagram to help you solve the problem.

- Draw a strip for Nina and a strip for Jolene.

Nina $\quad$ ← $\frac{1}{2}$ pound

- Make the length of Jolene's strip 4 times the length of Nina's strip.

Jolene

4. How many pieces in all are in the combined strips? _____

5. One small piece represents $\frac{1}{2}$ pound.

   How many pounds do 5 small pieces represent? _____ $\times \frac{1}{2}$ = _____

Show the Solution

6. Nina and Jolene bought _____ pounds of grapes in all.

Try This Draw a diagram to solve the problem.

7. Marty and David ran a total of $2\frac{1}{4}$ miles yesterday. Marty ran twice the distance David ran. How many miles did they each run?

Marty

David

$2\frac{1}{4}$ miles

Solution Marty ran _____ miles. David ran _____ mile.

Name _____ Date _____

Fractions and Decimals

You can use fractions and decimals to describe the shaded part.

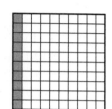 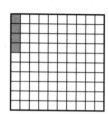 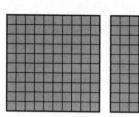

Fraction: $\frac{10}{100}$ Fraction: $\frac{4}{100}$ Mixed Number: $1\frac{7}{10}$

Decimal: 0.10   Decimal: 0.04   Decimal: 1.7

Write a fraction or mixed number and a decimal
to describe the shaded part of the model.

1.

Fraction: _____

Decimal: _____

2.

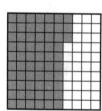

Fraction: _____

Decimal: _____

3.

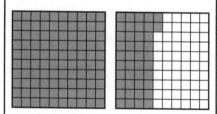

Fraction: _____

Decimal: _____

Write each as a decimal.

4.

$\frac{8}{10}$ _____

5.

$\frac{79}{100}$ _____

6.

$7\frac{1}{10}$ _____

Write each as a fraction or mixed number.

7.

0.5 _____

8.

0.27 _____

9.

5.45 _____

Objective: Write fractions and mixed numbers as decimals.
Chapter Intervention   — 158 —   Use with Chapter 11.
Grade 5

Name _____ Date _____

Add and Subtract Decimals

> Add and subtract decimals as you would add and subtract whole numbers.

You can use place value to add and subtract decimals.

---

1. Add $0.63 + 3.29$.

Line up the decimal points. Add hundredths.

ones	.	tenths	hundredths
	.	☐	
0	.	6	3
+ 3	.	2	9
	.		☐

Add tenths.

ones	.	tenths	hundredths
	.	1	
0	.	6	3
+ 3	.	2	9
	.	☐	2

Add ones. Write the decimal point in the answer.

ones	.	tenths	hundredths
	.	1	
0	.	6	3
+ 3	.	2	9
☐	☐	9	2

---

2. Subtract $4.65 - 1.48$.

Line up the decimal points. Subtract hundredths.

ones	.	tenths	hundredths
	.	5	15
4	.	6̸	5̸
− 1	.	4	8
	.		☐

Subtract tenths.

ones	.	tenths	hundredths
	.	5	15
4	.	6̸	5̸
− 1	.	4	8
	.	☐	7

Subtract ones. Write the decimal point in the answer.

ones	.	tenths	hundredths
	.	5	15
4	.	6	5
− 1	.	4	8
☐	☐	1	7

Add or subtract using a place-value chart.

3. $2.71 + 0.43$

ones	.	tenths	hundredths
	.		
+	.		
	.		

4. $8.93 - 0.47$

ones	.	tenths	hundredths
	.		
+	.		
	.		

Add or subtract.

5. $1.8 + 0.3 =$ _____

6. $2.19 + 5.36 =$ _____

7. $0.74 - 0.27 =$ _____

Objective: Add and subtract decimals.
Chapter Intervention

Use with Chapter 11.
Grade 5

Estimate Decimals

Use rounding rules to estimate decimals.

> • If the digit to the right of the rounding place is 5 or more, round up.
> • If the digit is less than 5, round down.

Round to the nearest **tenth**. Then estimate the *sum*.

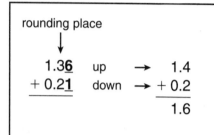

	1.	**2.**
rounding place ↓	↓	↓
1.3**6** up → 1.4	0.2**7** 0.___	2.4**3** 2.___
+ 0.2**1** down → + 0.2	+ 0.3**9** + 0.___	+ 0.7**5** + 0.___
1.6		

Round to the nearest **whole number.** Then estimate the *difference.*

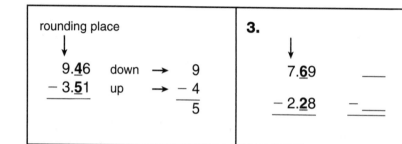

	3.	**4.**
rounding place ↓	↓	↓
9.**4**6 down → 9	7.**6**9 ___	11.**8**1 ___ ___
− 3.**5**1 up → − 4	− 2.**2**8 − ___	− 6.**4**3 − ___ ___
5		

Round to the place shown. Then estimate the *sum* or *difference.*

5.	**6.**	**7.**	**8.**
tenths ↓	ones ↓	tenths ↓	ones ↓
0.86	48.48	0.82	5.92
+ 1.71	− 12.63	− 0.36	+ 0.75
9.	**10.**	**11.**	**12.**
tenths ↓	ones ↓	tenths ↓	ones ↓
2.74	92.63	0.54	14.38
− 1.23	+ 7.71	+ 3.26	− 5.62

Name _____ Date _____

Relate Fractions and Decimals

You can use fractions to help you add and subtract decimals.

Use fractions to write an addition sentence for the model.
Then write a decimal for each fraction.

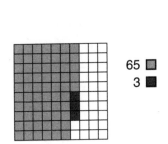

65 ☐
3 ■

$$\frac{65}{100} + \frac{3}{100} = \frac{68}{100}$$

↓ ↓ ↓

$0.65 + 0.03 = 0.68$

1.

$\frac{\Box}{\Box} + \frac{\Box}{\Box} = \frac{\Box}{\Box}$

↓ ↓ ↓

$0.\_\_ + 0.\_\_ = 0.\_\_$

2.

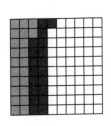

$\frac{\Box}{\Box} + \frac{\Box}{\Box} = \frac{\Box}{\Box}$

↓ ↓ ↓

$0.\_\_ + 0.\_\_ = 0.\_\_$

Use fractions to write a subtraction sentence for the model.
Then write a decimal for each fraction.

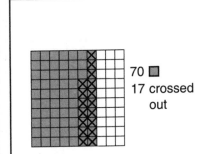

70 ☐
17 crossed
out

$$\frac{70}{100} - \frac{17}{100} = \frac{53}{100}$$

↓ ↓ ↓

0.70

↓

$0.7 - 0.17 = 0.53$

3.

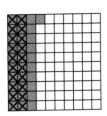

$\frac{\Box}{\Box} - \frac{\Box}{\Box} = \frac{\Box}{\Box}$

↓ ↓ ↓

$0.\_\_ - 0.\_ = 0.\_\_$

4.

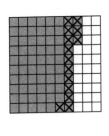

$\frac{\Box}{\Box} - \frac{\Box}{\Box} = \frac{\Box}{\Box}$

↓ ↓ ↓

$0.\_\_ - 0.\_\_ = 0.\_\_$

Objective: Relate addition and subtraction of fractions and decimals.
Chapter Intervention

Use with Chapter 11.
Grade 5

Name _____ Date _____

Add Decimals

When you add decimals, use the decimal points to line up the digits. Then add from right to left.

Find 2.7 + 4.38.

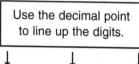

Use the decimal point to line up the digits.

ones	.	tenths	hundredths
1			
2	.	7	**0**
+ 4	.	3	8
7	.	0	8

← Write zero to have the same number of places to add.

---

1. Find 6.53 + 4.2.

Think
Write 4.2 as 4.20.

o	.	t	h
6	.	5	3
+ 4	.	2	**0**
	.		

Add. Use the gridlines to help you.

2. 3.49 + 2.1

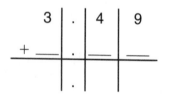

3. 2.13 + 3.4

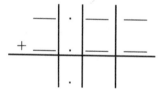

4. 7.7 + 4.65

5. 4.401 + 0.78

4	.	4	0	1
+ 0	.	7	8	0
	.			

6. 2.357 + 1.6

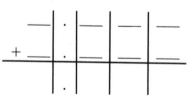

7. 2.384 + 0.6

Add.

8. 3.59 + 0.4 = _____

9. 1.245 + 5.8 = _____

10. 3.173 + 2.46 = _____

Objective: Add and subtract decimals through thousandths.
Chapter Intervention

Use with Chapter 11.
Grade 5

Name _____ Date _____

Subtract Decimals

When you subtract decimals use the decimal points to
align the digits. Then subtract, place by place from right to left.

Find 9.7 − 1.54.

Use the decimal points to align the digits.	There are not enough **hundredths** to subtract. Regroup. Then subtract.	Subtract tenths. Then subtract ones.
Write a zero to have the same number of places in each number.		
9.7**0** − 1.5**4**	^{610} 9.$\not7\not0$ − 1.5**4** ──── 6	^{610} 9.$\not7\not0$ − 1.5**4** ──── 8.16

Subtract.

1. 7.36 − 3.239	**2.** 4.25 − 1.34	**3.** 7.8 − 1.24
7 . 3 6 0 − 3 . 2 3 9 ──────── __ . __ __ __	4 . 2 5 − __ . __ __ ────── __ . __ __	__ . __ __ − __ . __ __ ────── __ . __ __
4. 6.985 − 2.406	**5.** 3.764 − 0.63	**6.** 8.484 − 2.375
__ . __ __ __ − __ . __ __ __ ────────── .	__ . __ __ __ − __ . __ __ __ ────────── .	__ . __ __ __ − __ . __ __ __ ────────── .

Subtract.

7. 7.27 − 0.5 = _____	**8.** 3.764 − 0.206 = _____	**9.** 6.659 − 3.13 = _____

Objective: Subtract decimals through thousandths.
Chapter Intervention

Use with Chapter 11.
Grade 5

Estimate With Decimals

You can use rounding rules to
estimate sums and differences.

Round to the nearest *tenth.* Then add to estimate the sum.

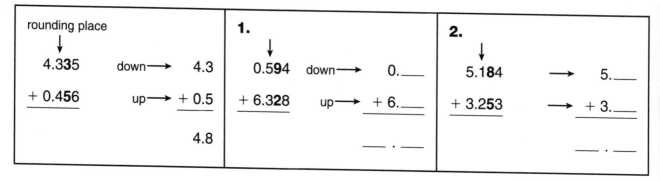

| rounding place
↓
4.335   down⟶   4.3
+ 0.456   up⟶ + 0.5
                4.8 | **1.**
↓
0.594 down⟶ 0.___
+ 6.328 up⟶ + 6.___
    ___ . ___ | **2.**
↓
5.184   ⟶ 5.___
+ 3.253   ⟶ + 3.___
    ___ . ___ |

Round to the nearest *whole number.* Then subtract to estimate the difference.

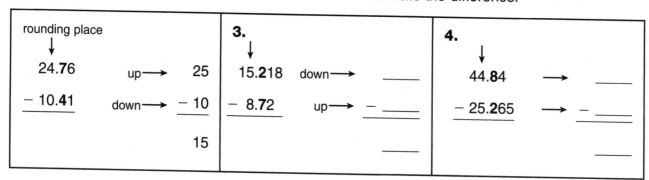

| rounding place
↓
24.76   up⟶   25
− 10.41   down⟶ − 10
                15 | **3.**
↓
15.218 down⟶ _____
− 8.72 up⟶ − _____
    _____ | **4.**
↓
44.84   ⟶ _____
− 25.265 ⟶ − _____
    _____ |

Round to the place indicated.
Add or subtract to estimate the *sum* or *difference.*

5. nearest tenth	**6.** nearest whole number	**7.** nearest tenth
0.873 − 0.501	19.61 + 43.7	17.43 − 9.39
___ − ___ = ___	___ + ___ = ___	___ − ___ = ___
0.873 − 0.501 is about ___.	19.61 + 43.7 is about ___.	17.43 − 9.39 is about ___.

Objective: Estimate decimal sums and differences.
Chapter Intervention   **− 164 −**   Use with Chapter 11.
Grade 5

Choose a Computation Method

Problem   Sue's car averages 26.42 miles per gallon of gasoline on the highway and 19.78 miles per gallon in the city. How many more miles per gallon does Sue's car average on the highway than in the city?

Read to Understand

1. How many miles per gallon does Sue's car average on the highway?   _____ miles per gallon

2. How many miles per gallon does Sue's car average in the city?   _____ miles per gallon

Choose a Way to Solve the Problem

3. What numbers should you subtract to solve the problem?   _____ – _____

To solve the problem, decide whether you should use **mental math, pencil and paper,** or a **calculator.**

- It is not easy to subtract these numbers in your head. So do not use mental math.

- It is faster to subtract using pencil and paper than a calculator.

> Show your work.

Show the Solution

4. Sue's car gets _____ more miles per gallon on the highway than in the city.

Try This   Solve. Tell which method you used.

Fernando worked for 3.5 hours on Saturday and 4 hours on Sunday. How many hours did he work in all during those two days?

5. **Solution**   Fernando worked _____ hours in all.

6. Which method did you use? _____

7. Why did you make that choice? _____

Name _____ Date _____

Fractions and Mixed Numbers

You can find equivalent fractions by multiplying or dividing the numerator and the denominator of a fraction by the same number.

1.
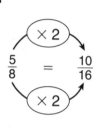
$\frac{5}{8} = \frac{10}{16}$ with $\times 2$ and $\times 2$

2.
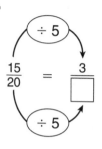
$\frac{15}{20} = \frac{3}{\square}$ with $\div 5$ and $\div 5$

3.
$\frac{2}{3} = \frac{8}{\square}$

4.
$\frac{6}{20} = \frac{\square}{10}$

To change a mixed number to an **improper fraction,** you can multiply and add.

> An improper fraction has a numerator that is greater than or equal to its denominator.

Think
Multiply. $3 \times 2 = 6$
Add. $6 + 1 = 7$

$2\frac{1}{3} = \frac{7}{3}$ ← $(3 \times 2) + 1$
← Use the same denominator.

5.
$2\frac{3}{8} = \dfrac{\blacksquare}{\blacksquare}$

$(8 \times 2) + 3 = \underline{\quad}$

$2\frac{3}{8} = \dfrac{\square}{\square}$

6.
$4\frac{5}{6} = \dfrac{\blacksquare}{\blacksquare}$

$(6 \times 4) + 5 = \underline{\quad}$

$4\frac{5}{6} = \dfrac{\square}{\square}$

To change an improper fraction to a **mixed number,** you can divide.

$\frac{14}{4} = 14 \div 4$

$\begin{array}{r} 3 \leftarrow \text{wholes} \\ 4\overline{)14} \\ -12 \\ \hline 2 \end{array}$

$\frac{14}{4} = 3\frac{2}{4}$ or $3\frac{1}{2}$

Remember
Write the fraction part in simplest form.

7. $\frac{10}{3} = 10 \div 3$

$= \dfrac{\square}{\square}$

$= \underline{\quad}$

8. $\frac{20}{5} = 20 \div 5$

$= \dfrac{\square}{\square}$

$= \underline{\quad}$

9. $\frac{39}{6} = \blacksquare$

$= \underline{\quad}$

10. $\frac{54}{8} = \blacksquare$

$= \underline{\quad}$

Name _____ Date _____

Part of a Number

You can use division and multiplication to find a fractional part of a number.

Find the fractional part of each number.

Divide by the denominator of the fraction.	**1.** $\frac{1}{2}$ of 8 is ___.	**2.** $\frac{1}{3}$ of 18 is ___.
Find $\frac{1}{3}$ of 15.		

Think
$8 \div 2 = ?$

Think
$18 \div 3 = ?$

$$15 \quad \div \quad 3 \quad = \quad 5$$

↑ number   ↑ denominator   ↑ part of the number

So, $\frac{1}{3}$ of 15 is 5.

3. $\frac{1}{5}$ of 10 is ___.

4. $\frac{1}{6}$ of 24 is ___.

Divide. Find $\frac{2}{3}$ of 15.

5. $\frac{2}{5}$ of 20 is ___.

6. $\frac{5}{8}$ of 24 is ___.

$$15 \quad \div \quad 3 \quad = \quad 5$$

↑ total   ↑ denominator   ↑ number in each group

Multiply the result by the numerator of the fraction to find the answer.

Divide. $20 \div 5$
Then multiply by 2.

Divide. $24 \div 8$
Multiply by 5.

7. $\frac{3}{4}$ of 16 is ___.

8. $\frac{7}{8}$ of 32 is ___.

$5 \times 2 = 10$ ← answer

So, $\frac{2}{3}$ of 15 is 10.

Name _____ Date _____

Multiply Fractions

When you multiply fractions,
decide if the product is in simplest form.

Find $\frac{3}{4} \times \frac{2}{5}$.

Multiply the numerators. ⟶ $\frac{3}{4} \times \frac{2}{5} = \frac{3 \times 2}{4 \times 5} = \frac{6}{20}$ or $\frac{3}{10}$
Multiply the denominators. ⟶

Write the answer in simplest form.

Multiply. Write the answer in simplest form.

1. $\frac{2}{3} \times \frac{5}{6} = \frac{2 \times 5}{3 \times 6} = \frac{\square}{\square} = \frac{\square}{\square}$

simplest form

2. $\frac{3}{8} \times 2 = \frac{3 \times 2}{8 \times 1} = \frac{\square}{\square} = \frac{\square}{\square}$

Think

$2 = \frac{2}{1}$

simplest form

3. $\frac{5}{12} \times \frac{1}{2} = \frac{5 \times 1}{12 \times 2} = \frac{\square}{\square}$

4. $\frac{4}{5} \times \frac{3}{8} = \frac{4 \times 3}{5 \times 8} = \frac{\square}{\square} = \frac{\square}{\square}$

5. $\frac{1}{2} \times \frac{1}{4} =$ _____

6. $\frac{7}{8} \times \frac{4}{5} =$ _____

Simplest form _____

Multiply. Write the answer in simplest form.

7. $\frac{1}{6} \times \frac{2}{3} =$ _____

8. $\frac{5}{6} \times \frac{3}{4} =$ _____

9. $\frac{1}{8} \times 6 =$ _____

Name _____ Date _____

Multiply With Mixed Numbers

When you multiply with mixed numbers,
first write the mixed numbers as improper fractions.

Find $1\frac{1}{3} \times \frac{3}{5}$.

- Write the mixed number as an improper fraction.

$$1\frac{1}{3} = \frac{3}{3} + \frac{1}{3}$$

Think
$1 = \frac{3}{3}$

$$= \frac{4}{3}$$

- Simplify and multiply.

$$1\frac{1}{3} \times \frac{3}{5} = \frac{4 \times \overset{1}{\cancel{3}}}{\underset{1}{\cancel{3}} \times 5}$$

$$= \frac{4}{5}$$

So, $1\frac{1}{3} \times \frac{3}{5} = \frac{4}{5}$.

Multiply. Write each product in simplest form.

1. $\frac{1}{3} \times 2\frac{1}{4}$

Divide by 3 to simplify.

$$\frac{1}{3} \times \frac{9}{4} = \frac{1 \times \overset{3}{\cancel{9}}}{\underset{1}{\cancel{3}} \times 4} = \frac{\square}{\square}$$

$$\frac{1}{3} \times 2\frac{1}{4} = \underline{\qquad}$$

2. $1\frac{2}{3} \times \frac{1}{5}$

$$\frac{\square}{3} \times \frac{1}{5} = \frac{\square \times 1}{3 \times 5} = \frac{\square}{\square}$$

$$1\frac{2}{3} \times \frac{1}{5} = \underline{\qquad}$$

3. $1\frac{1}{4} \times \frac{1}{2}$

$$\frac{\square}{4} \times \frac{1}{2} = \frac{\square \times 1}{4 \times 2} = \frac{\square}{\square}$$

$$1\frac{1}{4} \times \frac{1}{2} = \underline{\qquad}$$

4. $\frac{1}{5} \times 3\frac{1}{2}$

$$\frac{1}{5} \times \frac{\square}{\square} = \frac{1 \times \square}{5 \times \square} = \frac{\square}{\square}$$

$$\frac{1}{5} \times 3\frac{1}{2} = \underline{\qquad}$$

Objective: Find products of fractions and mixed numbers.
Chapter Intervention

Use with Chapter 12.
Grade 5

Name _____ Date _____

Divide Fractions

When you divide with fractions, you can use multiplication.

> Two fractions that have a product of 1 are **reciprocals.**

Divide. Write the answer in simplest form.

1.

Find the reciprocal of the divisor.

$$6 \div \frac{3}{5}$$

The reciprocal of $\frac{3}{5}$ is $\frac{5}{3}$.

Write a multiplication expression using the reciprocal.

$$6 \div \frac{3}{5} = \frac{6}{1} \times \frac{5}{3}$$

 reciprocals

Multiply. Simplify the answer.

$$\frac{6}{1} \times \frac{5}{3} = \frac{30}{3} = \underline{\quad}$$

↑ simplest form

2.

$$6 \div \frac{2}{3} = \frac{6}{1} = \frac{\square}{\square} = \frac{\square}{\square} = \underline{\quad}$$

reciprocals

3.

$$3 \div \frac{10}{3} = \frac{3}{1} \times \frac{\square}{\square} = \underline{\quad}$$

reciprocals

4.

Find the reciprocal of the **divisor.**

$$\frac{3}{4} \div 6$$

The reciprocal of 6 is $\frac{1}{6}$.

Write a multiplication expression using the reciprocal.

$$\frac{3}{4} \div \frac{6}{1} = \frac{3}{4} \times \frac{1}{6}$$

 reciprocals

Multiply. Simplify the answer.

$$\frac{3}{4} \times \frac{1}{6} = \frac{3}{24} = \underline{\quad}$$

↑ simplest form

5.

$$\frac{2}{3} \div 10 = \frac{2}{3} \times \frac{1}{\square} = \frac{\square}{\square} = \underline{\quad}$$

reciprocals

6.

$$\frac{4}{5} \div 8 = \frac{4}{5} \times \frac{\square}{\square} = \frac{\square}{\square} = \underline{\quad}$$

reciprocals

7.

$$\frac{4}{5} \div \frac{11}{10} = \frac{4}{5} \times \frac{10}{11} = \underline{\quad}$$

reciprocals

8.

$$\frac{2}{3} \div \frac{6}{5} = \frac{2}{3} \times \frac{\square}{\square} = \underline{\quad}$$

reciprocals

Objective: Use the reciprocal to divide fractions.
Chapter Intervention

Use with Chapter 12.
Grade 5

Name _____ Date _____

Divide Mixed Numbers

When you divide with mixed numbers, you can write the mixed numbers as improper fractions.

$$4\frac{2}{3} = \frac{12}{3} + \frac{2}{3} = \frac{14}{3}$$

↑ mixed number   ↑ improper fraction

Divide. Write the answer in simplest form.

1.

Write both mixed numbers as improper fractions.

$$2\frac{3}{4} \div 3\frac{1}{2}$$

$$\frac{11}{4} \div \frac{7}{2}$$

Write a multiplication expression using the reciprocal of the divisor.

$$\frac{11}{4} \div \frac{7}{2} = \frac{11}{4} \times \frac{2}{7}$$

└ reciprocals ┘

Multiply. Simplify the answer.

$$\frac{11}{4} \times \frac{2}{7} = \frac{22}{28} = \underline{\qquad}$$

↑ simplest form

2.

$$1\frac{1}{2} \div 2\frac{2}{3} = \frac{3}{2} \div \frac{8}{3} = \frac{3}{2} \times \frac{\square}{\square} = \underline{\qquad}$$

└ reciprocals ┘

3.

$$2\frac{1}{2} \div 3\frac{1}{3} = \frac{\square}{\square} \div \frac{\square}{\square} = \frac{\square}{\square} \times \frac{\square}{\square} = \underline{\qquad}$$

└ reciprocals ┘

4.

Write the divisor as an improper fraction.

$$3 \div 3\frac{3}{4}$$

$$3 \div \frac{15}{4}$$

Write a multiplication expression using the reciprocal.

$$\frac{3}{1} \div \frac{15}{4} = \frac{3}{1} \times \frac{4}{15}$$

└ reciprocals ┘

Multiply. Simplify the answer.

$$\frac{3}{4} \times \frac{4}{15} = \frac{12}{15} = \underline{\qquad}$$

↑ simplest form

5.

$$2 \div 2\frac{2}{3} = \frac{2}{1} \div \frac{8}{3} = \frac{2}{1} \times \frac{\square}{\square} = \underline{\qquad}$$

└ reciprocals ┘

6.

$$\frac{3}{5} \div 2\frac{1}{4} = \frac{\square}{\square} \div \frac{\square}{\square} = \frac{\square}{\square} \times \frac{\square}{\square} = \underline{\qquad}$$

└ reciprocals ┘

7.

$$\frac{1}{2} \div 1\frac{1}{2} = \frac{1}{2} \div \frac{3}{2} = \frac{1}{2} \times \frac{\square}{\square} = \underline{\qquad}$$

└ reciprocals ┘

8.

$$\frac{4}{5} \div 2\frac{2}{5} = \frac{\square}{\square} \div \frac{\square}{\square} = \frac{\square}{\square} \times \frac{\square}{\square} = \underline{\qquad}$$

└ reciprocals ┘

Objective: Use the reciprocal to divide fractions.
Chapter Intervention

Use with Chapter 12.
Grade 5

Choose the Operation

Problem   A trail is $5\frac{3}{4}$ miles long. Martin has $\frac{1}{3}$ of the trail left to hike.
How many miles does Martin have left to hike?

Read to Understand

1. How long is the trail? _____ miles

2. What fractional part of the trail does Martin have left to hike? _____ of the trail

3. What does the question ask? _____

Choose a Way to Solve the Problem
Before you can solve the problem, you need to decide which operation
to use. For Exercises 4–8, decide which item below describes what
you need to find.

Write **Yes** or **No.**

4. You need to add to find the amount that is $\frac{1}{3}$ more than $5\frac{3}{4}$. _____

5. You need to subtract to find the amount that is $\frac{1}{3}$ less $5\frac{3}{4}$. _____

6. You need to multiply to find the amount that is $\frac{1}{3}$ of $5\frac{3}{4}$. _____

7. You need to divide to find how many $\frac{1}{3}$s are in $5\frac{3}{4}$. _____

8. Choose the operation that you should use
to solve the problem. Write a number sentence.   _____ ◯ _____ = _____

Show the Solution

9. Martin has _____ miles left to hike.

Try This   Choose the operation to solve.

10. Rowena studied for $2\frac{1}{4}$ hours. She spent the same amount of time on
each of 3 subjects. How much time did Rowena spend on each subject?

   Solution   What operation should you use? _____

   Rowena spent _____ on each subject.

Name _____ Date _____

Multiply by 1-Digit Numbers

Sometimes you need to regroup when you multiply.

Multiply 4 × 238.

• Multiply ones. $4 \times 8 = 32$ Regroup.	

H	T	O
	3	
2	3	8
×		4
		2

• Multiply tens.
$4 \times 30 = 120$
Add the 3 tens.
$120 + 30 = 150$
Regroup.

H	T	O
1	3	
2	3	8
×		4
	5	2

• Multiply hundreds.
$4 \times 200 = 800$
Add the 1 hundred.
$800 + 100 = 900$

H	T	O
1	3	
2	3	8
×		4
9	5	2

Multiply. Regroup when necessary.

1.

H	T	O
	☐	
1	3	5
×		2
___	___	___

2.

H	T	O
	☐	
2	1	6
×		4
___	___	___

3.

H	T	O
☐	☐	
2	6	8
×		3
___	___	___

4.

H	T	O
☐	☐	
	5	3	9
×		6
___ , ___	___	___

5.

H	T	O
3	2	7
×		3
___	___	___

6.

H	T	O
4	3	2
×		4
___ , ___	___	___

7.

H	T	O
5	0	9
×		9
___ , ___	___	___

8.

H	T	O
3	3	3
×		4
___ , ___	___	___

Objective: Multiply by 1-digit numbers.
Chapter Intervention

Use with Chapter 3.
Grade 5

Name _____ Date _____

Estimate Products

You can use rounding to estimate products.

Round the decimal to the nearest **whole number**.
Then estimate the product.

> • If the digit to the right of the rounding place is 5 or more, round up.
>
> • If the digit is less than 5, round down.

1. rounding place
$\downarrow$

12 × 4.**3** ← round down
$\downarrow$

12 × **4** = ___

So, 12 × 4.3 is about _____.

2. rounding place
$\downarrow$

4 × 6.**62** ← round up
$\downarrow$

4 × ___ = ___

So, 4 × 6.62 is about _____.

3.

22 × 3.**2**
$\downarrow$

22 × ___ = ___

22 × 3.2 is about _____.

4.

11 × 3.**81**
$\downarrow$

11 × ___ = ___

11 × 3.81 is about _____.

5.

3 × 5.7

3 × ___ = ___

3 × 5.7 is about ___.

6.

20 × 3.82

20 × ___ = ___

20 × 3.82 is about ___.

7.

11 × 7.34

11 × ___ = ___

11 × 7.34 is about ___.

8.

9 × 4.4 is about ___.

9.

3 × 9.83 is about ___.

10.

7 × 5.12 is about ___.

11.

13 × 9.6 is about ___.

12.

21 × 2.3 is about ___.

13.

12 × 5.72 is about ___.

Name _____ Date _____

Relate Fraction and Decimal Products

You can use fractions to help you multiply decimals.
Use the product of the fractions to help you find the
product of the decimals.

Write each decimal as a fraction and multiply.
Write each answer as a decimal.

Think: 0.8 is 8-tenths or $\frac{8}{10}$.

1.3 is 1 and 3-tenths or $1\frac{3}{10} = \frac{13}{10}$.

Multiply Decimals

0.7×0.8

$\frac{7}{10} \times \frac{8}{10} = \frac{56}{100}$

$= 0.56$

$0.7 \times 0.8 = 0.56$

1.

0.4×0.3

$\frac{4}{10} \times \frac{\boxed{}}{10} = \frac{\boxed{}}{100}$

$= 0.\underline{}$

$0.4 \times 0.3 = \underline{}$

2.

0.5×0.7

$\frac{\boxed{}}{10} \times \frac{\boxed{}}{10} = \frac{\boxed{}}{100}$

$= 0.\underline{}$

$0.5 \times 0.7 = \underline{}$

Multiply Whole Numbers

0.8×3

$\frac{8}{10} \times \frac{3}{1} = \frac{24}{10}$ or $2\frac{4}{10}$

$= 2.4$

$0.8 \times 3 = 2.4$

3.

0.6×2

$\frac{6}{10} \times \frac{2}{1} = \frac{\boxed{}}{10}$

$= 1.\underline{}$

$0.6 \times 2 = 1.\underline{}$

4.

7×0.8

$\frac{7}{1} \times \frac{\boxed{}}{\boxed{}} = \frac{\boxed{}}{\boxed{}}$

$= \underline{}$

$7 \times 0.8 = \underline{}$

Multiply Decimals Greater Than 1

0.2×1.3

$\frac{2}{10} \times \frac{13}{10} = \frac{26}{100}$

$= 0.26$

$0.2 \times 1.3 = 0.26$

5.

0.4×1.2

$\frac{4}{10} \times \frac{\boxed{}}{10} = \frac{\boxed{}}{100}$

$= 0.\underline{}$

$0.4 \times 1.2 = \underline{}$

6.

1.4×0.2

$\frac{14}{10} \times \frac{\boxed{}}{\boxed{}} = \frac{\boxed{}}{\boxed{}}$

$= 0.\underline{}$

$1.4 \times 0.2 = \underline{}$

Estimate Products

You can use rounding to estimate products.

- Round **whole numbers and decimals greater than 1** to the greatest place value.
- Round **decimals less than 1** to the nearest tenth.

Estimate. 0.67 × 421

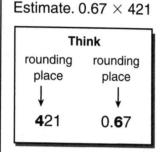

| Think |
rounding place	rounding place
↓	↓
421	0.**6**7

$$\begin{array}{r} 421 \\ \times\,0.67 \end{array}$$ nearest hundred → 400 ← 0 decimal places
nearest tenth → $\times\,0.7$ ← + 1 decimal place
280.0 ← 1 decimal place

So, 0.67 × 421 is about 280.

Estimate each product.

1. 0.65 × 23

$$\begin{array}{r} 23 \\ \times\,0.65 \end{array}$$ nearest ten → $\begin{array}{r} 2\;0 \\ \times\,0.7 \end{array}$

nearest tenth →

___ ___ . ___

So, 0.65 × 23 is about _____.

2. 0.51 × 32

32 → _____

$\times\,0.51$ → × _____

___ ___ . ___

So 32 × 0.51 is about _____.

3.

$$\begin{array}{r} 15.9 \\ \times\;\;21 \end{array}$$ → $$\begin{array}{r} 16 \\ \times\,20 \end{array}$$

So, 21 × 15.9 is about _____.

4.

2.38 → _____

$\times\;\;18$ → × _____

So, 18 × 2.38 is about _____.

5.

1.98 → ___

$\times\;\;26$ → × _____

___ ___

Estimate _____

6.

57 → _____

$\times\,3.89$ → × _____

___ ___ ___

Estimate _____

Multiply Whole Numbers and Decimals

You can multiply decimals the same way that
you multiply whole numbers.

Find 3 × 4.79.

Multiply the hundredths.	Multiply the tenths.	Multiply the ones.	Place the decimal point.
2 4.79 × 3 ——— 7	2 2 4.79 × 3 ——— 37	2 2 4.79 × 3 ——— 1437	4.79 ← 2 decimal places × 3 ——— 14.37 ← 2 decimal places

---

Multiply.

1.

$$\begin{array}{r} 5\ .\ 8 \\ \times\qquad 4 \\ \hline \end{array}$$ ← 1 decimal place

___ ___ . ___ ← 1 decimal place

2.

$$\begin{array}{r} 9\ .\ 2\ 1 \\ \times\qquad 8 \\ \hline \end{array}$$ ← 2 decimal places

___ ___ . ___ ___ ← 2 decimal places

3.

$$\begin{array}{r} 5\ .\ 1\ 8\ 5 \\ \times\qquad\quad 3 \\ \hline \end{array}$$ ← 3 decimal places

___ ___ . ___ ___ ___ ← 3 decimal places

Multiply. Place the decimal point.

4.

3.9 ← 1 decimal place
× 2
———

5.

7.65 ← 2 decimal places
× 5
———

6.

1.937 ← 3 decimal places
× 6
———

7.

2.7
× 3
———

8.

8.26
× 2
———

9.

4.454
× 7
———

10.

3.94
× 6
———

11.

1.641
× 9
———

12.

6.5
× 7
———

Objective: Find the product of a whole number and a decimal.

Chapter Intervention

— 177 —

Use with Chapter 13.
Grade 5

Name _____ Date _____

Multiply Decimals

You can multiply decimals the same way
that you multiply whole numbers.
Remember to place the decimal point in the product.

Find 0.3×1.2.

• Multiply.	• Count the number of decimal places in both factors.	• Place the decimal point. • Write a zero in the ones place.
$\begin{array}{r} 1.2 \\ \times\, 0.3 \\ \hline 36 \end{array}$	$\begin{array}{r} 1.2 \leftarrow \quad\text{1 decimal place} \\ \times\, 0.3 \leftarrow +\text{1 decimal place} \\ \hline 36 \leftarrow \quad\text{2 decimal places} \end{array}$	$\begin{array}{r} 1.2 \leftarrow \quad\text{1 decimal place} \\ \times\, 0.3 \leftarrow +\text{1 decimal place} \\ \hline 0.36 \leftarrow \quad\text{2 decimal places} \end{array}$

Multiply.

1.	2.
$\begin{array}{r} 5\,.\,2 \leftarrow \quad\text{1 decimal place} \\ \times\, 0\,.\,3 \leftarrow +\text{1 decimal place} \\ \hline \underline{\quad}\,.\,\underline{\quad}\,\underline{\quad} \leftarrow \quad\text{2 decimal places} \end{array}$	$\begin{array}{r} 7\,.\,9 \leftarrow \quad\text{1 decimal place} \\ \times\, 0\,.\,4 \leftarrow +\text{1 decimal place} \\ \hline \underline{\quad}\,.\,\underline{\quad}\,\underline{\quad} \leftarrow \quad\text{2 decimal places} \end{array}$

Multiply. Place the decimal point.

3.	4.	5.
$\begin{array}{r} 0.8 \leftarrow \text{1 decimal place} \\ \times\, 0.2 \leftarrow \text{1 decimal place} \\ \hline \end{array}$	$\begin{array}{r} 3.32 \leftarrow \text{2 decimal places} \\ \times\,\ \ 0.4 \leftarrow \text{1 decimal place} \\ \hline \end{array}$	$\begin{array}{r} 4.32 \leftarrow \text{2 decimal places} \\ \times\, 0.13 \leftarrow \text{2 decimal places} \\ \hline \end{array}$
6. $\begin{array}{r} 0.52 \\ \times\,\ \ 0.6 \\ \hline \end{array}$	7. $\begin{array}{r} 2.34 \\ \times\,\ \ 0.7 \\ \hline \end{array}$	8. $\begin{array}{r} 10.56 \\ \times\,\ \ \ \ 0.3 \\ \hline \end{array}$

Zeros in the Product

Sometimes, when you multiply with decimals,
you may need to write zeros in a product to
place the decimal point correctly.

Find 0.3 × 0.08.

• Multiply.	• Count the number of decimal places in the factors.	• Write as many zeros as you need.	• Place the decimal point. Write a zero in the ones place.
	You need 3 decimal places.		
0.08 × 0.3 ―― 24	0.08 ← 2 decimal places × 0.3 ← + 1 decimal place ―――― 24 ← 3 decimal places	0.08 × 0.3 ―― **0**24	0.08 × 0.3 ―― **0.0**24 3 decimal places

Multiply.

1.
0 . 4 ← 1 decimal place
× 0 . 2 ← + 1 decimal place
――――
0.___ ___ ← 2 decimal places

2.
0 . 0 6 ← 2 decimal places
×   0 . 4 ← + 1 decimal place
――――
0.___ ___ ___ ← 3 decimal places

3.
0 . 0 4
× 0 . 0 7
――――
0.___ ___ ___ ___

Multiply. Place the decimal point.

4.
0.07 ← 2 decimal places
× 0.05 ← 2 decimal places
――――

5.
0.07 ← 2 decimal places
× 0.7 ← 1 decimal place
――――

6.
1.27 ← 2 decimal places
× 0.02 ← 2 decimal places
――――

7.
0.04
× 0.4
――――

8.
0.05
× 0.05
――――

9.
3.14
× 0.03
――――

Reasonable Answers

Problem Maggie has read 50 pages of a book. The book is 200 pages long. Maggie says she has read 0.4 of the book. Is Maggie's answer reasonable? Explain your answer.

Read to Understand

1. How long is Maggie's book? _____ pages

2. How many pages has Maggie read? _____ pages

3. What part of the book does Maggie say she has read? _____ of the book

4. Restate the question in another way: <u>Is 0.4 of the book a reasonable answer for 50 out of 200 pages?</u>

Choose a Way to Solve the Problem

To solve the problem, decide if Maggie's answer is reasonable.

5. What operation can you use to find 0.4 of 200 pages?_____

6. Write a number sentence to find 0.4 of 200 pages. _____ × _____ = _____

Compare your calculation to the number of pages that Maggie has read.

Show the Solution

7. Is Maggie's statement that she has read 0.4 of the book reasonable? _____

Why or why or not? _____

Try This Solve. Explain why the answer is reasonable or unreasonable.

8. Barry's summer job pays $75 each week. Barry's father wants him to save 0.3 of his pay. Barry figures that he must save $2.25 each week. Is Barry's answer reasonable? Explain your answer.

Solution _____

_____

Name _____ Date _____

Divide by Whole Numbers

When you divide, first decide where to place
the first digit of the quotient.

first digit of the quotient
↓
$28\overline{)6\ 5\ 4}$ 28 > 6, but 28 < 65

Divide.

	1.	2.
• Divide the tens. • Bring down the ones. • Divide the ones. • Write the remainder. $\begin{array}{r} 23\ \text{R}10 \\ 28\overline{)654} \\ -56 \\ \hline 94 \\ -84 \\ \hline 10 \end{array}$	$\begin{array}{r} 7\ \_\_\ \text{R}\_\_ \\ 4\overline{)2\ 9\ 5} \\ -2\ 8 \\ \hline \end{array}$	$\begin{array}{r} 3\ \_\_\ \text{R}\_\_ \\ 7\overline{)2\ 5\ 8} \\ -2\ 1 \\ \hline \end{array}$
3. $\begin{array}{r} \_\_\ \_\_\ \text{R}\_\_ \\ 32\overline{)5\ \ 7\ \ 9} \end{array}$	**4.** $\begin{array}{r} \_\_\ \_\_\ \text{R}\_\_ \\ 14\overline{)7\ \ 6\ \ 5} \end{array}$	**5.** $\begin{array}{r} \_\_\ \_\_\ \text{R}\_\_ \\ 19\overline{)3\ \ 2\ \ 5} \end{array}$
6. $\begin{array}{r} \_\_\ \_\_\ \text{R}\_\_ \\ 52\overline{)7\ \ 7\ \ 5} \end{array}$		
7. $\begin{array}{r} \_\_\ \_\_\ \_\_\ \text{R}\_\_ \\ 3\overline{)2,\ 8\ \ 7\ \ 5} \end{array}$	**8.** $\begin{array}{r} \_\_\ \_\_\ \_\_\ \text{R}\_\_ \\ 2\overline{)1,\ 9\ \ 9\ \ 5} \end{array}$	**9.** $\begin{array}{r} \_\_\ \text{R}\_\_ \\ 86\overline{)6\ \ 6\ \ 3} \end{array}$
10. $\begin{array}{r} \_\_\ \text{R}\_\_ \\ 21\overline{)1\ \ 5\ \ 5} \end{array}$		

Skill 109

Name _____ Date _____

Divide Money

You divide money just as you would whole numbers.

Find $7.32 ÷ 3.

• Divide as with whole numbers.
• Multiply to check.

Write the dollar sign and decimal point directly above the dollar sign and decimal point in the dividend.

$$\frac{\$\ .}{3)\$7.35}$$

```
    $2.45
3)$7.35
   - 6
   ─────
    1 3
   - 1 2
   ─────
      15
    - 15
   ─────
       0
```

```
  $2.45  ← quotient
×     3  ← divisor
───────
  $7.35  ← dividend
```

It checks.

Write a dollar sign and decimal point in each quotient to make it correct.

1.	2.	3.	4.
$\frac{2\ 8\ 6}{2)\$5.7\ 2}$	$\frac{1\ 3\ 2}{7)\$9.2\ 4}$	$\frac{1\ 1\ 0}{9)\$9.9\ 0}$	$\frac{0\ 8\ 6}{5)\$4.3\ 0}$

Divide. Multiply to check the answer.

5.	6.	7.	8.
$8)\$9.4\ 4$	$5)\$7.4\ 5$	$9)\$20.3\ 4$	$3)\$28.3\ 2$
Check:	Check:	Check:	Check:

Objective: Divide money.
Chapter Intervention

— 182 —

Use with Chapter 14.
Grade 5

Name _____ Date _____

Estimate Quotients

You can use basic facts and multiples of 10 to estimate quotients.

---

1. Estimate 172 ÷ 8.

- Find a new dividend that is close to 172 and easy to divide by 8.

Think: $8 \times 2 = 16$ ←basic fact
$8 \times 20 = 160$ ←multiple of 10

Divide: $160 \div 8 = 20$

So, 172 ÷ 8 is about _____.

2. Estimate 464 ÷ 5.

- Find a new dividend that is close to 464 and easy to divide by 5.

Think: $5 \times 9 = 45$ ←basic fact
$5 \times 90 = 450$ ←multiple of 10

Divide: $450 \div 5 =$ _____

So, 464 ÷ 5 is about _____.

---

3. Estimate 281 ÷ 6.

Think: $6 \times$ _____ $= 24$ ←basic fact

$6 \times$ _____ $= 240$ ←multiple of 10

Divide: $240 \div 6 =$ _____

So, 281 ÷ 6 is about _____.

4. Estimate 155 ÷ 4.

Think: $4 \times$ _____ $= 16$ ←basic fact

$4 \times$ _____ $= 160$ ←multiple of 10

Divide: $160 \div 4 =$ _____

So, 155 ÷ 4 is about _____.

---

5. Estimate 481 ÷ 7.

_____ × _____ = _____ ←basic fact

_____ × _____ = _____ ←multiple of 10

_____ ÷ _____ = _____ ←divide

So, 481 ÷ 7 is about _____.

6. Estimate 488 ÷ 6.

_____ × _____ = _____ ←basic fact

_____ × _____ = _____ ←multiple of 10

_____ ÷ _____ = _____ ←divide

So, 488 ÷ 6 is about _____.

---

7. Estimate 711 ÷ 8.

711 ÷ 8 is about _____.

8. Estimate 312 ÷ 8.

312 ÷ 8 is about _____.

Name _____ Date _____

Relate Fraction and Decimal Division

Fractions and decimals can name the same number.
So you can use fractions to divide decimals.

Find 6 ÷ 0.5.   Think 6 ÷ $\frac{1}{2}$.

• Model 6 wholes. Then show $\frac{1}{2}$s.

• To find 6 ÷ $\frac{1}{2}$, count the $\frac{1}{2}$s in 6.

There are 12 halves in 6.

6 ÷ $\frac{1}{2}$ = 12 and 6 ÷ 0.5 = 12

Divide.

1. 4 ÷ 0.4 ⟶ 4 ÷ $\frac{4}{10}$

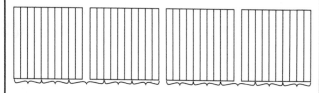

There are ___ $\frac{4}{10}$ parts in 4.

So, 4 ÷ 0.4 = ___.

2. 3 ÷ 0.25 ⟶ 3 ÷ $\frac{1}{4}$

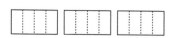

There are ___ $\frac{1}{4}$ parts in 3.

So, 3 ÷ 0.25 = ___.

3. 8 ÷ 0.25 ⟶ 8 ÷ ___

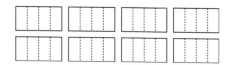

8 ÷ 0.25 = ___.

4. 6 ÷ 0.3 ⟶ _____

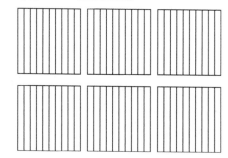

6 ÷ 0.3 = ___.

5.

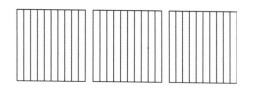

3 ÷ 0.6 = ___.

6.

5 ÷ 0.5 = ___.

Objective: Relate division of fractions to division of decimals.
Chapter Intervention

Use with Chapter 14.
Grade 5

Name _____ Date _____

Estimate Decimal Quotients

You can use unit fractions and compatible numbers
to estimate some decimal quotients.

Decimals and Equivalent Unit Fractions
$0.1 = \frac{1}{10}$ $0.25 = \frac{1}{4}$ $0.125 = \frac{1}{8}$ $0.3 \approx \frac{1}{3}$ $0.2 = \frac{1}{5}$ $0.5 = \frac{1}{2}$

Estimate $74 \div 0.18$.

• Round the decimal to a unit fraction. 0.18 is close to 0.2. $0.2 = \frac{1}{5}$ • Then write the dividend as a *compatible number.* 74 is close to 70	• Rewrite the division as a multiplication by using the reciprocal of the divisor. $70 \div \frac{1}{5} = 70 \times 5$ The reciprocal of $\frac{1}{5}$ is $\frac{5}{1}$.	• Multiply to estimate the quotient. $70 \div \frac{1}{5} = 70 \times 5$ $= 350$ So, $74 \div 0.18$ is about 350.

Use unit fractions to estimate the quotients.

1. $57 \div 0.46$

60   0.5 ⟶ $\frac{1}{2}$

$60 \div \frac{1}{2} = 60 \times$ _____

$=$ _____

$57 \div 0.46$ is about _____.

2. $9 \div 0.24$

10   0.25 ⟶ $\frac{1}{4}$

$10 \div \frac{1}{4} = 10 \times$ _____

$=$ _____

$9 \div 0.24$ is about _____.

3. $38 \div 0.32$

_____ _____ ⟶ _____

_____ $\div$ _____ $=$ _____ $\times$ _____

$=$ _____

$38 \div 0.32$ is about _____.

4. $11 \div 0.09$

_____ _____ ⟶ _____

_____ $\div$ _____ $=$ _____ $\times$ _____

$=$ _____

$11 \div 0.09$ is about _____.

Divide Decimals and Whole Numbers

When you divide a decimal by a whole number, place the decimal point in the quotient **directly above** the decimal point in the dividend.

Find 4.26 ÷ 6.

• Place the decimal point in the quotient.	• Divide as if you were dividing whole numbers.	• Multiply to check.
$6\overline{)4.26}$ with decimal point above	$\begin{array}{r} 0.71 \\ 6\overline{)4.26} \\ -4.2\downarrow \\ \hline 06 \\ -6 \\ \hline 0 \end{array}$	$\begin{array}{r} 0.71 \leftarrow\text{quotient} \\ \times\quad 6 \leftarrow\text{divisor} \\ \hline 4.26 \leftarrow\text{dividend} \end{array}$

Divide. Multiply to check.

1. $3\overline{)2.55}$ Check:	2. $4\overline{)4.96}$ Check:	3. $7\overline{)3.78}$ Check:
4. $5\overline{)7.05}$ Check:	5. $6\overline{)5.34}$ Check:	6. $9\overline{)5.67}$ Check:

Name _____ Date _____

Divide Decimals

When the divisor is a decimal, change it to a whole number
by multiplying by a power of ten.

Find $8.28 \div 0.6$.

• Multiply the divisor and dividend by the same power of ten. 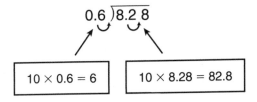 $10 \times 0.6 = 6$ $10 \times 8.28 = 82.8$	• Place a decimal point in the quotient directly above the decimal point in the dividend. • Divide. $$\begin{array}{r} 13.8 \\ 6\overline{)82.8} \\ -6\downarrow \\ \hline 22 \\ -18\downarrow \\ \hline 48 \\ -48 \\ \hline 0 \end{array}$$

Multiply by the same power of ten.

1.	2.	3.	4.
$0.05\overline{)3.20}$ $5\overline{)}$	$1.3\overline{)23.57}$ $13\overline{)}$	$60.3\overline{)26.05}$ $\_\_\overline{)}$	$1.32\overline{)5.315}$ $\_\_\overline{)}$

Divide.

5.	6.	7.
$0.4\overline{)2\ \ 4\ .\ 4}$	$1.5\overline{)9\ \ 1\ .\ 0\ \ 5}$	$2.7\overline{)5\ .\ 6\ \ 7}$

Name _____ Date _____

Repeating Decimals

You can divide to change a fraction to a decimal. Sometimes when you do this the remainder is not 0, and one or more digits in the quotient keep repeating.

$$\frac{6}{11} = 11\overline{)6}$$

Write $\frac{6}{11}$ as a decimal.

Write a decimal point in the dividend and enough zeros so you can divide.

```
        0.5454  ←
   11 )6.0000
      - 5 5
      ─────
        50
       - 44
       ─────
         60
        - 55
        ─────
          50
         - 44
         ─────
           6
```

Show the quotient as a **repeating decimal.**

The digits 5 and 4 **repeat.**
    0.5454 ...

Write a bar over the digits 5 and 4 to show they repeat.
    $6 \div 11 = \overline{54}$

---

1. Write $\frac{7}{9}$ as a decimal.

```
      0. _ _ _
   9 )7. 0 0 0
    - 6   3
```

repeating decimal:

_____

---

2. Write $\frac{5}{6}$ as a decimal.

```
      0. _ _ _
   6 )5. 0 0 0
    - 4   8
```

repeating decimal:

_____

Divide.

3.
```
      0. _ _ _
  12 )4. 0 0 0
```

repeating decimal:

_____

4.
```
      0. _ _ _
   9 )6. 0 0 0
```

repeating decimal:

_____

5.
```
      0. _ _ _
  11 )2. 0 0 0
```

repeating decimal:

_____

Objective: Use division to find repeating decimals.
Chapter Intervention

Use with Chapter 14.
Grade 5

Express the Quotient

Problem Students are buying decorations for a school dance. They estimate that they will need 350 feet of streamers. The streamers are sold in rolls of 40 feet. How many rolls will they need?

Read to Understand

1. How many feet of streamers are needed? _____

2. How many feet are in each roll? _____

3. Restate the problem another way.
   The students need 350 feet of streamers.
   The rolls come in lengths of 40 feet. How many rolls are needed?

Choose a Way to Solve the Problem

You can divide 350 feet by 40 to find the number of rolls.

4. How many rolls of 40 feet are in 350 feet? _____ rolls

$$\begin{array}{r} 8 \text{ R}30 \\ 40\overline{)350} \\ -\ 320 \\ \hline 30 \end{array}$$

Show the Solution

The next step is to decide what to do with the remainder.

> • **Use the remainder to decide on the answer.** Sometimes you need to increase the quotient. Sometimes the remainder is the answer.
>
> • **Write the remainder as a fraction.**
>
> • **Write the remainder as a decimal.**

5. Are 8 rolls enough? _____ Should you increase the quotient? _____

6. How many rolls should the students buy? _____

Try This Solve. Tell what to do with the remainder.

A softball league has 104 members. Each team in the league has exactly 12 players. The players not on a team are umpires. How many umpires are there?

Show your work.

7. There are _____ umpires.

8. What did you decide to do with the remainder?

_____

Points, Lines, and Angles

You can use words to name figures.

A **point** is a location in space.	A **line** extends without end in two directions.	A **line segment** is part of a line. It has two endpoints.	The **endpoint** of a **ray** is always the first letter.	An **angle** is formed by two rays with a common endpoint.
• D	A ←•———•→ B	J •———• K	C / D	R S T
point *D*	line *AB* or *BA*	line segment *JK* or *KJ*	ray *CD*	angle *S* or *RST* or *TSR*

Circle the correct name for each figure.

1.	**2.**	**3.**	**4.**
a. line *AB*	**a.** ray *XY*	**a.** angle *STU*	**a.** line *CD*
b. line segment *BA*	**b.** ray *YX*	**b.** angle *TUS*	**b.** ray *CD*

Name each figure.

5.	**6.**	**7.**	**8.**
_____	_____	_____	_____

Name _____ Date _____

Identify Plane Figures

A **polygon** is a closed figure made up of **three or more sides**.

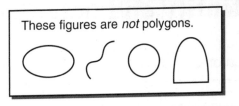

These figures are *not* polygons.

You can classify a polygon by the number of its sides.

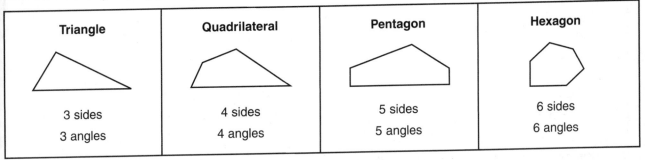

Triangle	Quadrilateral	Pentagon	Hexagon
3 sides 3 angles	4 sides 4 angles	5 sides 5 angles	6 sides 6 angles

Write the number of sides and angles. Then name the polygon.

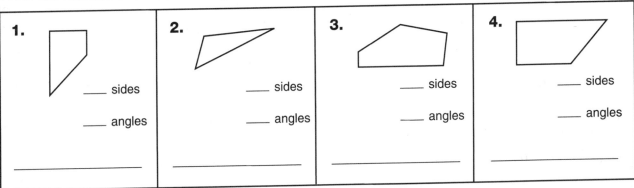

1. ___ sides ___ angles _____

2. ___ sides ___ angles _____

3. ___ sides ___ angles _____

4. ___ sides ___ angles _____

You can classify a triangle by the lengths of its sides.

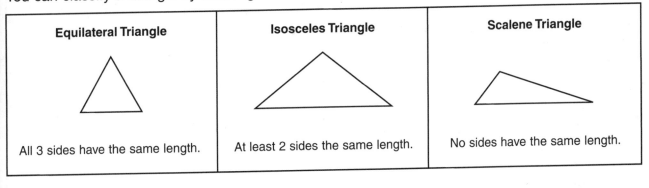

Equilateral Triangle	Isosceles Triangle	Scalene Triangle
All 3 sides have the same length.	At least 2 sides the same length.	No sides have the same length.

Name the triangle by the lengths of its sides.

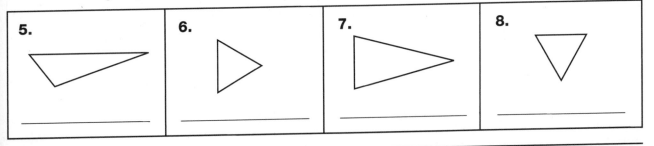

5. _____

6. _____

7. _____

8. _____

Objective: Identify and classify plane geometric figures.
Chapter Intervention

Use with Chapter 15.
Grade 5

Identify and Describe Lines

A **pair of lines** in the same plane can **intersect** or be **parallel** to each other.

Remember

• A **point** is an exact location in space.

• A **line** extends in two directions without end.

• An **angle** is made up of 2 rays with a common endpoint.

1.

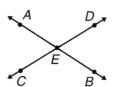

Line *AB* intersects line *CD*.
Intersecting lines have 1 point in common.

Name the point at which line *AB* intersects

line *CD*. _____

2.

Parallel lines lie in the same plane. They do not intersect.

Does line *DE* intersect line *HJ*?

_____

Is line *DE* parallel to line *HJ*? _____

3.

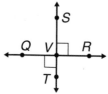

Perpendicular lines intersect at right angles.

Is line *QR* perpendicular to

line *ST*? _____

Name one right angle. _____

Write *intersects, parallel,* or *perpendicular* to describe the lines.

4.

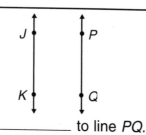

Line *AB* is _____ to line *CD*.

5.

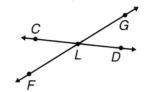

Line *CD* _____ line *FG*.

6.

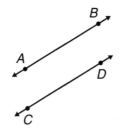

Line *JK* is _____ to line *PQ*.

7.

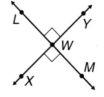

Line *LM* is _____ to line *XY*.

Name and Classify Angles

Angles are classified by the size of the opening between the rays.

Right Angle	Acute Angle	Obtuse Angle	Straight Angle
Measure is equal to 90°.	Measure is less than 90°.	Measure is greater than 90° and less than 180°.	Measure is equal to 180°.
Name: ∠ABC or ∠CBA	Name: ∠PQR or ∠RQP	Name: ∠RST or ∠TSR	Name: ∠XYZ or ∠ZYX

Classify each angle.

1.

Classify: _____

Name: ∠RST or ∠TSR

2.

Classify: _____

Name: ∠LMN or ∠NML

Classify and name each angle.

3.

Classify: _____

Name: ∠EFG or ∠ _____

4.

Classify: _____

Name: ∠ABC or ∠ _____

5.

Classify: _____

Name: ∠ _____ or ∠ _____

6.

Classify: _____

Name: ∠ _____ or ∠ _____

Triangles

Types of Triangles

Classify by Sides
Equilateral
4 cm 4 cm 4 cm
all sides the same length
Isosceles
8 ft 8 ft 6 ft
2 sides the same length
Scalene
3 m 4 m 5 m
no sides the same length

Classify by Angles
Right
Right angle: 90°
45° 90° 45°
1 right angle
Acute
Acute angle: **less** than 90°
80° 60° 40°
all acute angles
Obtuse
Obtuse angle: **greater** than 90°
110° 30° 40°
1 obtuse angle

Classify the triangles by the lengths of the **sides**.

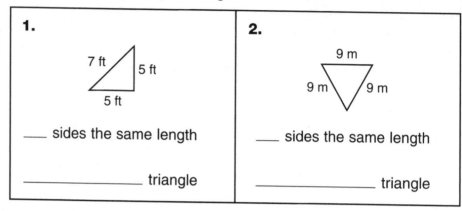

1.
7 ft 5 ft 5 ft

____ sides the same length

_____ triangle

2.
9 m 9 m 9 m

____ sides the same length

_____ triangle

Classify the triangles by the measures of the **angles**.

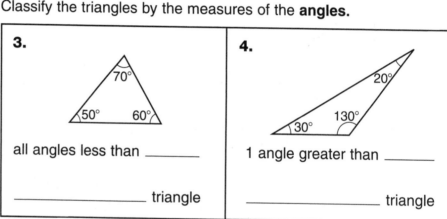

3.
70° 50° 60°

all angles less than _____

_____ triangle

4.
20° 30° 130°

1 angle greater than _____

_____ triangle

The **sum** of the angles of a triangle is **180°**.

Find the missing measure.

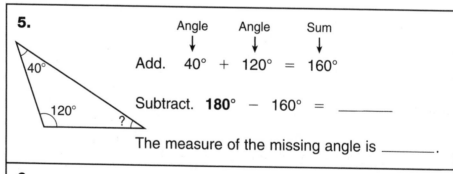

5.
40° 120° ?

Angle	Angle	Sum
↓	↓	↓

Add.   40° + 120° = 160°

Subtract. **180°** − 160° = _____

The measure of the missing angle is _____.

6.
? 100° 40°

Angle	Angle	Sum
↓	↓	↓

Add. _____ + _____ = _____

Subtract. **180°** − _____ = _____

The measure of the missing angle is _____.

Name _____ Date _____

Circles

Use the circle below for Exercises 1–2.
Underline the correct answer.

> A **circle** is the set of all points that are the same distance from the **center** point

Point *A* is the **center**.

$\overline{AC}$ is a radius.

$\overline{BC}$ is a diameter.

$\overline{DE}$ is a chord.

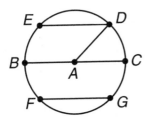

> **Remember**
>
> The **radius** connects the center to any point on the circle.
>
> The **diameter** connects any two points on the circle and passes through the center.
>
> A **chord** connects two points on a circle.

1. $\overline{AD}$ is a ___?___. radius   diameter

2. $\overline{FG}$ is a ___?___. chord   radius

Use the circle below for Exercises 3–5.
Underline the correct answer.

3. $\overline{PS}$ is a ___?___. radius   diameter

4. $\overline{RT}$ is a ___?___. chord   radius

5. $\overline{QR}$ is a ___?___. diameter   radius

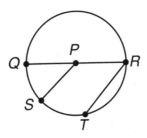

Use the circle below for Exercises 6–8.

6. Name a diameter. _____

7. Name a chord. _____

8. Name a radius. _____

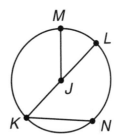

Congruence

Plane figures that have the same size and shape are **congruent.**

These figures are congruent.	These figures are not congruent.
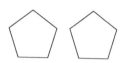 They are the **same size.** They are the **same shape.**	 They are the same size. They are **not** the same shape.

Decide whether the figures are congruent.
Trace one of each figure. Then place your drawing over the other figure.

1.

Are the figures the same size? _____

Are they the same shape? _____

Are they congruent? _____

2.

Are the figures the same size? _____

Are they the same shape? _____

Are they congruent? _____

3.

Figures can face different directions and still be the same size and shape.

Are the figures the same size and shape? _____

Are they congruent? _____

4.

Are the figures the same size and shape? _____

Are they congruent? _____

5.

Are the figures congruent? _____

6.

Are the figures congruent? _____

Name _____ Date _____

Symmetry

A figure has **line symmetry** if it can be folded in half so that the two parts match.

The fold line is a **line of symmetry.**

	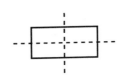	
one line of symmetry	two lines of symmetry	three lines of symmetry

For Questions 1–3, write *yes* or *no.*

1.	**2.**	**3.**
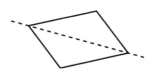		
If you fold the figure across the dashed line, will the halves match? ____	If you fold the figure across the dashed line, will the halves match? ____	If you fold the figure across the dashed line, will the halves match? ____
Is the dashed line a line of symmetry? ____	Is the dashed line a line of symmetry? ____	Is the dashed line a line of symmetry? ____

Trace each figure, fold it, and draw the lines of symmetry.
Then answer the question.

4.	**5.**	**6.**
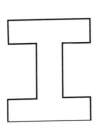	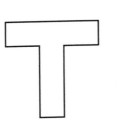	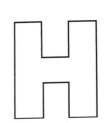
How many lines of symmetry are there? ____	How many lines of symmetry are there? ____	How many lines of symmetry are there? ____

Objective: Identify line symmetry.
Chapter Intervention

Use with Chapter 15.
Grade 5

Transformations

Transformations are different ways to move a figure.

> **Reflections, translations,** and **rotations** are transformations.

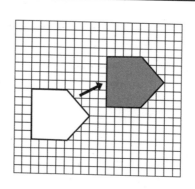

In a **reflection,** a figure *flips* over a line

In a **translation,** a figure *slides* in a straight line.

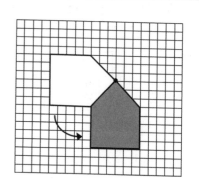

In a **rotation,** a figure *turns* around a point.

Circle the type of transformation that the figure shows.

1.

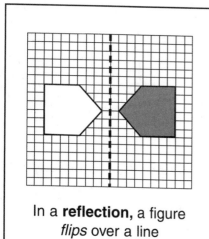

rotation   translation

2.

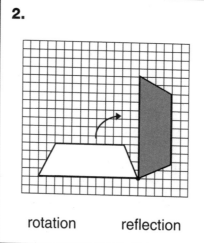

rotation   reflection

3.

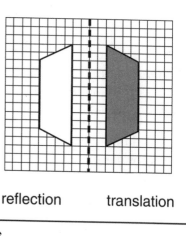

reflection   translation

4.

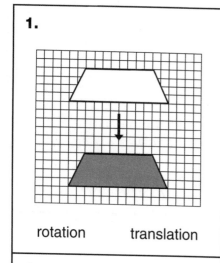

translation   rotation

5.

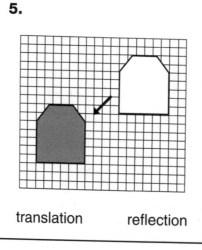

translation   reflection

6.

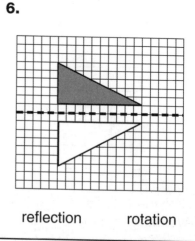

reflection   rotation

Name _____ Date _____

Make a Model

Problem Allie wants to use the triangle at the right to make a **tessellation.** Will the triangle tessellate?

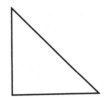

Read to Understand

1. What figure does Allie want to use? _____

2. What kind of pattern
does Allie want to make? _____

Choose a Way to Solve the Problem

A model will help you see if the triangle tessellates. So, the strategy to use is *Make a Model.*

> A **tessellation** is a repeating pattern that covers a plane without gaps or overlaps.

- Trace the triangle eight times.
  Cut out the triangles you have drawn.

- Use transformations to make a repeating pattern.
  Flip the triangle to begin the tessellation.
  Try turns and slides as well.

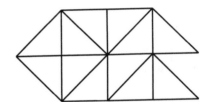

- Repeat the pattern.
  Make sure there are no gaps or overlaps.

Show the Solution

3. Can you repeat the pattern of
triangles without gaps or overlaps? _____

4. Will the triangle tessellate? _____

Try This Ryan wants to use the parallelogram at the right to make a tessellation. Will the figure tessellate?

5. Trace and cut out the figure eight times.
Then try to tessellate the figure.

This strategy is called Make a _____ .

6. Solution Will the figure tessellate? _____

Plane Figures

A **polygon** is a flat, closed figure that has three or more sides.

You can name a polygon by the number of sides it has.

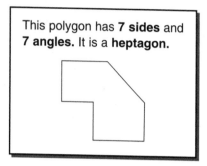

This polygon has **7 sides** and **7 angles.** It is a **heptagon.**

Name of Polygon	Number of Sides	Number of Angles
Triangle	3	3
Quadrilateral	4	4
Pentagon	5	5
Hexagon	6	6
Heptagon	7	7
Octagon	8	8
Nonagon	9	9
Decagon	10	10

1.

How many sides? _____

How many angles? _____

Name the polygon.

_____

2.

How many sides? _____

How many angles? _____

Name the polygon.

_____

3.

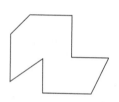

How many sides? _____

How many angles? _____

Name the polygon.

_____

Name each polygon.

4.

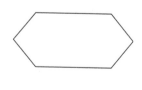

_____

5.

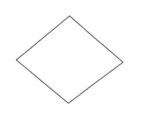

_____

6.

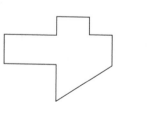

_____

Objective: Identify, classify, and describe plane geometric figures.
Chapter Intervention

Use with Chapter 16.
Grade 5

Perimeter and Area

Perimeter is the distance around a figure.
Area is the number of square units in a region.

1.

6 units

4 units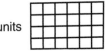

You can measure **perimeter** by adding the lengths of its sides.

Find the perimeter of the rectangle. Count the number of units along each side.

   6 + 4 + ___ + ___ = ___

| A **square unit** is a square with sides one unit long. |

The perimeter is ___ units.

You can measure **area** by counting the square units in a rectangle.

Find the area of the rectangle. Count the number of square units in the rectangle.

There are ___ square units inside the rectangle.

| **Remember** Area is expressed in square units. |

The area is ___ square units.

Find the perimeter and area.

2.

Perimeter: ___ + ___ + ___ + ___ = ___

The perimeter is ___ units.

There are ___ square units in the rectangle.

The area is ___ square units.

3.

Perimeter: ___ + ___ + ___ + ___ = ___

The perimeter is ___ units.

There are ___ square units in the rectangle.

The area is ___ square units.

4.

The perimeter is ___ units.

The area is ___ square units.

5.

The perimeter is ___ units.

The area is ___ square units.

Perimeter of Rectangles

You can use a formula to find the **perimeter** of rectangles.

Find the perimeter of each rectangle.

1.

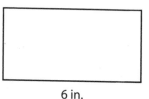

3 in.

6 in.

$P = 2l + 2w$
$\downarrow \qquad \downarrow$
$= (2 \times 6) + (2 \times 3)$
$\qquad \downarrow \qquad \downarrow$
$= \quad 12 \quad + \quad 6$
$= \quad 18$

> **Think**
> Perimeter equals 2 times length plus 2 times width.

The perimeter is _____ in.

2.

2 yd [rectangle]

5 yd

$P = 2l + 2w$

$= (2 \times \text{\_\_\_\_}) + (2 \times \text{\_\_\_\_})$

$= \text{\_\_\_\_} + \text{\_\_\_\_}$

$= \text{\_\_\_\_}$

The perimeter is _____ yd.

3.

[rectangle] 1 cm

8 cm

$P = 2l + 2w$

$= (\text{\_\_\_\_} \times \text{\_\_\_\_}) + (\text{\_\_\_\_} \times \text{\_\_\_\_})$

$= \text{\_\_\_\_} + \text{\_\_\_\_}$

$= \text{\_\_\_\_}$

The perimeter is _____ cm.

4.

[rectangle] 3 ft

4 ft

> **Remember**
> $P = 2l + 2w$

The perimeter is _____.

5.

[rectangle] 1 m

3 m

The perimeter is _____.

Name _____ Date _____

Area of Parallelograms

You can use a formula to find the **area** of a parallelogram.

Area = **b**ase × **h**eight
$A = bh$
$= 10 \times 5$
$= 50$

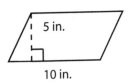
5 in.
10 in.

The area is 50 square inches or 50 in.²

Find the area of each parallelogram.

1.

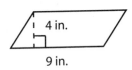
4 in.
9 in.

base = _____ height = _____

$A = bh$

$A =$ _____ × _____

$A =$ _____ in.²

2.

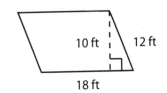
10 ft   12 ft
18 ft

base = _____ height = _____

$A = bh$

$A =$ _____ × _____

$A =$ _____ ft²

3.

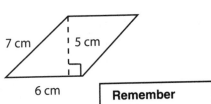
7 cm   5 cm
6 cm

$A = bh$

$A =$ _____ cm²

Remember
Include the square units of measurement when you write the area.

4.

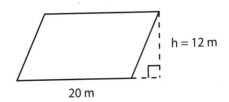
h = 12 m
20 m

$A = bh$

$A =$ _____ m²

5.

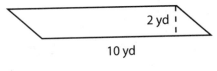
2 yd
10 yd

$A =$ _____

6.

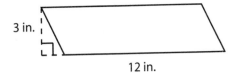
3 in.
12 in.

$A =$ _____

Objective: Use a formula for the areas of parallelograms.
Chapter Intervention

Use with Chapter 16.
Grade 5

Area of Triangles

You can use a formula to find the **area** of a triangle.

Area $= \frac{1}{2} \times$ base $\times$ height

$A = \frac{1}{2} bh$

$\quad = \frac{1}{2} \times 6 \times 7$

$\quad = \frac{1}{2} \times 42 = 21$

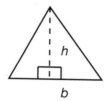

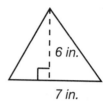

6 in.

7 in.

The area is 21 square inches or 21 in.²

| **Remember** to include the square units of measurement when you write the area. |

Find the area of each triangle.

1.

base = _____

height = _____

5 in.

4 in.

6 in.

$A = \frac{1}{2} bh$

$A = \frac{1}{2} \times$ ___ $\times$ ___ $= \frac{1}{2} \times$ _____

$A =$ _____ in.²

2.

base = _____

height = _____

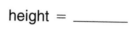

13 ft

5 ft

12 ft

$A = \frac{1}{2} bh$

$A = \frac{1}{2} \times$ ___ $\times$ ___ $= \frac{1}{2} \times$ _____

$A =$ _____ ft²

3.

14 cm

7 cm

$A =$ _____

4.

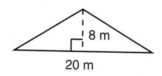

8 m

20 m

$A =$ _____

5.

20 m

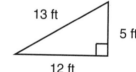

30 m

$A =$ _____

6. base = 10 ft
height = 6 ft

$A =$ _____

7. base = 22 in.
height = 12 in.

$A =$ _____

8. base = 15 cm
height = 30 cm

$A =$ _____

Name _____ Date _____

Perimeter and Area of Irregular Figures

Find the **perimeter** and **area** of each figure.

1. Add the lengths of the sides
   to find the perimeter.

   $P = 2 + 3 + 4 + 5 + 6 + 8$

   $= \underline{\hspace{2cm}}$ in.

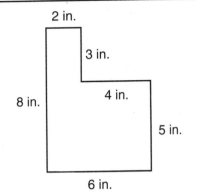

2 in.
3 in.
8 in.
4 in.
5 in.
6 in.

2. You can separate an irregular figure into
   squares, rectangles, or triangles
   to find the area.

   $A = $ area of $M + $ area of N

   $= (8 \times 2) + (4 \times 5)$

   $= \underline{\hspace{2cm}} + \underline{\hspace{2cm}}$

   $= \underline{\hspace{2cm}}$ in.^{2}

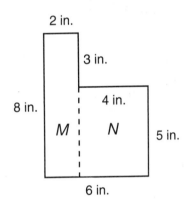

2 in.
3 in.
8 in.
4 in.
M N
5 in.
6 in.

3. Perimeter: $P = \underline{\hspace{2cm}}$ cm

   Area: $A = $ area of $R + $ area of S

   $= (\underline{\hspace{0.5cm}} \times \underline{\hspace{0.5cm}}) + (\underline{\hspace{0.5cm}} \times \underline{\hspace{0.5cm}})$

   $= \underline{\hspace{2cm}} + \underline{\hspace{2cm}}$

   $= \underline{\hspace{2cm}}$ cm^2

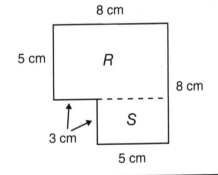

8 cm
5 cm R
8 cm
S
3 cm
5 cm

Remember The formula for the area of a triangle is $A = \dfrac{1}{2} bh$.

4. Perimeter: $P = \underline{\hspace{2cm}}$ m

   Area: $A = $ area of rectangle $+$ area of triangle

   $= \underline{\hspace{0.5cm}} \times \underline{\hspace{0.5cm}} + \dfrac{1}{2} \times 4 \times \underline{\hspace{0.5cm}}$

   $= \underline{\hspace{2cm}} + \underline{\hspace{2cm}}$

   $= \underline{\hspace{2cm}}$ m^2

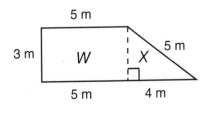

5 m
3 m W X 5 m
5 m   4 m

Objective: Find perimeters and areas of irregular figures.
Chapter Intervention

Use with Chapter 16.
Grade 5

Name _____ Date _____

Circumference of a Circle

The **circumference** of a circle is the distance around the circle. The circumference is equal to π times the diameter.

Use the diameter. Find the circumference of each circle.

1. Think Use 3.14 for pi.

2 ft

$C = \pi d$
$\approx 3.14 \times 2$
$\approx$ _____

The circumference is about _____ ft.

2.

3 m

$C = \pi d$
$\approx 3.14 \times$ ___
$\approx$ _____

The circumference is about _____ m.

3.

5 cm

$C = \pi d$
$\approx 3.14 \times$ ___
$\approx$ _____

The circumference is about _____ cm.

Use the radius. Find the circumference of each circle.

4. Think Use $\frac{22}{7}$ for pi.

14 in.

$C = 2\pi r$
$\approx 2 \times \frac{22}{7} \times 14$

$\approx 2 \times \frac{22}{7} \times \overset{2}{14}$

$\approx$ _____

The circumference is about _____ in.

5.

$3\frac{1}{2}$ ft

$C = 2\pi r$
$\approx 2 \times \frac{22}{7} \times \square$

$\approx 2 \times \frac{22}{7} \times \square$

$\approx \frac{\square}{\square}$ or ___

The circumference is about _____ ft.

6.

7 cm

$C = 2\pi r$
$\approx 2 \times \frac{22}{7} \times \square$

$\approx 2 \times \frac{22}{7} \times \square$

$\approx \frac{\square}{\square}$ or ___

The circumference is about _____ cm.

Find the circumference of each circle.

7. Use 3.14 for π.

10 m

$C \approx$ _____

8. Use 3.14 for π.

1.5 in.

$C \approx$ _____

9. Use $\frac{22}{7}$ for π.

$1\frac{3}{4}$ ft

$C \approx$ _____

Name _____ Date _____

Find Patterns

Problem Nadine uses square tiles to make the figures on the right. If the pattern continues, how many tiles will Nadine use in the sixth figure in the pattern?

Read to Understand

1. What shapes does Nadine use to make the figures? _____

2. How many figures are in the pattern? _____

3. Which figure do you need to find? _____

Choose a Way to Solve the Problem

Nadine used a pattern to make the shapes. To find the sixth figure in the pattern, the strategy to use is *Find a Pattern*.

- Make a table that shows the number of square tiles in each figure.

- Study the table to find a pattern.

- Continue the pattern.

Figure	1st	2nd	3rd	4th	5th	6th
Tiles	1	3	6	10	?	?

+2   +3   +4   +5   +6

Show the Solution

4. How many tiles does Nadine use to make the fifth figure? _____

5. How many tiles does Nadine need to make the sixth figure? _____

Try This Find a pattern to solve.

Wayne uses square tiles to make the figures on the right. If the pattern continues, how many tiles will Wayne use in the sixth figure in the pattern?

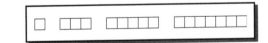

6. Complete the table to find a pattern.

Figure	1st	2nd	3rd	4th	5th	6th
Tiles	1	3	5			

7. Solution Wayne uses _____ tiles in the sixth figure.

Name _____ Date _____

Solid Figures

Solid figures are objects that take up space. Prisms and pyramids are solid figures that have faces, edges, and vertices.

> The **face** of solid figure is a flat surface.
> Two faces meet to form an **edge**.
> The point where three edges meet is a **vertex**.

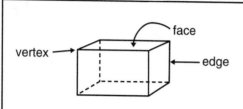

Rectangular Prism

Number of faces: 6
Number of edges: 12
Number of vertices: 8

Triangular Pyramid

Number of faces: 4
Number of edges: 6
Number of vertices: 4

Cylinder

Number of faces: 2
Number of edges: 0
Number of vertices: 0

Use each figure to answer the questions.

1.

Cube

How many faces? _____

How many edges? _____

How many vertices? _____

2.

Square Pyramid

How many faces? _____

How many edges? _____

How many vertices? _____

3.

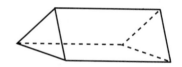

Triangular Prism

How many faces? _____

How many edges? _____

How many vertices? _____

Name each figure.

4.

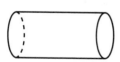

Solid figure: _____

5.

Solid figure: _____

6.

Solid figure: _____

Area of Figures

You can use a formula to find the area of a **parallelogram**.

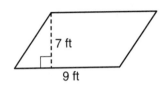

$A = b \times h$
$A = 9 \text{ ft} \times 7 \text{ ft}$
$A = 63 \text{ ft}^2$

Remember Area is measured in square units. You write 3 square inches as 3 in.^{2}

You can use a formula to find the area of a **triangle**.

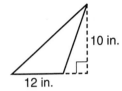

$A = \frac{1}{2} \times b \times h$

$A = \frac{1}{2} \times 12 \text{ in.} \times 10 \text{ in.}$

$A = 60 \text{ in.}^2$

Find the area of each parallelogram.

1.

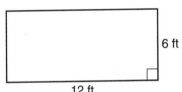

$A = b \times h$

$A = 12 \text{ ft} \times$ _____

$A =$ _____

2.

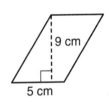

$A = b \times h$

$A =$ _____ $\times$ _____

$A =$ _____

3.

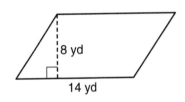

$A =$ _____

Find the area of each triangle.

4.

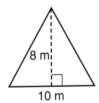

$A = \frac{1}{2} \times b \times h$

$A = \frac{1}{2} \times$ _____ $\times 8 \text{ m}$

$A =$ _____

5.

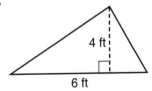

$A = \frac{1}{2} \times b \times h$

$A =$ ___ $\times$ ___ $\times$ ___

$A =$ _____

6.

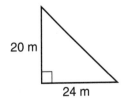

$A =$ _____

Name _____ Date _____

Volume of Solid Figures

Volume is the amount of space a figure occupies.
You can use a formula to find the volume of a rectangular prism.

Find the volume of the rectangular prism at the right.

Volume = length × width × height

$V = l \times w \times h$

$V = 6 \times 2 \times 4$

$V = 48 \text{ ft}^3$

Remember Volume is measured in cubic units. You write 48 cubic feet as 48 ft³.

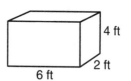

4 ft
2 ft
6 ft

Find the volume of each rectangular prism.

1.

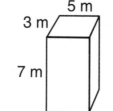

5 m
3 m
7 m

$V = l \times w \times h$

$V = 5 \times 3 \times$ _____

$V =$ _____ m³

2.

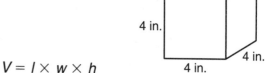

4 in.
4 in.
4 in.

$V = l \times w \times h$

$V =$ _____ × _____ × _____

$V =$ _____ in.³

3.

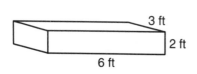

3 ft
2 ft
6 ft

$V =$ _____

4.

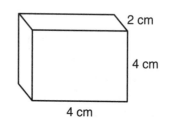

2 cm
4 cm
4 cm

$V =$ _____

5.

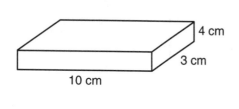

4 cm
3 cm
10 cm

$V =$ _____

6.

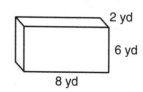

2 yd
6 yd
8 yd

$V =$ _____

Identify Solid Figures

| Types of Figures | Name the figures. |

Prisms

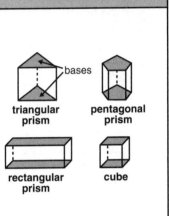

triangular prism · pentagonal prism · rectangular prism · cube

Pyramids

triangular pyramid · pentagonal pyramid · rectangular pyramid · square pyramid

Curved

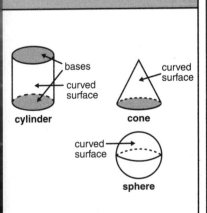

cylinder · cone · sphere

1.

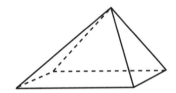

shape of base: triangle

solid figure: _____ prism

2.

shape of base: _____

solid figure: _____

3.

shape of base: rectangle

solid figure: _____ pyramid.

4.

shape of base: _____

solid figure: _____

5.

type of surface: curved

solid figure: _____

6.

type of surface: _____

solid figure: _____

Name _____ Date _____

Nets

A **net** is a flat pattern of the faces of a solid figure.

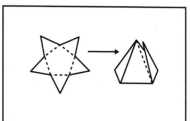

<table>
<tr><td colspan="2" align="center">**Some Solid Figures**</td></tr>
<tr><td align="center">**Pyramids**</td><td align="center">**Prisms**</td></tr>
<tr><td>Pyramids have triangular faces and *one base*.

Each pyramid is named by the shape of the base.
  triangular pyramid
  square pyramid
  rectangular pyramid
  pentagonal pyramid</td><td>Prisms have rectangular faces and *two parallel bases*.

Each prism is named by the shape of the bases.
  triangular prism
  cube or *square* prism
  rectangular prism
  pentagonal prism</td></tr>
</table>

Name the solid figure each net will make.

1. The net to the right has ____triangular____ faces.

The shape of the base is a _____.

The figure is a _____ pyramid.

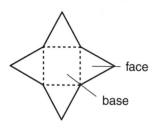

2.

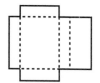

What is the shape of the faces? _____

What is the shape of the base? _____

The figure is a _____.

3.

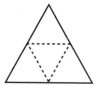

What is the shape of the faces? _____

What is the shape of the base? _____

The figure is a _____.

4.

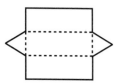

The figure is a _____.

5.

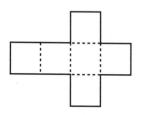

The figure is a _____.

Name _____ Date _____

Surface Area of Solid Figures

You can find the **surface area** of any solid figure by adding the areas of all its faces.

---

1. For rectangular prisms, determine the areas of opposite faces to find the surface area.

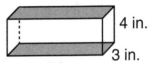

top and bottom   front and back   left and right

↓   ↓   ↓

2 × (6 × 3) = ___   2 × (6 × 4) = ___   2 × (3 × 4) = ___

4 in.
3 in.
6 in.

Add. ___ + ___ + ___ = ___ in.² | square inches |

Find the surface area of each solid figure.

2.

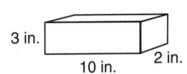

3 in.
10 in.   2 in.

top and bottom: 2 × (10 × 2) = ___

front and back: 2 × (10 × ___) = ___

left and right: 2 × (2 × ___) = ___

Add. ____ + ____ + ____ = ___ in.²

3.

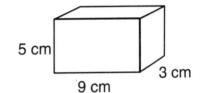

5 cm
9 cm   3 cm

top and bottom: 2 × (___ × ___) = ___

front and back: 2 × (___ × ___) = ___

left and right: 2 × (___ × ___) = ___

Add. ____ + ____ + ____ = ___ cm²

4.

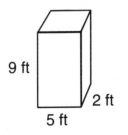

9 ft
2 ft
5 ft

surface area = _____

5.

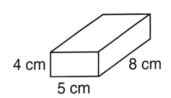

4 cm   8 cm
5 cm

surface area = _____

Name _____ Date _____

Volume

You can use a formula to find the **volume** of a
rectangular prism, a cube, and a triangular prism.

> **Remember**
> You measure volume in cubic units.
> 3 cubic feet = 3 ft³

Find the volume of each retangular prism.

---

1. The volume of a **rectangular prism**
is the length times width times height.

$$V = l \times w \times h$$

$$= 9 \times 6 \times 5$$

9 in.   6 in.   5 in.

$$= \underline{\quad\quad} \text{ in.}^3$$

2.

$$= \underline{\ } \times \underline{\ } \times \underline{\ }$$

$$= \underline{\quad\quad} \text{ cm}^3$$

3.

$$= \underline{\quad\quad} \text{ ft}^3$$

Find the volume of each cube.

---

4. In a cube, all faces have the same
measure. So the volume of a **cube**
is one side to the third power.

$$V = s^3$$

$$= 4 \times 4 \times 4$$

4 in.   4 in.   4 in.

$$= \underline{\quad\quad} \text{ in.}^3$$

5.

$$= \underline{\ } \times \underline{\ } \times \underline{\ }$$

$$= \underline{\quad\quad} \text{ ft}^3$$

6.

6 cm   6 cm   6 cm

$$= \underline{\quad\quad} \text{ cm}^3$$

Find the volume of each triangular prism.

---

7. The volume of a **triangular prism**
is one half times length times width
times height.

$$V = \tfrac{1}{2} \times l \times w \times h$$

$$= \tfrac{1}{2} \times 3 \times 2 \times 4$$

$$= \tfrac{1}{2} \times 24$$

2 ft   3 ft   4 ft

$$= \underline{\quad\quad} \text{ ft}^3$$

8.

8 cm   8 cm   2 cm

$$= \tfrac{1}{2} \times \underline{\ } \times \underline{\ } \times \underline{\ }$$

$$= \underline{\quad\quad} \text{ in.}^3$$

9.

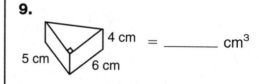

5 cm   6 cm   4 cm

$$= \underline{\quad\quad} \text{ cm}^3$$

Solve a Simpler Problem

Problem

Andy is building this solid figure.

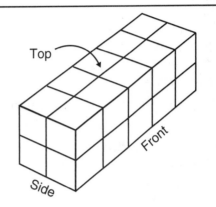

- The figure is 5 cubes long, 2 cubes wide, and 2 cubes tall.
- He paints the front, back, top, and sides of the figure.

What is the total number of faces that he paints?

Read to Understand

1. How long is the figure? _____ How wide? _____ How tall? _____

2. Which parts of the figure does Andy paint? _____

Choose a Way to Solve the Problem

Smaller Figure

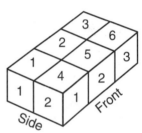

The figure has some hidden sides.

- To help solve the problem, you can use a smaller figure to count sides that you see and those that are hidden.
- So, the strategy to use is *Solve a Simpler Problem.*

Show the Solution

Start with the **small figure.** Read Questions 3–5 to fill in the correct column in the table at the right.

3. How many faces are painted on the **top?**

4. How many faces are painted on the **side?**

5. Fill in the table. What is the total number of faces that are painted on the figure? _____

6. Now try the **large figure.** Read Questions 3–5 again. Fill in the rest of the table. What is the total number of faces that are painted? _____

View	Small Figure	Large Figure
Front	3	10
Top		
Side		
Back	3	
Hidden side		
Total		

Try This Use Questions 3–5 to help you count the painted faces on the figure at the right.

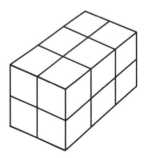

7. What is the total number of faces that are painted? _____

Objective: Solve problems by solving a simpler problem first.
Chapter Intervention

– 215 –

Use with Chapter 17.
Grade 5

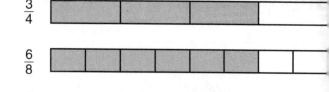

Find Equivalent Fractions

Equivalent fractions name the same number.

The models show that $\frac{3}{4}$, $\frac{6}{8}$, and $\frac{9}{12}$ are equivalent fractions.

$\frac{3}{4}$

$\frac{6}{8}$

$\frac{9}{12}$

You can multiply or divide to find equivalent fractions.

To find $\frac{2}{3} = \frac{}{12}$, multiply the numerator
and denominator by the same number.
- First think, what number times 3 equals 12?
- Then, multiply.

$$\frac{2 \times 4}{3 \times 4} \rightarrow \frac{8}{12}$$

$$\frac{2}{3} = \frac{8}{12}$$

1.

$\frac{3}{8} = \frac{}{16}$ $\frac{3 \times 2}{8 \times 2} \rightarrow \frac{\square}{16}$ So, $\frac{3}{8} = \frac{\square}{16}$

2.

$\frac{5}{6} = \frac{}{18}$ $\frac{5 \times 3}{6 \times 3} \rightarrow \frac{\square}{18}$ So, $\frac{5}{6} = \frac{\square}{18}$

To find $\frac{6}{9} = \frac{}{3}$, divide the numerator
and denominator by the same number.
- First think, 9 divided by what number is 3?
- Then, divide.

$$\frac{6 \div 3}{9 \div 3} \rightarrow \frac{2}{3}$$

$$\frac{6}{9} = \frac{2}{3}$$

3.

$\frac{10}{12} = \frac{}{6}$ $\frac{10 \div 2}{12 \div 2} \rightarrow \frac{\square}{6}$ So, $\frac{10}{12} = \frac{\square}{6}$

4.

$\frac{12}{16} = \frac{}{4}$ $\frac{12 \div 4}{16 \div 4} \rightarrow \frac{\square}{4}$ So, $\frac{12}{16} = \frac{\square}{4}$

Multiply or divide to find equivalent fractions.

5.

$$\frac{3 \times 5}{4 \times 5} = \frac{\square}{20}$$

6.

$$\frac{2}{7} = \frac{\square}{14}$$

7.

$$\frac{6 \div 3}{15 \div 3} = \frac{\square}{5}$$

8.

$$\frac{12}{18} = \frac{\square}{3}$$

Name _____ Date _____

Write Fractions as Decimals

To write a fraction as a decimal, you can write an equivalent fraction with a denominator of 10 or 100.

Write each fraction as a decimal. Use 10 for the denominator.

Write $\frac{1}{2}$ as a decimal.

The denominator is **2**.
2 is a factor of **10**.

Write an equivalent fraction with a denominator of **10**.

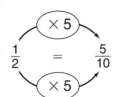

or, $\frac{1 \times 5}{2 \times 5} = \frac{5}{10}$

5 tenths = 0.5

1. $\frac{1}{5} = \frac{1 \times \boxed{}}{5 \times 2} \rightarrow \frac{\boxed{}}{10} = 0.\rule{1cm}{0.4pt}$

2. $\frac{3}{5} = \frac{3 \times \boxed{}}{5 \times 2} \rightarrow \frac{\boxed{}}{10} = 0.\rule{1cm}{0.4pt}$

3. $\frac{4}{5} = \frac{4 \times \boxed{}}{5 \times \boxed{}} \rightarrow \frac{\boxed{}}{10} = 0.\rule{1cm}{0.4pt}$

Write each fraction as a decimal. Use 100 for the denominator.

Write $\frac{3}{4}$ as a decimal.

The denominator is **4**.
4 is a factor of **100**.

Write an equivalent fraction with a denominator of **100**.

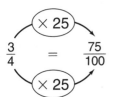

or, $\frac{3 \times 25}{4 \times 25} = \frac{75}{100}$

75 hundredths = 0.75

4. $\frac{7}{50} = \frac{7 \times \boxed{}}{50 \times 2} \rightarrow \frac{\boxed{}}{100} = 0.\rule{1cm}{0.4pt}$

5. $\frac{13}{20} = \frac{13 \times \boxed{}}{50 \times 2} \rightarrow \frac{\boxed{}}{100} = 0.\rule{1cm}{0.4pt}$

6. $\frac{6}{50} = \frac{6 \times \boxed{}}{50 \times \boxed{}} \rightarrow \frac{\boxed{}}{100} = 0.\rule{1cm}{0.4pt}$

Objective: Write fractions as decimals.
Chapter Intervention

Use with Chapter 18.
Grade 5

Name _____ Date _____

Ratios

You can use a **ratio** to compare two quantities.

Word Form	**1.**	**2.**
☐☐☐ ○○	△ △ ☐	☐ △ △
3 squares **2** circles	triangles to rectangle	rectangle to triangles
Ratio → **3 to 2**	Ratio → ___ to ___	Ratio → ___ to ___

Ratio Form	**3.**	**4.**
◆ ◆ ◇ ◇ ◇ ◇	● ○ ○ ○ ○ ○	○ ○ ○ ○ ○ ●
2 shaded **4** unshaded	shaded to unshaded	unshaded to shaded
Ratio → **2 : 4**	Ratio → ___ : ___	Ratio → ___ : ___

Fraction Form	**5.**	**6.**
◺◺ ☐☐☐ ◺◺ ☐☐☐		
4 triangles **6** squares	rectangles to ovals	ovals to rectangles
Ratio → $\frac{4}{6}$	Ratio → ☐/☐	Ratio → ☐/☐

Write each in ratio and fraction form.

○ ○ ○ ○ ○ ○ ☐ ☐ ☐ ☐ ☐ ☐ ☐		
13 figures in all		
7. circles to squares	**8.** squares to circles	**9.** squares to all figures
____ ____	____ ____	____ ____

Name _____ Date _____

Find Equivalent Ratios

You can find **equivalent ratios** by multiplying or dividing each term of the ratio by the same number.

Find an equivalent ratio.

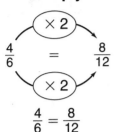

Multiply.

$$\frac{4}{6} = \frac{8}{12}$$

1.

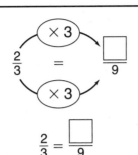

$$\frac{2}{3} = \frac{\square}{9}$$

2.

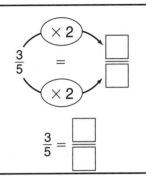

$$\frac{3}{5} = \frac{\square}{\square}$$

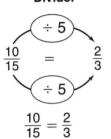

Divide.

$$\frac{10}{15} = \frac{2}{3}$$

3.

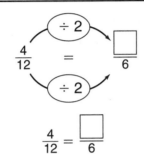

$$\frac{4}{12} = \frac{\square}{6}$$

4.

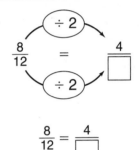

$$\frac{8}{12} = \frac{4}{\square}$$

To find the **simplest form** for a ratio, divide each term by their GCF (greatest common factor).

Find the simplest form for each ratio.

5. $\frac{12}{16}$ The GCF of 12 and 16 is **4.**
Divide each term by 4.

$$\frac{12}{16} = \frac{3}{\square}$$

simplest form _____

6. $\frac{14}{35}$ The GCF of 14 and 35 is **7.**
Divide each term by 7.

$$\frac{14}{35} = \frac{2}{\square}$$

simplest form _____

7. $\frac{9}{24}$ The GCF of 9 and 24 is _____.

Divide each term by _____.

$$\frac{9}{24} = \frac{\square}{\square}$$

simplest form _____

8. $\frac{8}{32}$ The GCF of 8 and 32 is _____.

Divide each term by _____.

$$\frac{8}{32} = \frac{\square}{\square}$$

simplest form _____

9. $\frac{6}{10}$ The GCF of 6 and 10 is _____.

simplest form _____

10. $\frac{15}{20}$ The GCF of 15 and 20 is _____.

simplest form _____

Objective: Use multiplication and division to find equivalent ratios.
Chapter Intervention

Use with Chapter 18.
Grade 5

Name _____ Date _____

Rates

A **rate** is a special type of ratio. It compares quantities expressed
in different units, such as **miles** and **hours.**

A car travels 100 **miles** in 2 hours.

How far will it travel in 4 hours?

• Use equivalent ratios to solve.

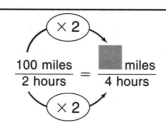

$$\frac{100 \text{ miles}}{2 \text{ hours}} = \frac{\square \text{ miles}}{4 \text{ hours}}$$

Think
What number times 2 is 4?
Multiply 100 by 2 to solve.

$$\frac{100 \text{ miles}}{2 \text{ hours}} = \frac{\mathbf{200} \text{ miles}}{\mathbf{4} \text{ hours}}$$

The car will travel 200 miles in 4 hours.

Find how far each car will travel in **12** hours.

---

1. A car travels 270 miles in 6 hours.

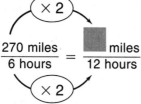

$$\frac{270 \text{ miles}}{6 \text{ hours}} = \frac{\square \text{ miles}}{12 \text{ hours}}$$

The car will travel _____ miles in
12 hours.

2. A car travels 100 miles in 2 hours.

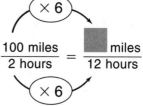

$$\frac{100 \text{ miles}}{2 \text{ hours}} = \frac{\square \text{ miles}}{12 \text{ hours}}$$

The car will travel _____ miles in
12 hours.

A **unit rate** is a rate in which the second term is **1.** Find each unit rate.

---

3. 300 miles in 5 hours

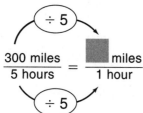

$$\frac{300 \text{ miles}}{5 \text{ hours}} = \frac{\square \text{ miles}}{1 \text{ hour}}$$

The unit rate is _____ miles in 1 hour.

4. 140 pages in 20 days

$$\frac{140 \text{ pages}}{20 \text{ days}} = \frac{\square \text{ pages}}{1 \text{ day}}$$

The unit rate is _____ pages in 1 day.

---

5. $40 in 8 hours

$ _____ in 1 hour

6. 120 words in 5 minutes

_____ words in 1 minute

Name _____ Date _____

Proportions

A **proportion** is a statement that two ratios are equal. You can use **cross products** to find the missing term in a proportion.

> The two ratios are equal.
> Their cross products are equal.
> $$\frac{1}{2} \times \frac{3}{6}$$
> $2 \times 3 = 6$
> $1 \times 6 = 6$

Solve the proportion. Find n.	Identify the cross products.	Write an equation to show the cross products are equal. Find n.
$$\frac{3}{2} = \frac{n}{4}$$	$$\frac{3}{2} \times \frac{n}{4}$$ **Think** 3×4 $2 \times n$	$3 \times 4 = 2 \times n$ $12 = 2n$ $$\frac{12}{2} = \frac{2n}{2}$$ ← Divide each side by 2. $6 = n$ **Think** Undo multiplication by dividing.

So, $n = 6$ because $3 \times 4 = 2 \times 6$.

1. $$\frac{5}{n} = \frac{2}{6}$$

Write the cross products.   ____ × ____ = ____ × n

Simplify.   ____ = ____ × n

Solve for n.   ____ = ____

____ = n

2. $$\frac{n}{6} = \frac{5}{3}$$

Write the cross products.   ____ × ____ = n × ____

Simplify.   ____ = n × ____

Solve for n.   ____ = ____

____ = n

3. $$\frac{3}{4} = \frac{12}{n}$$

____ × ____ = ____ × ____

____ = ____

____ = ____

$n =$ ____

4. $$\frac{n}{15} = \frac{2}{5}$$

____ × ____ = ____ × ____

____ = ____

____ = ____

$n =$ ____

Proportions and Scale Drawings

A **scale** is a ratio that compares two different measurements.

You use a scale to create a **scale drawing.** A scale drawing can be an enlargement or a reduction of the actual object.

When you know the scale of a drawing, you can use a **proportion** to find the actual length of an object.

A scale of 1 in. : 2 ft means that 1 inch in a drawing represents 2 feet of the actual object.

← 10 ft →   ← 5 in. →

Scale of the drawing ⟶ 1 in. : 2 ft

Length in the drawing ⟶ 3 in. = ▢ ft

- Write a proportion.

- Solve.

Think
1 n = 2 × 3
n = 6

×3

length in drawing ⟶ $\dfrac{1 \text{ in.}}{2 \text{ ft}} = \dfrac{3 \text{ in.}}{\boxed{}}$
▮ actual length ⟶

$\dfrac{1 \text{ in.}}{2 \text{ ft}} = \dfrac{3 \text{ in.}}{6 \text{ ft}}$

×3

The actual length is 6 ft.

Use the scales to find the actual lengths.

1. 1 cm : 5 m 8 cm : ▮ m $\times \boxed{}$ $\dfrac{1 \text{ cm}}{5 \text{ m}} = \dfrac{8 \text{ cm}}{\boxed{} \text{m}}$ Actual length: _____	**2.** 1 in. : 6 yd 30 in. : ▮ yd $\times \boxed{}$ $\dfrac{1 \text{ in.}}{6 \text{ yd}} = \dfrac{30 \text{ in.}}{\boxed{}}$ Actual length: _____	**3.** 1 m : 5 cm 25 m : ▮ cm $\times \boxed{}$ $\dfrac{1 \text{ m}}{5 \text{ cm}} = \dfrac{25 \text{ m}}{\boxed{}}$ Actual length: _____
4. 1 cm : 20 km 8 cm : ▮ km $\dfrac{\boxed{} \text{ cm}}{\boxed{} \text{ km}} = \dfrac{\boxed{} \text{ cm}}{\boxed{} \text{ km}}$ Actual length: _____	**5.** 1 ft : $\frac{1}{4}$ in. 3 ft : ▮ in. Actual length: _____	**6.** 1 in. : 150 mi 3 in. : ▮ mi Actual length: _____

Choose Exact or Estimated Amounts

Problem   A box of 6 Crunchy granola bars costs $3.18.
A box of 8 Nutty granola bars costs $3.84.
Which is the better buy?

Read to Understand

1. How many Crunchy bars are in 1 box? _____   **2.** cost of 1 box of Crunchy bars: _____

3. How many Nutty bars are in 1 box? _____   **4.** cost of 1 box of Nutty bars: _____

Choose a Way to Solve the Problem

You can find the unit prices and then compare them.
You may be able to estimate, or you may need to find exact amounts.

> The **unit price** is the cost of one unit of an item.

5. Use compatible numbers to estimate the unit prices.

Crunchy bars: $3.18 ÷ 6   Nutty bars: $3.84 ÷   8

$$\downarrow \quad \downarrow \qquad\qquad\qquad \downarrow \qquad\qquad \downarrow$$

$3.00 ÷ 6 = _____ $4.00 ÷ _____ = _____

These estimates are the same, so they cannot tell you which box is the better buy.

6. Use actual numbers to find the exact unit prices.
Round each price to the nearest cent.

Crunchy bars: $3.18 ÷ 6 = _____   Nutty bars: _____ ÷ _____ = _____

7. Compare the unit prices. _____ is less than _____ .

8. Show the Solution   The better buy is _____ granola bars.

Try This   Solve. Tell whether you used an estimate or an exact answer.

9. Film Follies rents 5 movies for $18.95.
Movie Master rents 4 movies for $12.88.
Which store has the better buy?

_____ has the better buy.

I used an _____.

10. Office Place sells 6 pens for $5.95.
Supplies Central sells 4 pens for $3.85.
Which store has the better buy?

_____ has the better buy.

I used an _____.

Name _____ Date _____

Place Value Through Thousandths

The number 3.927 is in the place-value chart.
Each digit in the number has a different value.
The number can be written in different ways.

- Standard Form: 3.927
- Short Word Form: 3 and 927 *thousandths.*
- Word Form: three **and** nine hundred
  twenty-seven *thousandths.*

Say **"and"** for the decimal point.

ones	.	tenths	hundreths	thousandths
3	.	9	2	7

Use the chart. Write the value of each digit.

1. 2   value: _____0.02_____   **2.** 9   value: _____   **3.** 7   value: _____

Write the value of the *underlined* digit.

4. 16.44<u>5</u>   _____0.005_____   **5.** 18.7<u>5</u>   _____   **6.** 0.43<u>9</u>   _____

7. 3<u>2</u>.5   _____   **8.** 73.<u>9</u>6   _____   **9.** <u>8</u>6.209   _____

10. 6.5<u>7</u>7   _____   **11.** 3.8<u>6</u>5   _____   **12.** 72.<u>5</u>48   _____

13. 7<u>5</u>0.2   _____   **14.** <u>5</u>4.7   _____   **15.** 33.06<u>2</u>   _____

Write the short word form for each number.

16. 1.43   ___1 and 43 hundredths___   **17.** 7.699 _____

18. 65.27 _____   **19.** 12.385 _____

20. 355.4 _____   **21.** 0.2 _____

22. 30.09 _____   **23.** 99.508 _____

Name _____ Date _____

Change Fractions and Decimals

Write each decimal as a fraction or mixed number.

Make sure your answers are in **simplest form.**

---

1. 0.2

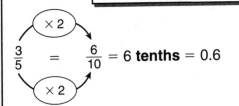

2 **tenths** = $\frac{2}{10}$ = $\frac{1}{5}$

Remember to simplify.

So 0.2 = _____

2. 1.75

1 and 75 **hundredths** = $1\frac{75}{100}$ = $1\frac{3}{4}$

So 1.75 = _____

---

3. 0.4

_____

4. 0.8

_____

5. 0.16

_____

6. 1.25

_____

7. 2.36

_____

Write each fraction or mixed number as a decimal.

8. $\frac{3}{5}$

Write an equivalent fraction with a denominator that is a power of 10.

$\frac{3}{5}$ = $\frac{6}{10}$ ×2 = 6 **tenths** = 0.6

So $\frac{3}{5}$ = _____

9. $1\frac{1}{20}$

Think $\frac{1}{20}$ = $\frac{5}{100}$

$1\frac{1}{20}$ = $1\frac{5}{100}$ = 1 and 5 **hundredths** = 1.05

So $1\frac{1}{20}$ = _____

---

10. $\frac{4}{5}$

_____

11. $\frac{1}{4}$

_____

12. $\frac{3}{20}$

_____

13. $2\frac{3}{4}$

_____

14. $3\frac{2}{5}$

_____

Objective: Convert fractions, mixed numbers, and decimals.
Chapter Intervention

Use with Chapter 19.
Grade 5

Name _____ Date _____

Relate Fractions, Decimals, and Percents

You can use a 10 × 10 grid to write percents
in fraction or decimal form.

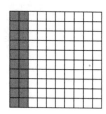

20 out of 100 is shaded.

$\frac{20}{100} = 20\%$ ← percent form

$\frac{20}{100} = 0.20$ ← decimal form

$\frac{20}{100} = \frac{1}{5}$ ← fraction form

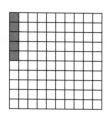

5 out of 100 is shaded.

$\frac{5}{100} = 5\%$ ← percent form

$\frac{5}{100} = 0.05$ ← decimal form

$\frac{5}{100} = \frac{1}{20}$ ← fraction form

Write each shaded region as a percent, decimal, and fraction.

1.

40 out of 100 is shaded.

Percent: _____

Decimal: _____

Fraction: _____

2.

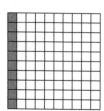

10 out of 100 is shaded.

Percent: _____

Decimal: _____

Fraction: _____

3.

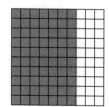

70 out of 100 is shaded.

Percent: _____

Decimal: _____

Fraction: _____

4. 15 out of 100 is shaded.

Percent: 15%

Decimal: _____

Fraction: $\frac{3}{20}$

5. 30 out of 100 is shaded.

Percent: _____

Decimal: 0.30

Fraction: $\frac{3}{10}$

6. 18 out of 100 is shaded.

Percent: 18%

Decimal: 0.18

Fraction: _____

Objective: Relate fractions, decimals, and percents.
Chapter Intervention

Use with Chapter 19.
Grade 5

Name _____ Date _____

Order Fractions, Decimals, and Percents

Sometimes you may need to write fractions, decimals, and
percents in the same form so you can compare and order them.

---

1. Order $\frac{1}{8}$, 34%, and 0.15 from least to greatest.

a. Rewrite $\frac{1}{8}$ as a decimal.

Divide the numerator
by the denominator.

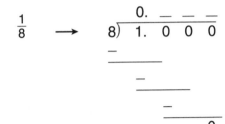

b. Rewrite 34% as a decimal.
- First, think of the percent
  as **hundredths.**
- Write it as a fraction with
  a denominator of 100.
- Then write the decimal.

34% = _____ hundredths

34 hundredths = $\dfrac{\text{_____}}{100}$ = 0.___ ___

c. Order the three decimals. _____, 0.15, _____

Rewrite the fractions and percents as decimals.
Then order the three decimals from least to greatest.

2. $\frac{2}{8}$, 48%, 0.11

3. $\frac{4}{5}$, 63%, 0.08

4. $\frac{3}{25}$, 51%, 0.75

5. $\frac{8}{20}$, 96%, 0.88

Percent of a Number

To find the percent of a number, you can write the percent as a fraction or as a decimal.

Write the percent as a fraction and multiply.

Find 5% of 80.	**1.** 10% of 30	**2.** 30% of 50
$5\% = \dfrac{5}{100}$ $\dfrac{5}{100} \times \dfrac{80}{1} = \dfrac{400}{100}$ $= 4$ 5% of 80 is 4.	$10\% = \dfrac{10}{\Box}$ $\dfrac{10}{\Box} \times \dfrac{30}{1} = \dfrac{\Box}{\Box}$ $= \underline{\ \ }$ 10% of 30 is ___.	$10\% = \dfrac{\Box}{100}$ $\dfrac{\Box}{100} \times \dfrac{\Box}{\Box} = \dfrac{\Box}{\Box}$ $= \underline{\ \ }$ 30% of 50 is ___.
3. 12% of 50 _____	**4.** 25% of 20 _____	**5.** 20% of 15 _____

Write the percent as a decimal and multiply.

Find 24% of 50.	**6.** 15% of 60	**7.** 58% of 50
$24\% = 0.24$ $\begin{array}{r} 50 \\ \times\ 0.24 \leftarrow \text{2 decimal places} \\ \hline 2\,00 \\ +\ 10\,0 \\ \hline 12.00 \leftarrow \text{2 decimal places} \end{array}$ 24% of 50 is 12.	$15\% = 0.\underline{\ \ }\,\underline{\ \ }$ Multiply: 15% of 60 is ___.	$58\% = \underline{\ \ \ \ \ \ }$ Multiply: 58% of 50 is ___.
8. 16% of 75 _____	**9.** 15% of 20 _____	**10.** 65% of 80 _____

Use Circle Graphs

Problem   Craig tosses 3 coins and records the number of heads on the toss. He does this 80 times. The results are in the frequency table at the right. Show the data as a circle graph.

number of heads	frequency
3	16
2	24
1	32
0	8

Read to Understand

1. How many times did Craig toss the coins?

$16 + 24 + 32 + 8 =$ _____

2. How many times did Craig toss 3 heads? _____

3. When Craig tossed 0 heads, he must have tossed _____ tails.

Choose a Way to Solve the Problem

You can show the data in a circle graph.

1 part = 10%

- Write each frequency as a percent of the total number of tosses.

- Shade parts of the circle to match each percent.

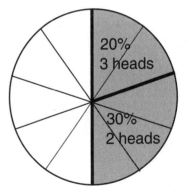

4. What percent of the tosses resulted in 3 heads?

16 out of 80 tosses or $\frac{16}{80} = \frac{2}{10} = \frac{20}{100} =$ _____ %

5. What percent of the tosses resulted in 2 heads? _____

1 head? _____ 0 heads? _____

Show the Solution

6. Complete the circle graph. Shade the parts in the circle to match each percent.

Try This   Use Craig's results to answer Questions 7 and 8.

7. What is the sum of the percents in the circle? _____

8. How many times would you expect to toss at least one head

when you toss 3 coins 100 times? _____

Name _____ Date _____

Add and Subtract Fractions

When you add or subtract fractions with like denominators,
add or subtract the numerators. Write the sum with the same denominator.

Denominators are the same. Add the numerators.	Simplify the answer, if necessary.	Denominators are the same. Subtract the numerators.	Simplify the answer, if necessary.

$$\frac{3}{8} + \frac{7}{8} = \frac{10}{8} = 1\frac{2}{8} = 1\frac{1}{4} \qquad\qquad \frac{5}{6} - \frac{1}{6} = \frac{4}{6} = \frac{2}{3}$$

Add or subtract. Write your answer in simplest form.

1. $\frac{9}{10} + \frac{3}{10} = \frac{\square}{10} = 1\frac{\square}{10} = 1\frac{\square}{5}$ **2.** $\frac{5}{6} + \frac{5}{6} = \frac{\square}{6} = 1\frac{\square}{6} = 1\frac{\square}{\square}$

3. $\frac{7}{8} - \frac{3}{8} = \frac{\square}{8} = \frac{\square}{2}$ **4.** $\frac{11}{12} - \frac{1}{12} = \frac{\square}{12} = \frac{\square}{\square}$

5. $\frac{3}{5} + \frac{4}{5} =$ _____ **6.** $\frac{7}{10} + \frac{3}{10} =$ _____ **7.** $\frac{5}{8} + \frac{1}{8} =$ _____

8. $\frac{8}{9} - \frac{7}{9} =$ _____ **9.** $\frac{5}{12} - \frac{1}{12} =$ _____ **10.** $\frac{4}{5} - \frac{2}{5} =$ _____

11. $\frac{7}{12} - \frac{5}{12} =$ _____ **12.** $\frac{3}{4} + \frac{1}{4} =$ _____ **13.** $\frac{7}{8} + \frac{7}{8} =$ _____

14. $\frac{11}{18} - \frac{7}{18} =$ _____ **15.** $\frac{10}{13} + \frac{4}{13} =$ _____ **16.** $\frac{9}{10} - \frac{3}{10} =$ _____

Name _____ Date _____

Outcomes and Probability

The spinner has four **equally likely** outcomes.

Outcomes: A, B, C, D

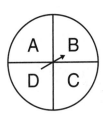

The probability of landing on D is **1 out of 4.**

Probability $= \frac{1}{4}$ ← favorable outcomes (D)
                              ← total outcomes (A, B, C, D)

Use the spinner for Exercises 1–2. Complete the sentence.
Then write the probability as a fraction in simplest form.

1. The probability of landing on **B** is ___ out of ___. Probability = _____	**2.** The probability of landing on **C** or **D** is ___ out of ___. Probability = _____

Find the **outcomes** and **probability.**

3. 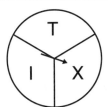 Outcomes: _____ The probability of landing on **T** is ___ out of ___. Probability = _____	**4.** 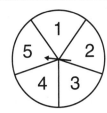 Outcomes: _____ The probability of landing on an **odd number** is ___ out of ___. Probability = _____

Use the spinner to write each probability in simplest form.

5. Landing on **C**: 2 out of ___

Probability = _____

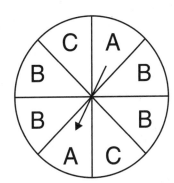

6. Landing on **B**: ___ out of ___

Probability = _____

7. Landing on **A** or **B**: ___ out of ___

Probability = _____

Name _____ Date _____

Combinations

You can multiply to help you find all the possible choices from a set of items.

1. Choose either white or wheat bread and one filling.

How many possible choices do you have?
You can multiply to find the number of choices.

Sandwiches	
Bread	**Filling**
white	turkey
wheat	tuna
	cheese

bread   filling   number of
choices   ×   choices   =   choices
  ↓   ↓   ↓
  2   ×   3   =   6

There are _____ possible sandwich choices.

You have one choice from each category.
Multiply to find the number of choices possible.

2. 5 colors, 3 sizes

Hats	
Colors	**Sizes**
purple	small
gray	medium
red	large
pink	
black	

color   size   number of
choices   ×   choices   =   choices
  ↓   ↓   ↓

_____ × _____ = _____

There are _____ possible choices.

3.

T-Shirts	
Design	**Color**
frog	green
baseball	red
	black

There are _____
possible choices.

4.

Earrings	
Style	**Material**
hoop	silver
stud	gold
clip-on	

There are _____
possible choices.

5.

Bicycles	
Style	**Color**
street	orange
off-road	red
comfort	black
racing	silver

There are _____
possible choices.

Objective: Determine combinations.
Chapter Intervention

Use with Chapter 20.
Grade 5

Name _____ Date _____

Probability

Probability describes the likelihood that an event will occur.

This spinner has 4 same-size sectors.
When the spinner is spun once, there are
3 possible outcomes: A, B, C.

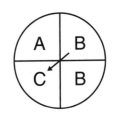

1. How many sectors are labeled D? _____
The probability of the spinner landing on D is **impossible.**

2. All the sectors are labeled A, B, or C. Can the spinner land on D? _____
The probability of the spinner *not* landing on D is **certain.**

3. How many sectors are labeled A? _____ How many are labeled B? _____
The spinner is **less likely** to land on A than B.

4. How many sectors are labeled B? _____ How many are labeled C? _____
The spinner is **more likely** to land on B than C.

5. How many sectors are labeled A? _____ How many are labeled C? _____
The spinner is **equally likely** to land on A or C.

This spinner has 8 same-size sectors.
The spinner is spun once. Choose the
best word to complete each sentence.

| certain |
| equally likely |
| impossible |
| less likely |
| more likely |

6. The probability of the spinner landing on W is _____ .

7. The probability of the spinner *not* landing on W is _____ .

8. The spinner is _____ to land on S than U.

9. The spinner is _____ to land on T than R.

10. The spinner is _____ to land on T or U.

Objective: Describe the probability of an event.
Chapter Intervention

Use with Chapter 20.
Grade 5

Name _____ Date _____

Fractions and Probability

You can find the probability of an event by comparing the number of favorable outcomes with the number of possible outcomes. You can write the probability of an event as a fraction.

These shapes are put in a bag.
One shape is picked without looking.
What is the probability of picking a square?

1. Count the squares to find the number of favorable outcomes. _____

2. Count all the shapes to find the number of possible outcomes. _____

3. Write the probability of picking a square as a fraction in **simplest form.**

$$P(\text{square}) = \frac{\text{number of squares}}{\text{total number of shapes}} \longrightarrow \frac{4}{8} = \frac{\square}{\square}$$

So, $P(\text{square}) = $ _____.

Use the spinner.
Write the probability of each event
as a fraction in simplest form.

4. $P(D) = \dfrac{\text{number of D's}}{\text{total number of letters}} \longrightarrow \dfrac{\square}{\square} = \dfrac{\square}{\square}$

5. $P(E) = \dfrac{\text{number of E's}}{\text{total number of letters}} \longrightarrow \dfrac{\square}{\square} = \dfrac{\square}{\square}$

6. $P(F) = $ _____

7. $P(G) = $ _____

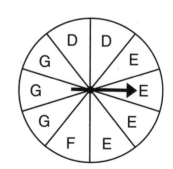

Objective: Use fractions to find probability.
Chapter Intervention

Use with Chapter 20.
Grade 5

Name _____ Date _____

Compound Events

A **compound event** is a combination of two or more events.

There are two envelopes.

- One envelope contains a green ticket, a red ticket, and a yellow ticket.

- A second envelope contains a black ticket and a white ticket.

G R Y   B W

A student picks a ticket from each envelope. What is the probability that the student picks a green ticket and a white ticket?

1. Use the tree diagram. Circle the favorable outcome, **green and white.**

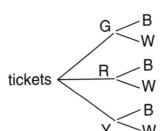

2. Count the outcomes.

Number of favorable outcomes: _____

Number of possible outcomes: _____

3. Write the probability.

P(green and white) = $\dfrac{1}{\boxed{}}$ ← number of favorable outcomes
← number of possible outcomes

Each spinner is spun once.

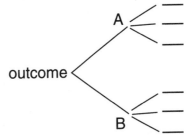

4. Complete the tree diagram for all the possible outcomes.

5. Find P(A and odd number). _____

6. Find P(B and even number). _____

Objective: Find the probability of compound events.
Chapter Intervention

Use with Chapter 20.
Grade 5

Make an Organized List

Problem   Mia wants to buy different colored t-shirts.
The colors of the shirts are blue, pink, and green.
Mia only has enough money to buy 2 t-shirts.
How many different ways can Mia choose the 2 t-shirts?

Read to Understand

1. How many t-shirts does Mia want to buy? _____

2. What are the possible colors of the t-shirts? _____, _____, _____

3. Restate the problem another way. <u>How many different combinations of 2 shirts can Mia choose out of 3 shirts?</u>

Choose a Way to Solve the Problem

You can make an organized list to show
all the possible ways Mia can buy 2 t-shirts.
Use letters to stand for each color shirt: blue (B), pink (P), green (G).

4. List all combinations of shirts that include blue.   **B** P   **B** G

5. List all combinations of shirts that include pink.   **P** G   **P** __

6. List all combinations of shirts that include green.   **G** B   ___

7. Draw lines to connect the pairs of shirts in the list above that have the same colors. The order of the colors does not matter.

8. How many matching pairs are there? _____

Show the Solution

9. There are _____ different ways Mia can choose 2 t-shirts.

Try This   Make an organized list to solve this problem.

A restaurant offers 4 vegetables: broccoli, corn, spinach, and peas.
How many different ways can a customer order 2 vegetables with
a meal?

10. Solution   A customer can order 2 vegetables in _____ ways.

Name _____ Date _____

Solve Equations

You can use a related fact to solve addition and
subtraction equations.

Use a related fact to find the missing number.

1. ☐ $+ 6 = 13$

Think
$13 - 6 = 7$

___ $+ 6 = 13$

2. $1 +$ ☐ $= 10$

Think
$10 - 1 = 9$

$1 +$ ___ $= 10$

3. ☐ $- 4 = 9$

Think
$4 + 9 = 13$

___ $- 4 = 9$

4. $15 -$ ☐ $= 6$

Think
$15 - 6 = 9$

$15 -$ ___ $= 6$

Find the missing number.

5. ☐ $+ 5 = 14$

Think
$14 - 5 =$ ☐

___ $+ 5 = 14$

6. ☐ $- 6 = 5$

Think
$6 + 5 =$ ☐

___ $- 6 = 5$

7. $7 +$ ☐ $= 15$

Think
$15 - 7 =$ ☐

$7 +$ ___ $= 15$

8. $12 -$ ☐ $= 7$

Think
$12 - 7 =$ ☐

$12 -$ ___ $= 7$

9. ___ $+ 4 = 11$

10. ___ $- 7 = 6$

11. $9 +$ ___ $= 17$

12. $10 -$ ___ $= 6$

13. $8 +$ ___ $= 14$

14. $16 -$ ___ $= 8$

15. ___ $- 3 = 9$

16. ___ $+ 9 = 16$

17. ___ $- 8 = 5$

Objective: Solve addition and subtraction equations.
Chapter Intervention

— 237 —

Use with Chapter 21.
Grade 5

Name _____ Date _____

Solve More Equations

You can use a related fact to solve multiplication
and division equations.

Use a related fact to find each missing number.

1. ▨ × 4 = 20

> **Think**
> 20 ÷ 4 = 5

___ × 4 = 20

2. 7 × ▨ = 21

> **Think**
> 21 ÷ 7 = 3

7 × ___ = 21

3. ▨ ÷ 6 = 4

> **Think**
> 6 × 4 = 24

___ ÷ 6 = 4

4. 30 ÷ ▨ = 5

> **Think**
> 30 ÷ 5 = 6

30 ÷ ___ = 5

Find the missing number.

5. ▨ × 3 = 27

> **Think**
> 27 ÷ 3 = ▨

___ × 3 = 27

6. ▨ ÷ 5 = 8

> **Think**
> 8 × 5 = ▨

___ ÷ 5 = 8

7. 7 × ▨ = 28

> **Think**
> 28 ÷ 7 = ▨

7 × ___ = 28

8. 36 ÷ ▨ = 4

> **Think**
> 36 ÷ 4 = ▨

36 ÷ ___ = 4

9. ___ × 4 = 20

10. ___ ÷ 6 = 3

11. 9 × ___ = 54

12. 32 ÷ ___ = 8

13. 5 × ___ = 35

14. ___ ÷ 8 = 6

15. 60 ÷ ___ = 10

16. ___ × 7 = 49

17. ___ ÷ 3 = 6

Objective: Solve multiplication and division equations.
Chapter Intervention

— 238 —

Name _____ Date _____

Use Inverse Operations

You can use **inverse operations** to solve equations.

Inverse Operations

addition ⟷ subtraction
multiplication ⟷ division

Solve using inverse operations.

Addition Equations

$$n + 16 = 40$$
$$n + 16 - 16 = 40 - 16$$
$$n + 0 = 24$$
$$n = 24$$

16 is **added** to n.
Subtract 16 from both sides.

1.

$$m + 8 = 39$$
$$m + 8 - \underline{} = 39 - \underline{}$$
$$m + 0 = \underline{}$$
$$m = \underline{}$$

2.

$$k + 14 = 23$$

$$k + 0 = \underline{}$$
$$k = \underline{}$$

Subtraction Equations

$$a - 5 = 15$$
$$a - 5 + 5 = 15 + 5$$
$$a + 0 = 20$$
$$a = 20$$

5 is **subtracted** from a.
Add 5 to both sides.

3.

$$w - 8 = 14$$
$$w - 8 + \underline{} = 14 + \underline{}$$
$$w + 0 = \underline{}$$
$$w = \underline{}$$

4.

$$c - 14 = 23$$

$$c - 0 = \underline{}$$
$$c = \underline{}$$

Multiplication Equations

$$7t = 70$$
$$7t \div 7 = 70 \div 7$$
$$1t = 10$$
$$t = 10$$

7 is **multiplied** by t.
Divide both sides by 7.

5.

$$8x = 56$$
$$8x \div 8 = 56 \div \underline{}$$
$$1x = \underline{}$$
$$x = \underline{}$$

6.

$$5y = 70$$

$$1y = \underline{}$$
$$y = \underline{}$$

Division Equations

$$w \div 9 = 11$$
$$w \div 9 \times 9 = 11 \times 9$$
$$1w = 99$$
$$w = 99$$

w is **divided** by 9.
Multiply both sides by 9.

7.

$$d \div 5 = 20$$
$$d \div 5 \times 5 = 20 \times \underline{}$$
$$1d = \underline{}$$
$$d = \underline{}$$

8.

$$y \div 7 = 30$$

$$1y = \underline{}$$
$$y = \underline{}$$

Name _____ Date _____

Use a Function Table

The function table shows some inputs and outputs for the rule $y = x + 3$.

Substitute each input in the expression. Simplify to find the output.

Input (x)	Expression ($x + 3$)	Output (y)
1	1 + 3	4
2	2 + 3	5
3	3 + 3	6
4	4 + 3	7
5	5 + 3	8

← When the input (x) is 1, the output (y) is 4.

Complete the function tables.

1. $y = x - 6$

Substitute 8 for x. Simplify.

Substitute 10 for x.

Substitute 12 for x.

Substitute 14 for x.

Input (x)	Expression ($x - 6$)	Output (y)
8	8 − 6	
10	10 − 6	
12	12 − 6	
14		

2. $y = 5x$

Input (x)	Expression (5x)	Output (y)
0		
1		
4		
5		
7		

3. $y = x \div 3$

Input (x)	Expression ($x \div 3$)	Output (y)
0		
6		
12		
15		
21		

Name _____ Date _____

Describe and Extend Patterns

You can extend function tables by looking for patterns.

Extend each function table.

1.

x	y
0	6
1	8
2	10
3	

y values are increasing by 2.

10 + 2 = 12

When x = 3, y = ___.

2.

x	y
2	10
4	13
6	16
8	

y values are increasing by 3.

16 + 3 = 19

When x = 8, y = ___.

3.

x	y
0	8
1	11
2	14
3	
4	

y values are increasing by 3.

← 14 + 3

← ___ + 3

When x = 4, y = ___.

4.

x	y
0	2
2	6
4	10
6	
8	

← 10 + ___

← ___ + ___

When x = 8, y = ___.

5.

x	y
0	1
1	4
2	7
3	10
4	
5	

← ___ + ___

← ___ + ___

When x = 5, y = ___.

6.

x	y
0	12
1	14
2	16
3	18
4	
5	

← 18 + ___

When x = 5, y = ___.

7.

x	y
0	10
3	14
6	18
9	
12	
15	

When x = 15, y = ___.

Write an Equation

Problem There are 168 books in Roberto's bookcase.
Each shelf holds 28 books. How many shelves are in the bookcase?

Read to Understand

1. How many books are on a shelf? _____

2. How many books are in the bookcase? _____

3. Restate the problem in another way. <u>I need to find how many shelves</u>
<u>are in the bookcase.</u>

Choose a Way to Solve the Problem

You can use a variable to represent what is unknown.
So, the strategy is to write an equation to solve a problem.

4. What operation can you use to find
the total number of books on the shelf? _____

5. Let s represent the total number of shelves.
Write an equation to solve the problem.

$$\underline{\hspace{2cm}} \times s = \underline{\hspace{2cm}}$$

Show the Solution

6. There are _____ shelves in Roberto's bookcase.

Try This Write and solve an equation to solve this problem.

For parades, the members of a band march in rows of 6.
There are 72 band members.
How many band members are there in each row?

7. Solution I can use the equation _____.

There are _____ band members in each row.

Name _____ Date _____

Use a Number Line

You can use a pattern to find missing numbers on a number line.

Use a pattern to find the missing numbers.

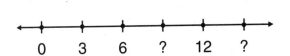

0   3   6   ?   12   ?

Think
Study the given numbers to find a pattern.

$0 + 3 = 3$ $3 + 3 = 6$

Add 3 to each number to find the next number.

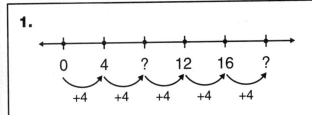

0   3   6   **9**   12   **15**
   +3   +3   +3   +3   +3

$6 + 3 = 9$
$12 + 3 = 15$

Write each missing number.

1.

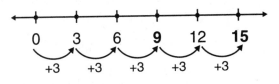

0   4   ?   12   16   ?
   +4   +4   +4   +4   +4

_____   _____

2.

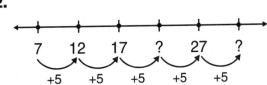

7   12   17   ?   27   ?
   +5   +5   +5   +5   +5

_____

3.

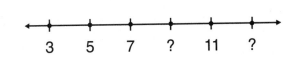

3   5   7   ?   11   ?

_____   _____

4.

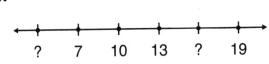

?   7   10   13   ?   19

_____   _____

5.

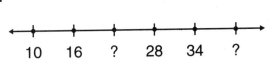

10   16   ?   28   34   ?

_____   _____

6.

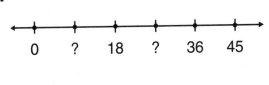

0   ?   18   ?   36   45

_____   _____

Objective: Find missing numbers on a number line.
Chapter Intervention

Use with Chapter 22.
Grade 5

Compare Whole Numbers

You can use a place-value chart to compare numbers.

Compare. Write > or < in each ◯.

> means *is greater than.*
< means *is less than.*

1. 402 ⬭ 420

- Begin at the greatest place.
- Find the place where the digits are different.
- Compare.

Hundreds	Tens	Ones
4	**0**	2
4	**2**	0

↑ same ↑ different

0 tens ◯< **2** tens

402 ◯ 420

2. 7,675 ⬭ 7,659

Thousands	Hundreds	Tens	Ones
7	6	**7**	5
7	6	**5**	9

↑ same ↑ same ↑ different

7 tens ◯> **5** tens

7,675 ◯ 7,659

3. 947 ⬭ 948

Hundreds	Tens	Ones
9	4	**7**
9	4	**8**

↑

7 ones ◯ **8** ones

94**7** ◯ 94**8**

4. 3,509 ⬭ 3,913

Thousands	Hundreds	Tens	Ones
3	**5**	0	9
3	**9**	1	3

↑

5 hundreds ◯ **9** hundreds

3,**5**09 ◯ 3,**9**13

5. 162 ⬭ 126

Hundreds	Tens	Ones
1	**6**	2
1	**2**	6

↑

_____ tens ◯ _____ tens

1**6**2 ◯ 1**2**6

6. 6,974 ⬭ 6,074

Thousands	Hundreds	Tens	Ones
6	**9**	7	4
6	**0**	7	4

↑

_____ hundreds ◯ _____ hundreds

6,**9**74 ◯ 6,**0**74

Name _____ Date _____

Addition and Subtraction

Sometimes you need to regroup when
you add or subtract whole numbers.

Find 218 + 344.

h	t	o
	1	
2	1	8
+ 3	4	4
5	6	2

Add the ones.
Regroup 12 ones as 1 ten 2 ones.

Add the tens.

Add the hundreds.

---

1. Find 461 + 287.

h	t	o
☐		
4	6	1
+ 2	8	8

Find 726 − 531.

h	t	o
6	**12**	
7	2	6
− 5	3	1
1	9	5

Subtract the ones.

Regroup 1 hundred as 10 tens.
Subtract the tens.

Subtract the hundreds.

---

2. Find 840 − 639.

h	t	o
	☐	☐
8	4	0
− 6	3	9

Add or subtract.

3.	4.	5.
764 + 220	351 + 350	156 + 456
6.	**7.**	**8.**
761 − 200	428 − 119	634 − 561
9.	**10.**	**11.**
545 + 372 = _____	754 − 82 = _____	967 − 474 = _____

Objective: Add and subtract whole numbers.
Chapter Intervention

Use with Chapter 22.
Grade 5

Locate Integers

The set of **integers** includes 0, the counting numbers
1, 2, 3, and so on, and their opposites.

Integers that are the same distance from zero, but are
on opposite sides of zero, are called opposites.

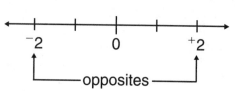

Use the number line. Write the opposite of each integer.

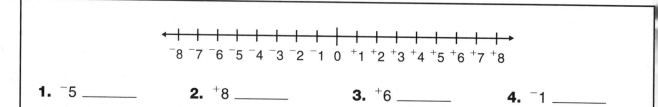

1. ⁻5 _____   **2.** ⁺8 _____   **3.** ⁺6 _____   **4.** ⁻1 _____

Write the opposite of each integer.

5. ⁺15 _____   **6.** ⁻30 _____   **7.** ⁻27 _____   **8.** ⁺95 _____

The **absolute value** of a number is its distance from 0.

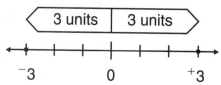

⁻3 is 3 units from 0.   ⁺3 is 3 units from 0.

The absolute value of ⁻3 is 3.   The absolute value of ⁺3 is 3.

Use the number line to write the absolute value of each integer.

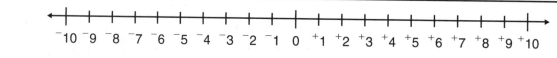

9. ⁻4 is _____ units from 0.   **10.** ⁺2 is _____ units from 0.

The absolute value of ⁻4 is _____.   The absolute value of ⁺2 is _____.

11. ⁻6 is _____ units from 0.   **12.** ⁺10 is _____ units from 0.

The absolute value of ⁻6 is _____.   The absolute value of ⁺10 is _____.

Write the absolute value of each integer.

13. ⁻85 _____   **14.** ⁺46 _____   **15.** ⁻27 _____   **16.** ⁺100 _____

Objective: Locate integers and their opposites on a number line and find absolute value.
Chapter Intervention

Use with Chapter 22.
Grade 5

Name _____ Date _____

Compare and Order Integers

You can use a number line to compare and order integers.

> is greater than
< is less than

Compare $^-4$ and $^+2$.

- Locate each integer on the number line.

- Compare. $^-4$ is to the **left** of $^+2$, so $^-4$ is **less** than $^+2$.

$$^-4 \;<\; ^+2$$

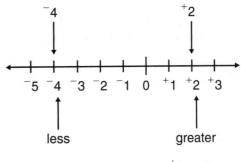

$^-4 < \,^+2 \qquad\qquad ^+2 > \,^-4$

---

1. Compare $^-3$ 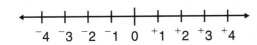 $^+1$.

$^-3$ is to the _____ of $^+1$.

$^-3$ is _____ than $^+1$.

$^-3$ ◯ $^+1$

2. Compare $^-2$ ⬭ $^-5$.

$^-2$ is to the _____ of $^-5$.

$^-2$ is _____ than $^-5$.

$^-2$ ◯ $^-5$

Order $^+2$, $^-5$, and $^-1$ from least to greatest.

- Locate each integer on the number line.

- Compare the integers on the number line. $^-5$ is least. $^+2$ is greatest.

$$^-5 < \,^-1 < \,^+2$$

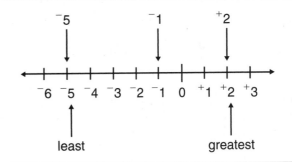

least   greatest

3. Order $^+3$, $^+4$, $^-2$ from least to greatest.

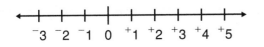

_____ is least.   _____ is greatest.

_____ < _____ < _____

4. Order $^-1$, $^-3$, $^+3$ from least to greatest.

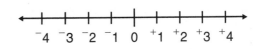

_____ is least.   _____ is greatest.

_____ < _____ < _____

Objective: Compare and order integers.
Chapter Intervention

Use with Chapter 22.
Grade 5

Add Integers

You can use a number line to add integers.

The sum of **two positive** integers is **positive**.	The sum of **two negative** integers is **negative**.

1. Find $^+2 + {}^+5$.
Start at 0.

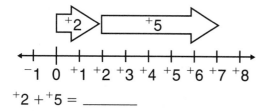

$^+2 + {}^+5 =$ _____

2. Find $^-2 + {}^-5$.
Start at 0.

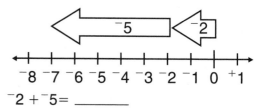

$^-2 + {}^-5 =$ _____

The sum of a **positive** integer and a **negative** integer will have the same sign as the integer with the **greater** absolute value.

3. Find $^-2 + {}^+5$.
Start at 0.

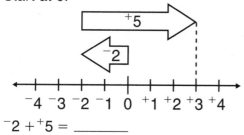

$^-2 + {}^+5 =$ _____

4. Find $^+2 + {}^-5$.
Start at 0.

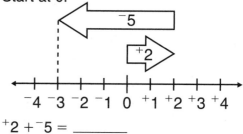

$^+2 + {}^-5 =$ _____

Find the sign of the sum. Then add.

5. $^-3 + {}^-4$

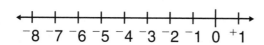

What is the sign of the sum? _____
$^-3 + {}^-4 =$ _____

6. $^-6 + {}^+2$

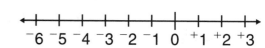

What is the sign of the sum? _____
$^-6 + {}^+2 =$ _____

7. $^+4 + {}^-1$

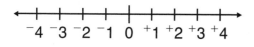

$^+4 + {}^-1 =$ _____

8. $^-5 + {}^+4$

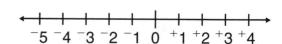

$^-5 + {}^+4 =$ _____

Name _____ Date _____

Subtract Integers

Subtracting an integer is the same as **adding its opposite.**

Find $^-2 - {}^+5$. • Change the operation sign. $\quad ^-2 - {}^+5$ • Write the opposite of the $\qquad \downarrow \quad \downarrow$ $\quad$ number. Add. $\qquad\qquad ^-2 + {}^-5$ $^-2 + {}^-5 = {}^-7$, so $^-2 - {}^+5 = {}^-7$	Find $^-3 - {}^-7$. • Change the operation sign. $\quad ^-3 - {}^-7$ • Write the opposite of the $\qquad \downarrow \quad \downarrow$ $\quad$ number. Add. $\qquad\qquad ^-3 + {}^+7$ $^-3 + {}^+7 = {}^+4$, so $^-3 - {}^-7 = {}^+4$

Write the related expressions to solve.

1. Find $^+4 - {}^-1$. $^+4 - {}^-1$ $\downarrow \quad \downarrow$ $^+4 + \underline{\quad}$ $^+4 + \underline{\quad} = \underline{\quad}$	**2.** Find $^-8 - {}^-2$. $^-8 - {}^-2$ $\downarrow \quad \downarrow$ $^-8 + \underline{\quad}$ $^-8 + \underline{\quad} = \underline{\quad}$	**3.** Find $^-4 - {}^+5$. $^-4 - {}^+5$ $\downarrow \quad \downarrow$ $^-4 + \underline{\quad}$ $^-4 + \underline{\quad} = \underline{\quad}$
4. Find $^-2 - {}^+3$. $^-2 - {}^+3$ $\downarrow \quad \downarrow$ $^-2 \bigcirc \underline{\quad}$ $^-2 \bigcirc \underline{\quad} = \underline{\quad}$	**5.** Find $^-1 - {}^-7$. $^-1 - {}^-7$ $\downarrow \quad \downarrow$ $^-1 \bigcirc \underline{\quad}$ $^-1 \bigcirc \underline{\quad} = \underline{\quad}$	**6.** Find $^+8 - {}^-3$. $^+8 - {}^-3$ $\downarrow \quad \downarrow$ $^+8 \bigcirc \underline{\quad}$ $^+8 \bigcirc \underline{\quad} = \underline{\quad}$

7. $^+6 - {}^-2$ Addition expression: _____ Difference: _____	**8.** $^-4 - {}^-3$ Addition expression: _____ Difference: _____
9. $^-7 - {}^+8$ Addition expression: _____ Difference: _____	**10.** $^-3 - {}^+5$ Addition expression: _____ Difference: _____

Use Integers to Solve

Problem The temperature at the beginning of the day was ⁻3°F.
The temperature had risen 8° by the afternoon.
By nightfall, the temperature had dropped 6°.
What was the temperature at nightfall?

Read to Understand

1. What was the temperature at the beginning of the day? _____°F

2. How many degrees did the temperature rise? _____ drop? _____

Choose a Way to Solve the Problem

You can use integers to represent the beginning temperature
and its changes.
Then add the integers to find the final temperature.

3. Write the temperature and change in temperature as integers.
   • Record a rise in temperature as a positive integer.
   • Record a drop in temperature as a negative integer.

   beginning temperature: ⁻**3**   8° rise: ⁺**8**   6° drop: _____

4. Use a number line to add the integers.
   • Start at zero. Show the beginning temperature.
   • Then show the temperature rise.
   • Finally, show the temperature drop.

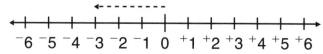

Show the Solution.

5. At nightfall, the temperature was _____°F.

Try This Use integers and the number line to solve this problem.
At bedtime, the temperature was ⁺5°F. The temperature dropped
10 degrees overnight. The temperature had risen 7° by noon
the next day.
What was the temperature at noon?

6. Solution

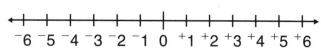

   At noon, the temperature was _____°F.

Name _____ Date _____

oints on a Grid

You can use an **ordered pair** such as (2, 1)
o name the location of points on a grid.

- The first number in an ordered pair tells
  how many units to move **right** from 0.

- The second number tells how many
  units to move **up** on the grid.

(2, 1) means move **2** units **right** from 0.
Then move **1** unit **up**.
   (2, 1) names **Point E.**

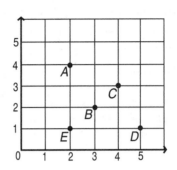

Use the graph for Exercises 1–4.

1. To reach Point *A,* start at 0. Move ___2___ units to the **right.** Then, move _____ units **up.** Point *A* is at (_2_ ,___).	**2.** To reach Point *B,* start at 0. Move ___3___ units to the **right.** Then, move _____ unit **up.** Point *B* is at (_3_ ,___).
3. To reach Point *C,* start at 0. Move _____ units to the **right.** Then, move _____ units **up.** Point *C* is at (___ ,___).	**4.** To reach Point *D,* start at 0. Move _____ units to the **right.** Then, move _____ unit **up.** Point *D* is at (___ ,___).

Use the grid. Name the ordered pair for each point.
Label each point with its letter.

5. Point *G*   (1 ,___)

6. Point *H*   (___,___)

7. Point *J*   (___,___)

8. Point *K*   (___,___)

> **Think**
> Start at 0.
> Move **right** 1 unit.
> Move **up** 5 units

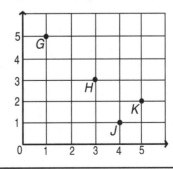

Objective: Identify points on a coordinate plane.

Chapter Intervention

Use with Chapter 23.
Grade 5

Name _____ Date _____

Write Integers

You can use a number line to find the **opposite** of an integer.

You can find the opposites.

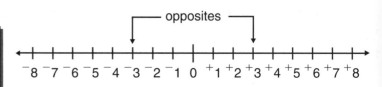

Integers that are the same distance from zero, but are on opposite sides of zero, are called **opposites.**

The opposite of ⁺3 is ⁻3.   The opposite of ⁻3 is ⁺3.

Write the opposite of each integer.

1. 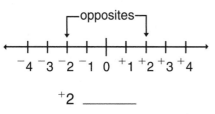 ⁺2 _____	2. 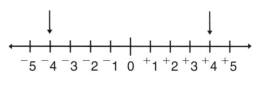 ⁻4 _____
3. ⁺5 _____	4. ⁻7 _____	5. ⁻16 _____	6. ⁺104 _____

The **absolute value** of a number is its distance from zero.

You can find the absolute value.

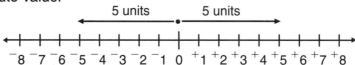

⁺5 is **5 units** from 0.
The absolute value of ⁺5 is 5.

⁻5 is **5 units** from 0.
The absolute value of ⁻5 is 5.

Find the absolute value of each integer.

7. 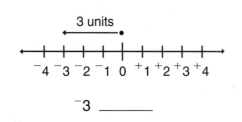 ⁻3 _____	8. 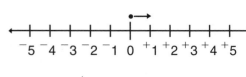 ⁺1 _____
9. ⁺8 _____	10. ⁻9 _____	11. ⁺82 _____	12. ⁻121 _____

Name _____ Date _____

Graph Ordered Pairs

Look at the coordinate plane at the right.
The horizontal axis is the *x*-axis.
The vertical axis is the *y*-axis.

You can use an ordered pair such as ($^+$4, $^+$2)
to describe points on the plane.

- The first number in an ordered pair tells
  how many units to move **left** or **right,**
  from 0, on the *x*-axis.

- The second number tells how many
  units to move **up** or **down** on the *y*-axis.

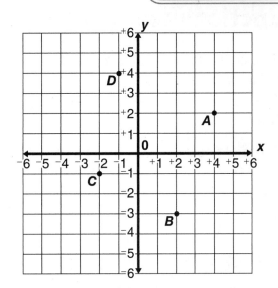

Use the graph for Exercises 1–4.

1. Point *A* is at ($^+$4, $^+$2). To reach Point *A*, start at 0 and move _____ units to the right. Then, move _____ units up.	**2.** Point *B* is at ($^+$2, $^-$3). To reach Point *B*, start at 0 and move 2 units to the _____. Then, move 3 units _____.
3. Point *C* is at ($^-$2, $^-$1). To reach Point *C*, start at _____ and move _____ units to the _____. Then move _____ unit _____.	**4.** Point *D* is at ($^-$1, $^+$4). To reach Point *D*, start at _____ and move _____ unit to the _____. Then move _____ units _____.

Use the ordered pairs to plot the points on the coordinate plane.
Label each point with its letter.

		x	y
5.	Point *W*	($^+$3,	$^+$4)
6.	Point *X*	($^+$2,	$^-$5)
7.	Point *Y*	($^-$1,	$^-$2)
8.	Point *Z*	($^-$4,	$^+$3)

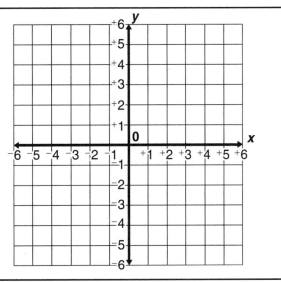

Name _____ Date _____

Functions and Ordered Pairs

Complete the function table for the function $y = 3x + 1$.
Write the ordered pairs.

1.

Substitute each value of x.	Solve to find the values of y.	Write the values of y in the function table.	Write the ordered pairs.
$y = 3x + 1$			(x, y)
$x = 1, (3 \times 1) + 1$	$(3 \times 1) + 1 = 4$		$(\underline{1}, \underline{4})$
$x = 2, (3 \times 2) + 1$	$(3 \times 2) + 1 = \underline{}$		$(\underline{2}, \underline{})$
$x = 3, (3 \times \underline{}) + 1$	$(3 \times \underline{}) + 1 = \underline{}$		$(\underline{}, \underline{})$
$x = 4, (3 \times \underline{}) + 1$	$(3 \times \underline{}) + 1 = \underline{}$		$(\underline{}, \underline{})$

x	y
1	4
2	
3	
4	

Complete the function table. Write the ordered pairs.

2. $y = x + 5$

$x = {}^-2,$	${}^-2 + 5$	${}^-2 + 5 = 3$
$x = {}^-1,$	$\underline{} + 5$	$\underline{} + 5 = \underline{}$
$x = 0,$	$\underline{} + \underline{}$	$\underline{} + \underline{} = \underline{}$
$x = 1,$	$\underline{} + \underline{}$	$\underline{} + \underline{} = \underline{}$

x	y
${}^-2$	3
${}^-1$	
0	
1	

(x, y)
$(\underline{{}^-2}, \underline{3})$
$(\underline{}, \underline{})$
$(\underline{}, \underline{})$
$(\underline{}, \underline{})$

3. $y = 7x$

x	y
1	7
2	
3	
4	

Ordered pairs

$(1, 7)$
$(2, \underline{})$
$(3, \underline{})$
$(\underline{}, \underline{})$

4. $y = 5x + 2$

x	y
0	
2	
4	
6	

Ordered pairs

$(\underline{}, \underline{})$
$(\underline{}, \underline{})$
$(\underline{}, \underline{})$
$(\underline{}, \underline{})$

Objective: Use a function rule to find the value of ordered pairs.
Chapter Intervention

Use with Chapter 23.
Grade 5

Name _____ Date _____

Graph Equations

Function tables and graphs are two ways to show the solutions of a function.

Graph the function $y = x + 3$ on the coordinate plane.

---

1. Make a function table. The value of y is $x + 3$. So you can **add 3** to each value of x to find y.

> When $x = 3$, substitute 3 in $x + 3$ to find that y equals $3 + 3$, or 6.

$y = x + 3$			
x	$x + 3$	y	Ordered Pairs
3	$3 + 3$	6	(3, 6)
2	___ + 3	___	(___ , ___)
1	___ + ___	___	(___ , ___)
0	___ + ___	___	(___ , ___)

2. Graph each ordered pair. Then draw a line that passes through all the points.

> To locate the point for the ordered pair **(3,6)**, start at the origin (0), move **3** units along the **x-axis,** and then move **6** units along the **y-axis.**

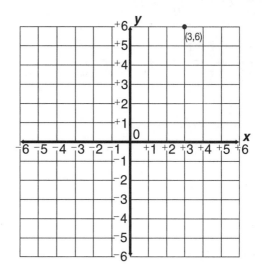

Graph the function $y = x - 3$ on the coordinate plane.

---

3. Complete the function table. Write the ordered pairs.

$y = x - 3$	
x	y
⁻1	
0	
3	
5	

Ordered Pairs

_____

_____

_____

_____

4. Graph each ordered pair. Then draw a line that passes through all the points.

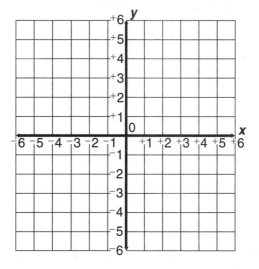

Objective: Graph an equation in the coordinate plane.

Chapter Intervention

Use with Chapter 23.

Grade 5

Name _____ Date _____

Coordinate Plane Transformations

You can **transform** a figure on the coordinate plane by changing its position. Transformations include **translations, reflections,** and **rotations.** Complete each transformation.

1. **Translation**	2. **Reflection**	3. **Rotation**
Translate, or **slide,** the point at ($^+$2, $^+$3) 5 units to the **left.**	Reflect, or **flip,** the point at ($^-$3, $^+$1) about the ***x*-axis.**	Rotate, or **turn,** the point at ($^+$1, $^+$3) a **half-turn** (180°) about the origin.
• Begin at the point and move left 5 units.	• Begin at the point and move down 2 units across the *x*-axis.	• Begin at the point. Make a **half circle** about the origin.
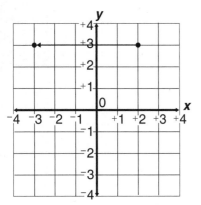	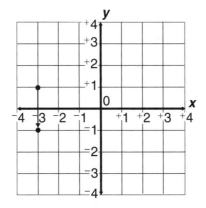	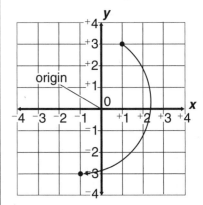
• To record the coordinates of the new point, **subtract 5** from the *x*-coordinate.	• To record the coordinates of the new point, write the **opposite** of the *y*-coordinate.	• To record the coordinates of the new point, write the **opposite** of the *x*- and *y*-coordinates.
The coordinates of the new point are (___, $^+$3).	The coordinates of the new point are ($^-$3, ___).	The coordinates of the new point are (___, ___).

Use a point with coordinates ($^+$5, $^+$2) for Exercises 4–9.
Find the coordinates of the new point after each transformation.

4. **Translate** right 2 units.	5. **Translate** left 1 unit.	6. **Reflect** about the *x*-axis.
Add ___ to the *x*-coordinate.	Subtract ___ from the *x*-coordinate.	Write the **opposite** of the *y*-coordinate.
New point: (___, $^+$2)	New point: (___, $^+$2)	New point: ($^+$5, ___)
7. **Reflect** about the *y*-axis.	8. **Rotate** a half-turn about the origin.	9. **Translate** up 3 units.
Write the **opposite** of the ___-coordinate.	Write the **opposite** of both the *x*- and *y*-coordinates.	Add ___ to the ___-coordinate.
New point: (___, ___)	New point: (___, ___)	New point: (___, ___)

Use a Graph

Problem The table shows the cost of renting a canoe at a state park. How much will it cost to rent a canoe for 7 hours?

Time (hours)	Cost (gallons)
1	12
2	15
4	21

Read to Understand

1. What is the cost to rent a canoe for the following times?

   1 hour _____ 2 hours _____ 4 hours _____

2. Restate the problem another way. <u>How much does it cost to rent a canoe for 7 hours when I know the costs for 1, 2, and 4 hours?</u>

Choose a Way to Solve the Problem

You can graph the data. Then extend the graph to find how much it costs to rent a canoe for 7 hours.

Show the Solution

3. Plot the three points on the graph. Draw a line through the points.

4. Extend the line so you can find the cost for 7 hours.

5. It will cost _____ to rent a canoe for 7 hours.

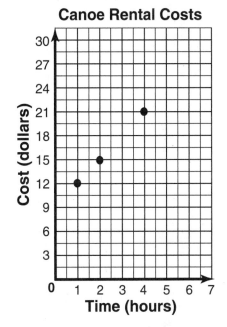

Canoe Rental Costs

Try This The table shows how much water was in the tank at hours 4, 5, and 6. Graph the data. Draw a line through the points to find how much water was in the tank at 1 hour.

Time (hours)	Cost (gallons)
4	6
5	4
6	2

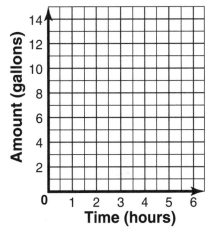

Amount of Water

6. At 1 hour there were _____ gallons in the tank.